20TH-CENTURY
ARMS AND
—ARMOR—

20TH-CENTURY
ARMS AND
-ARMOR-

STEPHEN BULL

FOREWORD BY
COLONEL HARRY G. SUMMERS, JR.

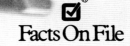

Facts On File

This edition first published in the United States and Canada in 1996 by
Facts On File, Inc., 11 Penn Plaza, New York, NY 10001, USA.

First published in 1996 by Studio
an imprint of Random House UK Ltd.
20 Vauxhall Bridge Road, London SW1V 2SA.

Library of Congress Cataloging-in-Publication Data

Bull, Stephen.
    20th-century arms and armor / Stephen Bull; foreword by Harry G.
Summers.
        p. cm.
    Includes bibliographic references and index.
    ISBN 0-8160-3349-8 (acid-free)
    1. Military weapons--History--20th century. 2. Armor-
-History--20th century.   I. Title
U815.B85 1995   95-12020
623.4'09'04--dc20

Facts On File books are available at special discounts when purchased in bulk
quantities for businesses, associations, institutions or sales promotions. Please call
our Special Sales Department in New York at 212/967-8800 or 800/322-8755.

You can find Facts On File on the World Wide Web
at http://www.factsonfile.com

Designed by Design Section/Butler and Tanner, Frome, Somerset, UK.

Printed and bound in Singapore.

Opening Illustrations

*(Page 1) A British airborne soldier checks his L85A1 rifle on a field exercise. This selective-fire
weapon fires the NATO 5.56mm round, and has a low-magnification optical sight as standard.
The bayonet attached to the muzzle is a tactical anachronism that lingers on with most armies.*

*(Pages 2–3) A US Navy SEAL (Sea, Air and Land) fires his M60E3 machine gun from the stand-
ing position. The M60E3 is a lighter and simpler variant of the standard 7.62mm weapon,
complete with a forward pistol grip under the barrel. It is more reliable and easier to use than
the normal M60, and is perhaps the weapon it should have been all along.*

*(Right) This trooper is from the 173rd Airborne Brigade, and is seen in action in Vietnam in
1969. He is with a jeep-mounted Browning M2HB .50in heavy machine gun, complete with belt
box clipped to the left side. The M2 was designed at the end of World War I, and looks set to
serve into the next century. Note the soldier is also wearing a protective jacket and steel helmet.*

*(Page 6) A sergeant of the US Army sometime in the mid-1980s. He is wearing full combat gear,
and is armed with the M16A1 lightweight assault rifle. The US Army is well equipped with sophisticated systems such as armored vehicles, helicopters, missiles and electronics — but in the end,
like every other army, it relies on men such as this to win a war.*

CONTENTS

FOREWORD 7

CHAPTER 1
TRENCHES AND EMPIRES 1900–1918 9

CHAPTER 2
THIRD REICH- ALLIES AND ENEMIES 1919–1945 47

CHAPTER 3
FROM KOREA TO VIETNAM 1946–1975 89

CHAPTER 4
FROM THE FALKLANDS TO THE GULF 1976–2000 119

CHAPTER 5
MEN AGAINST MACHINES 149

CHAPTER 6
LAW, CRIME AND TERROR 175

CHAPTER 7
SPORT AND LEISURE 201

INDEX 222

ACKNOWLEDGMENTS 224

BIBLIOGRAPHY 224

FOREWORD

'How quaint,' some would say, 'to come out with a volume on arms and armour just when the information age has rendered such industrial-age weaponry hopelessly anachronistic.' But Dr. Stephen Bull, Curator of the Lancashire County and Regimental museum has put together a work of interest to more than what he himself terms 'very rich or very eccentric' antiquarians.

A well-known expert on firearms and weaponry, Dr. Bull has produced a *tour d' horizon* of the weaponry of the 20th Century, of interest not only to collectors but to those concerned with the dynamics of modern war and post-Cold War conflicts. As he so correctly points out, 'the history of weaponry was not merely technological, but tactical.'

His first four chapters detail respectively the small arms and body armour of World War I, World War II, Korea and Vietnam, and the Falklands, Gulf Wars and beyond. Each chapter details the rifles, automatic rifles, pistols and revolvers, sub-machine guns, machine guns, grenades and mortars of each period, as well as the helmets and body armour. Further chapters examine anti-tank weapons, the use of weapons by criminals and terrorists, and sport and leisure weaponry.

As an infantry veteran of the Korean and Vietnam wars, it was fascinating to find how many of these 'antique' Great War weapons I had faced in battle, or, in the case of the M1911 .45cal automatic pistol, I had carried into battle myself. 'In terms of modernity,' Bull points out, 'it is noticeable that many weapons long since thought to have been past their sell-by date are still in service, or, in the mid 1990s are only just reaching the scrap yard.'

Although emphasising the importance of small arms on the battlefield, Bull also deflates some of the more extravagant claims for such weaponry. 'It is commonly supposed that it was the machine gun which led directly to the trench stalemate of 1914-1918,' he writes, 'but although it contributed in no small measure, artillery in sufficient quantity was quite capable of stopping mass attacks. Official German figures . . . suggest that 50% of their casualties in 1914-1915 were caused by artillery, and that the figure reached 85% in 1916-1918.'

Interestingly, US Army statistics show that artillery and mortar shell fragments were the primary cause of battlefield deaths in World War II and Korea, accounting for 53% and 59% respectively of those killed in action. In Vietnam, however, these losses fell to 39%, with small arms fire becoming the primary factor, accounting for 51% of those killed. One reason was the Soviet-designed AK 47 assault rifle, described by Bull as 'one of the most widespread and influential arms of the century.'

And the AK 47 and its counterparts will continue to be influential into the next century as well. 'In spite of all the technology of the industrial and post-industrial age,' noted the distinguished historian Sir Michael Howard, formerly the Regius Professor of Modern History at Oxford, in April 1994, 'does there not still lie at the core of all warfare a need to engage in the basic, primitive encounters of the agrarian age? And was not the lesson of Vietnam that, if the capacity to do so disappears, no amount of technology is going to help?'

In the pages that follow, Dr Bull has described the weaponry of those 'basic, primitive encounters.' And that is reason enough why it belongs in the libraries of those who are concerned with peace and stability in the post-Cold War world.

Colonel Harry G. Summers, Jr.
Bowie, Maryland
January 1995

Colonel Summers is a decorated combat veteran of the Korean and Vietnam wars. He is now a prolific writer, defence consultant, military lecturer and media analyst. He is currently editor of *Vietnam* magazine.

CHAPTER 1

TRENCHES AND EMPIRES 1900-1918

I N 1900 THE WORLD WAS DOMINATED by the great empires of Britain and France. Russia and Austria also possessed vast land masses, but their dominions, especially within Europe were less stable. The great unknowns at the dawn of the new century were Germany and the USA. The former, united at last in 1870, was growing quickly in industrial production and population, ready perhaps to demand its 'place in the sun'. America likewise was growing in stature, having confined the Native American to his reservations and achieved a Federal unity which completely eluded her southern neighbours. Two of the great powers were to learn lessons about modern warfare prior to 1914: the British in South Africa, and the Russians against the much underrated Japanese in Manchuria. The principal points to be assimilated were very different. From the Boers came an understanding of the importance of rapid accurate rifle fire and scouting, from the Japanese an inkling of the importance of earth works and machine guns. Dangerous rumblings and minor wars in the Balkans gave an idea of what was to come, even before the spark at Sarajevo ignited the war 'to end all wars'.

Though most experts still rated the sword, lance, and bayonet as important, the great armies relied on the bolt action rifle as their main weapon. This had existed, in embryonic form, using paper cartridges in single shot arms, since 1841. By the twentieth century the bolt action rifle was a very different species. It was still closed at the breech by a locking bolt, but this was now allied to a magazine and metallic cartridges. Working the bolt ejected any empty cartridge from the breech, pushed a new round into the chamber and cocked the rifle. A squeeze of the trigger let a striker fly forward under the power of a spring. The striker hit the base of the cartridge, setting off the primer, which instantly activated the main charge which propelled the bullet down the barrel. By working the bolt again, the next round could be fed from the magazine.

The general trend in bolt action rifles between 1880 and 1914 was towards

World War I saw the widespread use of machine guns as infantry weapons. Shown here is a group of French and British troops in co-operation. Readily distinguishable by their 'Adrian' helmets, three of the Frenchmen man a Hotchkiss 8mm, Model 1914 machine gun, on a 'Affut-Trepied' Model 1916 mount. The Hotchkiss was a light, air-cooled gun which remained in service for many years, and was used by many other armies.

smaller calibres and higher velocities. Smaller faster bullets increased range and flattened trajectory, but the theoretical increase in projectile energy was also seen as beneficial. Doubling the speed of a projectile quadruples its energy, whilst doubling its weight only doubles its energy.

The most influential type of bolt action was undoubtedly that perfected by Peter Mauser, an employee of the Wurttemberg government armoury at Oberndorf, Germany. As early as 1867 Mauser had produced a prototype which

Belgian troops manning a flimsy road barricade, 1914. The rifles are the 7.65mm, Model 1889, Mauser; which although manufactured by Fabrique Nationale, was based on a German design. Its most distinctive feature was a thin protective steel barrel jacket: this jacket was not a total success as it was expensive and could be a rust trap. The Model 1889 weighed 8.8lb (4kg) and had a five-round box magazine.

The extraordinary 7mm Mondragon semi-automatic rifle. With an action first patented by the Mexican General Mondragon in 1903, this weapon was one of the first practical self loaders. Manufactured in Switzerland it was imported to Germany during World War One, where it became known as the Model 1915. Too delicate for the trenches it saw limited use arming aircraft observers. The example illustrated is fitted with a 30-round drum magazine. (MOD Pattern Room)

linked a bolt with a 'centre fire' brass cartridge, but it was not until the adoption of the 'infanterie-Gewehr M1871' that his ideas were put into full scale production. Even then the barrel and rifling were essentially similar to the very successful French Chassepot rifle. About a million of the M1871 rifles were made, and they were followed by carbine and light infantry models using the same mechanism. In 1881 Mauser patented an under the barrel tube magazine system which led to a major modification of his service rifle from 1884 onward. Further revisions in 1888, 1896, and finally in 1898, produced a weapon using smokeless cartridges loading from an integral box magazine under the breech.

Both the 1888 and 1898 model Mauser rifles saw very widespread use well into the twentieth century, but it was the 'Gewehr 98' or G98 which was to have the most universal impact. Entering troop trials with the Prussian Guard and Spandau School of Arms in 1899, it was soon put into mass production. The first three Prussian Army Corps, the Navy and the 'Ostasiatisches Expeditionskorps' (or German Expeditionary Force in the Far East) were issued with the rifle soon after. By the outbreak of the Great War almost all of the reg-

The winners of the inter-platoon challenge cup, 6th Knutsford Battalion, Cheshire Volunteer regiment, c.1916. The rifles are US made .303in, 'P14' Enfields. The P14 was extremely accurate and was popular for sniping.

ular army was so equipped, but many reserve and Landwehr units still had older weapons. Worldwide at least 34 countries were equipped with Mauser-type rifles of various patterns, including the USA, China, Spain, Turkey, and most of South America.

In the US the Mauser-type rifle in use from 1903 was the Springfield, made both at the Rock Island Arsenal and Springfield, as well as by private contractors, and which replaced the old Norwegian designed Krag-Jorgensen, which had not performed particularly well in the Spanish-American War. The new Springfield was produced in one length for all types of troops, and took five rounds of .30in ammunition in an integral box magazine. It obtained the remarkably high muzzle velocity of 2,800ft/s (850m/s) and thus, like most Mauser types, had a good flat trajectory and excellent accuracy.

The major alternative to Mausers were Lee-type weapons. James Paris Lee was born in Scotland in 1831, but his family emigrated to Canada where he is reputed to have made his first gun at the age of 12. By the 1870s he was producing his own patents, and was working with the American firm of Remington. Subsequently his ideas were improved and adapted by several others, including William Ellis Metford and Joseph Speed, the assistant manager of the Royal Small Arms Factory at Enfield. The Lee-Metford rifle, approved for service in 1888, had all the main features of the later Lee-Enfields, including .303in ammunition and a detachable box magazine. At first, the new rifle was thought to be inferior to the Mauser. It was expensive, it had a lower muzzle velocity and the bolt-locking system was felt to be weaker. Practical use was to prove the worth of the

'Doughboys' armed with the Springfield rifle. Officially designated the 'US Magazine Rifle, Caliber .30, Model of 1903', the Springfield was designed as a replacement for the old Krag-Jorgensen. The new weapon, which was essentially Mauser inspired, originally took blunt nosed M1903 rounds, but minor modification fitted it for the new 'spitzer' 1906-type bullets. Both the rifle and the cartridge therefore became popularly known as the '.30-06'. The standard weapon had a five-round integral box magazine, but a rare 'Air Service' variant had a large 25-round box. Production of military 1903 Model Springfields ceased in 1940, when well over a million rifles had been made. Some 50 years later, the US military still retained a few examples for drill purposes.

weapon, however, as it turned out to be a fine, rugged design well able to be handled by soldiers. Improved rifling, smokeless cartridges and a shorter barrel produced the later Short Magazine Lee Enfield (SMLE) of 1904, a universal arm for cavalry, infantry and artillery.

At Mons in 1914 British troops armed with the SMLE were able to get off fifteen rounds a minute, leading some of those on the receiving end to believe they were facing machine guns. The 10-round magazine, short convenient bolt pull,

A British soldier observing through a sand bag covered trench periscope. The rifle, already cocked and with 1907 pattern 'sword' bayonet fitted, is the .303in, Short Magazine Lee Enfield, which was to serve British and Empire troops from 1904 onward. Total production of the 'Short' rifle would exceed seven million, the three major manufacturers being the Royal Ordnance Factory at Enfield, BSA, and the Indian Ishapore arsenal. Smaller numbers were also made elsewhere in Britain, and at the Australian Lithgow plant. The rifleman's pattern 1908 webbing has reserve ammunition capacity of up to 150 rounds in the pouches.

and handy length of the weapon all contributed to rapid use, but probably the main difference between British and German rates of fire was one of training. The Germans placed most value on slower deliberate accuracy with rifles, whilst by 1910 British training, instituted by Major McMahon, had moved towards rapidity of fire. In the words of the 1914 Musketry Regulations:

'Short bursts or rapid fire may surprise the enemy before he can take cover, they favour the observation of results and afford intervals of time for adjustment of sights and fire discipline . . . a well trained man should be able to fire from 2 to 15 rounds per minute without serious loss of accuracy.'

The standard French rifle of the period was the 8mm Lebel Model 86/93 that was designed in 1886, and modified in 1893. It was one of the first rifles to use smokeless cartridges and fed from an eight-round tubular magazine. It was an advanced design at the time of its introduction, but by 1914 was out of date. It was longer and heavier than the G98, with lower muzzle velocity. One notable feature of the Lebel was its long bayonet, cruciform in section, and well calculated for maximum reach and penetration, though useless for any other purpose. The basic Lebel rifle was supplemented by various carbines, including the Berthier, and although these were much handier and had more modern box magazines they all suffered from a ludicrously low ammunition capacity of three rounds. Modification of the Berthier in 1916 introduced a five-round model.

Both Russia and Italy had adopted new small calibre high velocity magazine

German infantryman c.1915 armed with the 8mm Mauser Gewehr 88. Designed as a counter to the French Lebel rifle the G88 was a standard issue from 1890 until replaced by the G98. Similar in general appearance to the Belgian service rifle, which it inspired, the G88 had an external barrel jacket, and was a clip loader with a five-round magazine. Modification in 1905 dispensed with the clip, and allowed loading from a charger. The G88 was still in use with the Landsturm and Landwehr in 1914, and even in 1918 over 100,000 remained in service.

rifles in 1891, and which were manufactured in their own state arsenals. The Russian gun was officially designated the 'Three Line Model 1891' (the line being an obsolete Russian unit of measurement) but it is often popularly known as the 'Moisin-Nagant' after its Russian and Belgian designers. It was serviceable, with a five-round magazine, and was fitted with a rather old-fashioned socket bayonet. Interestingly the point of the bayonet was chisel shaped, and apart from skewering the enemy could be used as an ad hoc screwdriver. The Italian weapon was the 'Fucile Modello 91' which was chambered for a rather weak 6.5 mm round. Again it is more commonly known after its designer as a Mannlicher, or more properly 'Mannlicher-Parravicino-Carcano'. Mannlicher designed the clip-loading system, Parravicino was the general in charge of adoption, and Carcano was a technician at the Turin arsenal instrumental in the rifle's development. The same Mannlicher clip-loading system was used in the Dutch and Romanian service rifles. The Italians also had a short light carbine, mechanically similar to the rifle, which sported a folding bayonet and had a turned down bolt handle for easy stowage on a saddle.

The story of rifles in the First World War might have stayed relatively simple were it not for the fact that production could not keep pace with the massively increasing size of armies in 1915. Many nations were therefore forced to use obsolete arms, captured weapons, and emergency imports to make up the shortfall. The Germans for example had to continue to use the old Model 1888 Mauser, and

Austro-Hungarian troops armed with the 8mm Mannlicher Steyr, Model 1888 rifle. In general use until replaced by the better known Model 1895, the Repetier Gewehr M88 was one of the last military weapons designed for a black powder cartridge. It was modified to smokeless powder in 1890, and had a five-round integral magazine.

to make use of large numbers of captured arms like the Russian Moisin-Nagant. They also began to cut corners in the making of the standard G98, and apart from bringing new factories into production introduced a 'star' marked model. This 'Stern Gewehr' was assembled from parts made in different places and its components could not be relied on for perfect interchangeability.

Britain likewise used the old pattern 'long' Lee-Enfield, especially for Territorials when supplies of new rifles ran short, and also issued a number of foreign imports. Perhaps the most important of these was the US-made P14 Enfield. This was an accurate and reliable longarm based on the Mauser system, whose only significant drawback was a five-round magazine capacity. Interestingly the design existed because the British War Office had been developing a new rifle on the eve of war, intending to adopt a very small, very powerful .276in cartridge. The war put an end to this scheme because a new cartridge and rifle would have meant total industrial dislocation, but it still proved possible to have the rifle made in .303in calibre in America. The scheme for the very small bore high velocity rifle would remain unfulfilled until after the Second World War. Probably the strangest supplementary rifle bought in by Britain to make up the shortfall in arms was the Japanese Arisaka. In British service the Arisaka was christened the 'Rifle, Magazine, .256in', but fortunately it seems to have seen little front line use, and was declared obsolete in 1921. 'British' Arisaka bayonets still turn up occasionally on the collectors' market, and are prized as something of a rarity.

When America entered the war in 1917 she likewise had difficulty finding enough Pattern 1903 Springfields; she too turned to the 'US Enfield' design, using a .30in version of it, known appropriately enough as the P17. The Canadian experience was almost the reverse, because by 1914 Canada had her own military rifle, the Ross. This had been designed by Sir Charles Ross in 1896, and was adopted between 1902 and 1910 by the Canadian Police and military. Though perfectly adequate as a sporting rifle, and indeed a very good peacetime target rifle, the Ross had not been designed for the hurly-burly of warfare in the hands of partially trained troops. In

A French infantryman using a periscope, or 'hyposcope' rifle on the Western Front c.1916. Often troops at the front or in base workshops manufactured these devices to their own specification, but in most cases the basics were similar, with either a shadow, or a 'set down' mechanism under the parapet, and the rifle on top sighted with mirrors and worked by means of levers.

The major US longarms of World War One; top to bottom are the Model 1903 Springfield rifle; the Model 1897 Winchester pump-action shot gun, with its distinctive barrel jacket and bayonet mounting for trench use; and the Model 1917, or 'US Enfield'. The Model 1917 was originally a British design, but was produced in the US as a supplementary arm in .30in calibre at the Remington, Winchester, and Eddystone facilities. The battered helmet was also a British design, adopted as US standard in June 1917.

the mud of the trenches malfunctions were common and on at least one occasion an incorrectly locked bolt flew out in the face of the firer. Simple failures to function were far more common and gave the weapon a poor reputation. Eventually the Canadian Army dropped the Ross in favour of the SMLE, although some leftovers would see service 25 years later in the hands of the British Home Guard. It also remained popular as a sniper rifle.

Special weapons for sniping came into their own as the war settled into trench stalemate. This development was not entirely new, since the earliest telescopes for use with firearms date back to at least the early nineteenth century, and military use of 'snipers' or 'sharpshooters' was familiar during the American Civil War and the Boer War. Contrary to popular opinion, many snipers operated at relatively close range, at under 200yd (183m), and a lot of the sniper's skill lay in self- concealment and in taking a swift shot at a fleeting target, rather than in hyper-accurate long range fire. Indeed one of the most successful sniper

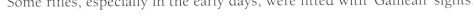

techniques consisted of crawling out of the line at night, perhaps camouflaged in a 'crawling suit' or with foliage, and then lying still after dawn. A relatively easy shot might then be taken, but the sniper would have to remain concealed until the cover of darkness returned. Many snipers operated in pairs from posts situated just in front of the main trench line, one of the two using a telescope to observe and record details of enemy movements and dispositions, the other sniping at any target of opportunity. Binoculars were sometimes used for observation but telescopes were preferred, as when rested they could give higher magnifications, and a steadier view, whilst presenting less of a target to the enemy. Many nations simply added telescopic sights to their service rifles, like the Zeiss, Goerz, and Luxor telescopes which were frequently fitted to German Mausers. Special training was also given to selected personnel, but there were other innovations.

Some rifles, especially in the early days, were fitted with 'Galilean' sights.

British troops on the Salonika front, Greece, armed with SMLE rifles. The man nearest the camera has an offset telescopic sight, and a slung leather case in which to carry the sniper scope when not in use. Offset scopes were intended to allow rapid charger reloading of the weapon without disturbing the sight, but had distinct disadvantages when the firer was aiming through narrow apertures.

These were simply two lenses mounted atop the rifle, but unlike a telescopic sight they were not joined by a tube. They had a narrow field of view, could not have cross hairs, and were easily broken, but unlike a proper telescope were cheap, easy to 'set up', and not difficult to use. Sometimes individual snipers procured their own high velocity civilian sporting rifles, such as the .333in Jeffery or the mighty .600 'Nitro Express'. 'Elephant' guns were especially useful when enemy snipers took refuge behind steel loopholes, as they were often powerful enough to penetrate this armour.

Eventually sniping would become a recognised discipline, with army 'schools' set up behind the lines. These schools taught accurate shooting and the use of telescopes but were equally useful in promulgating the tactics of concealment, loopholing, and intelligence gathering. An early German lead in sniping was later made up by the allies, especially the Canadians and Australians,

who proved particularly adept at the discipline. Britain also produced skilled snipers, especially amongst Yeomanry units like the Lovat Scouts, and the Duke of Lancaster's Own, which had detachments on the western front specifically earmarked for observation and sniping duties. The war also produced several notable theorists like Lord Cottesloe, and the well-known Major H. Hesketh-Pritchard of the First Army Sniping School.

Military pistols of the early twentieth century showed rather greater diversity than long arms. Though convenient to carry for long periods, and usually capable of operation with one hand, they tended to be prone to accidental discharge, and were inaccurate at all but very short ranges. They were usually carried as an officer's sidearm,

On the Western Front, cavalry were virtually useless on the battlefield, and were sometimes relegated to rear area security duties. These British troops are arresting a suspected spy in Belgium. The Lance Corporal has a Smith & Wesson revolver, while the man doing the searching has a Webley Mk VI.

The interior of a Royal Flying Corps Armourers' workshop. The rafters are weighed down with Webley Mark VI, .455in issue revolvers. The Mark VI, introduced in 1915, is identifiable even from this photograph by its squared off butt and six inch (152mm) barrel. On the lower level of the furthest rafter are 13 'Very' pistols for firing coloured signal flares.

A comparative selection of US Colt military semi-automatics, bottom to top; the .38in 'Military Model' 1902; the .45in 'Military Model' 1905; the ubiquitous .45in M1911A1; and a Model 1911 with a long London-made 'trench' magazine.

or as a weapon of last resort by specialist troops. The most basic division between the types of pistol, mechanically speaking, was between the semi-automatic and the revolver. The original rotating cylinder idea dated back to the sixteenth century, but was perfected by Samuel Colt in the 1830s and 1840s. The cylinder holds the rounds in axial chambers, and when the action is worked it rotates the cylinder to line up each round in turn with the hammer and the barrel. Auto-matics, or more properly semi-automatics, were a much more recent innovation, whose genesis dates to no earlier than the 1880s with the Austrian Schonberger-Laumann arms. An automatic holds the rounds in a magazine, which is usually a detachable narrow box which clips into the butt. The power of the discharge of one round is used to extract the empty case, reload the chamber from the magazine and cock the action. This energy can come from the empty case blowing back a bolt by gas pressure (blowback), or by the barrel and slide recoiling together for a short distance before unlocking and separating (recoil).

The debate between those in favour of revolvers and the supporters of automatics continues yet, and although in practical terms the twentieth century has seen the partisans of the automatic winning their argument there were advantages on both sides of the equation. Revolvers were usually very tough and reliable: accidents were fewer and a defective cartridge did not normally put the weapon out of action. Automatics, while less reliable, generally had higher magazine capacities and could be slightly swifter in use. Many armies used a mixture of both types, but revolvers were more common in British, French and Russian forces in 1914, whilst the Central Powers and America were already largely equipped with automatics. The American issue automatic, which would remain an influential design for much of the century, was the .45in Colt Model 1911. Developed from John Moses Browning's original design of 1900, this was one of the most successful handguns the world has seen. Muzzle velocity was low at about 820ft/s (250m/s), but stopping power was still high, due to the large calibre. The box magazine in the butt held only seven rounds. Some of these pistols, in .455in calibre, were also manufactured for the British Royal Navy and Royal Flying Corps during World War One. In the US forces the Model 1911 was intended to replace the Colt 'New Service' revolver but there were never enough to satisfy the demand caused by entry into the war. In 1917 it proved necessary to bring in another model of revolver, the M1917, made both by Colt, and Smith and Wesson.

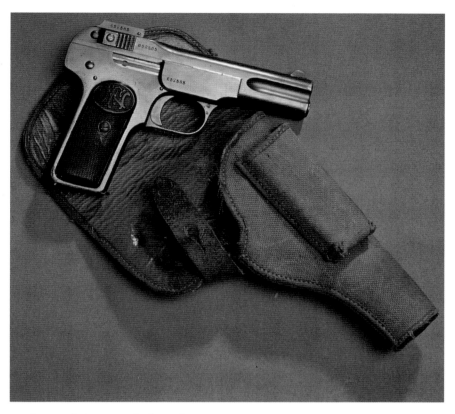

The German automatics of the period are now also widely regarded as classics. The Pattern '04' was the first 'Luger' model to be adopted, actually by the Navy, but in 1908 a new short-barrelled model was introduced for issue to the army. About 200,000 Luger types were in service by August 1914. Well balanced and easy to aim, the 'P 08' was a 9mm weapon with an eight round magazine. Very well made, it was perhaps a little too complex for the mud of the trenches. The design of the Luger actually owed a good deal to the earlier Borchardt pistol, which appears to have been Georg Luger's starting point when he set about developing a new gun in 1897. The most important technical feature of both weapons was the so-called 'toggle' mechanism; on firing the first round the barrel and

The Browning 7.65mm Model 1900 semi-automatic, manufactured by Fabrique Nationale of Belgium. Three quarters of a million of these seven-shot weapons had been made by the time production ended in 1911, and although of rather small calibre for military service, they saw use with Belgian and Russian forces.

Some of the more exotic German semi-automatic pistols illustrating their interest in long range military pistols, or pistols convertible to carbines. Top to bottom are the rare 1900 type Luger carbine with stock and forward hand grip; the 'Lange' Pistole Model 08, complete with its 32 shot 'Trommelmagazine', or drum magazine; and the influential, if not fully practical, Borchardt model of 1893. Underneath are the Lange Pistole and the Borchardt in their holsters, to which are attached their wooden shoulder stocks.

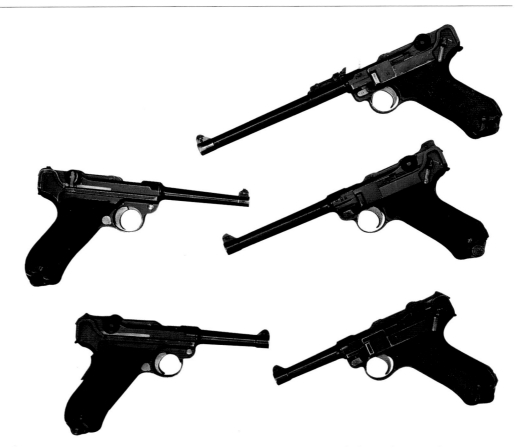

Some of the variations on the military Luger or Parabellum (described clockwise from top right); the 9mm Lange Pistole 08, here fitted with an ordinary eight-shot box magazine; the 9mm Pistole 04, which was used by the German Navy; a 9mm Pistole 08; an early 9mm model with a 'grip safety', which prevents the gun being fired unless firmly held in the hand; and a 7.65mm example, readily distinguished by its slender barrel.

The Italian 9mm Glisenti Model 1910 self loading pistol. Italy had began experiments with military self loaders by 1902, and enlisted the help of German and British arms makers as well as the Italian Glisenti company during the design stages. Having rejected a 7.65mm cartridge for service use the Italian authorities settled on a reduced power 9mm, which seemed to be the maximum practical for a not terribly robust weapon, with a mechanism which was a hybrid between a locked breech and a retarded blow back. Although production of the eight-shot Glisenti continued into the 1920s, it was effectively outclassed by the Model 1915 Beretta, and the excellent Model 1934 Beretta, both of which were adopted for army use. (MOD Pattern Room)

receiver of the pistol began to recoil, and as they did so the toggle joint was pushed upwards to unlock the breech. The spent cartridge was now ejected, whereupon a spring returned the mechanism to its original position, stripping a new round from the magazine and leaving the striker cocked as it did so. The effect of the workings was very similar to that of a Maxim machine gun, though of course the pistol required another squeeze of the trigger for the next round.

The 'P 08' replaced the 'Reichs-Commissions-Revolver' models 1879, and 1883. Massive expansion of the army meant that there were never enough new automatics to go round, so this pistol with its slow but hefty 10.66mm cartridge remained on issue to many second line units. Moreover 14 other pistol types were also taken into use, including Brownings, Dreyses, Frommers, and Bayards. Best known of these extra pistols is undoubtedly the Mauser C96, commonly known as the 'Broom Handle' after the shape of the grip. This automatic entered production in 1896, and was supplied to Italy, Turkey, and Russia. A few had even found their way to South Africa, in the hands of British officers, who had obtained them privately for service against the Boers. Formal adoption by the German military had to wait until 1915 when dire shortages led to quite widespread army use. The preferred service calibre was 9mm, rather than the original 7.63mm. An interesting feature of the C96 was its wooden holster; this can be clipped to the back of the gun, forming a shoulder stock.

The Austro-Hungarian Army was equipped with a variety of Mannlicher and Steyr automatic pistols in 1914. Indeed the Roth-Steyr 'Repetierpistole M07' was the first self loading pistol to be adopted by a major power for general service. It used an unusual 8mm short round, ten of which were held in a box magazine in the butt. A new model, the Steyr-Hahn 'Repetierpistole M12', was introduced in 1912. This had a larger 9mm round and could thus only hold eight shots in the magazine.

With certain exceptions British forces stuck pretty conservatively to large calibre revolvers all through the Great War. Most of these were various marks of the Webley which had been introduced in 1887. The decision to keep with revolvers for so long doubtless had much to do with simplicity and reliability, but the authorities also wanted something with a sufficiently massive round to lay out a charging tribesman with a single bullet. In the words of J. N. George, the outstanding features of the Webley were '. . . an utter imperviousness to damage by any form of neglect or rough usage, and the powerful man-stopping effect of its bullets at close quarters'. The .455in round was slow at only 600ft/s (183m/s) but it was not jacketed and deformed easily, transferring all its shock direct to the target. One version of the bullet, the Mark III, in use briefly between 1898 and 1900, had a hollow point and base and expanded so much that it was virtually an explosive bullet. It was rapidly withdrawn and a more conventional cartridge substituted. The gun itself went through six minor variations from inception to 1915, not counting police and target models. The most obvious difference between the types was barrel length, which was between three and six inches; details of the hammer, extractor and frame also varied.

Like many of the other powers Britain had to make up the numbers of pistols in service in the Great War with other types. These included several American varieties, most notably the Colt New Service, Colt M1911, and Smith and Wessons. The hefty Webley .455in automatic was purchased for the Navy, and is also believed to have been used, at least experimentally, by the Royal Horse Artillery. One unusual revolver to be seen with British service marks was the

The Austro-Hungarian Steyr 'Air Service' pistol. This was a fully automatic variant of the 9mm standard issue Steyr Model 1912 semi-automatic, which had an integral eight-round magazine. (MOD Pattern Room)

Webley & Scott made a series of heavy and robust automatic pistols from 1904 onwards. The .455in No. 1 saw service with the Royal Navy, while a stocked version was issued to the Royal Flying Corps. This is in fact the Model 1909, a slightly smaller and lighter variant in 9mm calibre which was used by the South African police.

Spanish Trocaola, which was a copy of a Smith and Wesson design, a quantity of which were purchased during the dark days of 1915.

The third major class of firearm in use in 1914 was the machine gun. It is commonly supposed that it was the machine gun which led directly to the trench stalemate of 1914-1918, but although it contributed in no small measure, artillery in sufficient quantity was quite capable of stopping massed attacks. Official German figures quoted by Winteringham and Blashford-Snell suggest that 50% of their casualties in 1914-1915 were caused by artillery, and that the figure reached 85% in 1916-1918. Nonetheless machine guns, especially when combined with barbed wire, were still very deadly against attacks which plodded across open ground. Exactly how useful they would be in breaking up attacks and allowing trench lines to be held with relatively few men was but ill appreciated before the war.

Prior to 1884 a number of nations had possessed volley, battery, or hand cranked multi-shot weapons like the Nordenfeldt, Gatling and Gardner guns. None of these, however, was a true 'machine' weapon which once loaded would carry on firing automatically by depressing a button or pulling a trigger. All required a motive power to be continued for the gun to keep firing. The true 'machine' action was invented by Hiram S. Maxim in 1884. Maxim had experimented with both escaping gases and recoil to unlock the breech mechanism of a gun, but it was with the forces of recoil that he had most success, combined with a breaking 'toggle' mechanism.

Most world powers had adopted Maxim-type guns by 1914, including Germany, Britain, Turkey, Russia, the United States, and most of the Balkan countries. France and Japan were to follow a different path, adopting instead the air-

A Colt Model 1895 machine gun in British service. This weapon, which saw limited action with British and Imperial forces in the Boer War, and in World War One, was actually first used in anger by the US Marine Corps at Guantanamo Bay, Cuba in 1898. It was also produced in Spain and Italy, and was made in several calibres. The gun was the brain child of J.M. Browning who managed to produce fully automatic fire by harnessing gas near the muzzle to operate a swinging arm, which worked the breech mechanism.

cooled, gas-operated Hotchkiss which had been invented in 1895. Austria also had a slightly different answer in the Schwarzlose, novel in the fact that it relied on the sheer mass of the breech block to keep the chamber closed until the round was out of the gun and the gas pressure had dropped to a safe level. The Schwarzlose was simple and strong but had a comparatively low muzzle velocity and rate of fire, managing a cyclic rate of fire of only 400 rounds per minute against the 600 of the British Vickers or American Browning.

In many ways it was the theory and the tactical applications of the machine gun which varied more from nation to nation, than the pure hardware. For example, despite recommendations to the contrary from musketry trainer McMahon, the British started the war with only two machine guns per battalion. The Germans had a machine gun company of six guns for each three battalion regiment, plus a machine gun company for each 'jäger' or light battalion. They were in the process of raising the allotment to six per battalion when war broke out. Up until 1914, many soldiers thought of the machine gun as a form of light artillery. When war started they were quickly disabused, for in fact these weapons were best employed dug in and covering a front with interlocking zones of enfilading

A tripod-mounted Austro-Hungarian Schwarzlose 8mm machine gun in action. The Schwarzlose had several interesting design peculiarities, for although water cooled and belt fed like most of its peers, it operated on the delayed blowback principle. When the first shot was fired, the mass of the breech block, aided by two levers, delayed the opening of the breech just enough to allow pressure to drop before the case was ejected and the new round chambered. Short barrel length was critical in allowing a rapid pressure decrease. The Schwarzlose fed from a 250-round belt, and the crew was often protected by a large shield.

A Russian 7.62mm Model 1910 Maxim machine gun. Though mechanically similar to their German counterpart, Russian Maxims were distinguished by a distinctive shield shape, and imaginative, though heavy, Solokov mountings. As originally planned the Solokov mount was both a wooden-wheeled carriage and a tripod, though the front legs, as seen here, were deleted after World War One.

The .303in Maxim in British service, c.1914. During the1880s and 1890s Hiram S. Maxim had travelled the world demonstrating and selling his famous machine gun, and in 1888 Maxim's company merged with Nordenfelt, with the result that many powers adopted variants of the Maxim. Early successes for the gun included Omdurman in 1898 and the Ashanti campaign of 1900. From the Maxim was developed the renowned Vickers machine gun.

German troops with a 7.92mm MG 08 machine gun, c.1914. Shown here on its 'Schlitten' or sledge mount, the water cooled MG 08 was the standard German machine gun of World War One, and over 72,000 were produced by 1918. Fed from a 250-round fabric belt it had a cyclic rate of about 450 rounds per minute. The soldier nearest to the camera wears a wide leather 'dragging strap' which was often the mark of a German machine gunner, and the firer is using the 'Zielfernrohr' or ZF12 optical sight.

Developed by Colonel Isaac Lewis of the United States Army, from an original design by Samual Maclean, the Lewis gun was rejected for American service. The weapon was then sold to Britain, where it entered service as the army's first infantry-portable light machine gun.

fire, or being carried up quickly behind an assault to give supporting fire.

The standard German machine gun, which was the scourge of allied attacks on both fronts, was the MG 08. This had been developed from the earlier 1901 model, which was itself the result of an earlier 'under licence' agreement to produce Maxim's gun. It was belt fed, water cooled, and was normally mounted on a 'Schlitten' or sledge mount. Though heavy this mounting was most versatile, since it allowed height adjustment for firing kneeling or prone, and could be carried like a stretcher, or dragged by one man in cases of necessity. Leather pads on the frame provided a rest for the firer's elbows whilst he grasped spade-type grips, between the handles of which was mounted the trigger. An optical sight was usually provided to aid long range fire. By 1915 a variety of smaller 'trench mounts' were in use for greater mobility and more flexible tactical use.

By the middle of the war it was often the case that the MG 08 teams kept their weapons in deep bunkers whilst enemy bombardments were in progress, and only brought their machine guns and attendant 250-round ammunition boxes to the surface when it was suspected that an attack was in progress. Such store was set by the abilities of this weapon that German standing orders entitled machine gunners to open fire when under attack, irrespective of the presence of any friendly troops in front of the position.

In 1915 all powers were seeking to add more machine guns to their infantry battalions, and to provide light machine guns, which were freely portable by one man, and capable of being brought into action without the encumbrances of tripod and water jacket. One of the best light machine guns introduced was the Lewis gun. Based on an idea by Samuel McLean and improved by Colonel Isaac Lewis in 1911, this was essentially an American design. It was taken up by the Belgians in 1913, but was not adopted by the US Army prior to 1916. It had distinct advantages in that it was air cooled, weighed only a little over half the weight of a Maxim, and had self-contained ammunition drums of 47 or 97 rounds. On the other hand it was not so good for sustained fire; and the Vickers (a Maxim type) was maintained in this role, where its 250-round belts and heavy tripod were more useful. By 1916 a clear tactical distinction had been drawn between the light Lewis gun, which remained on issue to the infantry battalions, and the Vickers, which was then grouped into companies of the 'Machine Gun Corps'. The Lewis was also used by various Empire forces, including the Australians who were noted as particularly skilled exponents. It was produced later in other calibres, and used by other nations including the Netherlands and Norway.

The German response to the requirement for a light machine gun was twofold. Danish Madsen guns were introduced – initially in 'Musketen' battalions – and a special lighter version of the old MG 08 was developed. This MG 08/15 was by far the most widespread German light machine gun of the Great War and a useful

The British .303 in, Vickers Mark I machine gun on the tripod Mark IVB. Adopted in November 1912, the Vickers, which was an improved version of the Maxim, would remain a standard issue for fifty years. Initially issued two per battalion, numbers were later increased, and then, in the winter of 1915-1916, the Vickers was withdrawn from infantry battalions to form machine gun companies of the Machine Gun Corps. Tactics improved from the pre-war situation where the machine gun was seen basically as a weapon of surprise and opportunity, to a position where the Vickers formed defended zones, and gave machine gun barrages at targets a mile or more distant, whilst lighter machine guns spearheaded the attack.

French troops with an 8mm St Etienne machine gun. As an attempt to improve on the original Hotchkiss the St Etienne models were no great success, their complex mechanisms being vulnerable to the mud of the trenches. Eventually the St Etienne would be removed to the colonies. This picture shows clearly both the strip feed of the St Etienne and the camouflaged helmet covers of the crew.

weapon, but it was very much a compromise. It still had a water jacket and belt feed, and the major components were identical to the standard machine gun, but it was fitted with a small bipod rather than a tripod. Not until 1918 were there experiments with an air-cooled version, and by then most platoons had two MG 08/15.

The French light machine gun was the Model 1915 or 'Chauchat', also known as the 'CSRG'. It was indeed light at 9kg, and air cooled, but hopelessly unreliable.

German assault troops c.1918. Most of the men are armed with the K98 AZ, a shortened and handier version of the standard Gewehr 98 service rifle. The light machine gun is a Danish 8mm Madsen, made by the Dansk Rekylriffel Syndikat AS, of Copenhagen. The Madsen was remarkable both in that it was arguably the first real 'light' machine gun, and in that it had a complex hinged block action. Nevertheless it was a considerable success, and was used in many countries, with production continuing until the 1950s.

The German MG 08/15 light machine gun in the trenches. The MG 08/15 was basically a simplified MG 08 on a small bipod, and, weighing 39lb (17.7kg), was a third heavier again than the Lewis gun. Nevertheless it was useful in mobile operations. The 08/15 was equipped with a sling, from which an interwar instruction manual even suggested it could be fired from the hip. The ammunition carrier standing in the trench wears a close combat knife at his belt.

This unreliability seems to have had several causes, the first of which was that rather than have a single designer it was the work of a four-man commission, and the mechanism they came up with left much to be desired. Secondly it was made at least in part from steel stampings, and whilst this technique was simple, and indeed foreshadowed some of the best mass production designs, it had not been honed enough at the time to give a trouble-free result. Lastly the magazine was an extraordinary semi-circular affair; this was because the 8mm Lebel rifle round was sharply tapered and wide rimmed, and naturally enough the authorities wished to retain standard ammunition. Surprisingly this weapon was also used by the US Army in 1917 and 1918, and by the Belgians and Greeks. It is interesting to note that a special shoulder strap and rest was patented in 1917, with the intention of allowing the Chauchat to be fired from the hip on the move. However impractical it did indicate at least some awareness of the tactical possibilities of the light machine gun in the French Army, and mirrored similar straps issued with the German MG 08, and the Lewis gun.

The ultimate in offensive personal firepower was a machine gun which was light enough for one man to carry and operate for long periods, even on the move, small enough to wield within the confines of a trench or bunker, and could easily be supplied and reloaded with large quantities of ammunition. Surprisingly only two 'sub-machine guns' saw use in the Great War. The most famous was the 'Maschinenpistole 18' or MP18 of the German Stormtroops. What made it light enough, and possible to use whilst mobile was the fact that it chambered a pistol cartridge, the standard 9mm parabellum round. It was fed from a 31-round 'snail' drum, also originally designed for pistols, and this was the only real weakness of the system. The MP18 was ideally suited to the assault tactics of 1918, being used by the troops of 'Storm' battalions in conjunction with small parties

US troops c.1918 with the French Chauchat light machine gun. The firer demonstrates the use of the bipod, pistol, and foward hand grips whilst the loader offers up a new 20 round magazine, in which the cartridges are clearly visible. The 8mm Chauchat had a very low cyclic rate of 250 rounds per minute, and was clearly something of a choice of desperation for America as it was less reliable than almost any other comparable arm of the period.

of bombers, light machine guns and riflemen, who would advance as loose strings or groups taking advantage of weaknesses in the enemy line rather than attacking in regimented waves.

The other sub-machine gun of the Great War, first produced in 1915, was the Italian Army's Vilar-Perosa. Though it could justifiably claim to have been the world's first sub-machine gun, it was used initially very much like any other light machine gun, and therefore took some time to realise its full potential. Until 1918 indeed it was double barrelled and fitted with a tripod; at that date a new single barrelled version was produced by Beretta, with a wooden stock and christened the 'Moschetto Automatica Beretta Modello 1918'. Perhaps more than any other

This Vickers team are making good use of cover in a wrecked building at Poellecapelle. The picture clearly shows the clouds of steam issued by the water-cooled gun once it had heated up, and which often negated the best attempts at camouflage and concealment.

weapon the Vilar-Perosa underlines just how much of the history of weaponry is not merely technological, but tactical.

It is interesting to relate that although the United States did not issue a sub-machine gun to her forces at this time, two other important innovations applicable to close assault tactics were investigated. The first was the use of shotguns as 'trench brooms': since the shotgun has great power at short range, and a degree of dispersal in its shot, it was ideal for rapid 'point and shoot' work in the confines of the trench. A relatively small number of Winchester pump-action Model 1897 weapons were issued for the purpose, and a 'shot shell' pouch, M1918, was made so that the user could conveniently carry 28 of the 12-bore cartridges. Arguably the Model 1897 was the progenitor of all subsequent 'combat shotguns' and their associated tactics. The second departure was perhaps even more significant, for the M1918 'Pedersen Device' was intended to convert the standard M1903 Springfield rifle to fully automatic fire for close range targets. The complete kit included the device itself which replaced the old rifle bolt, a special tool, and a pouch containing magazines for the short .30in cartridges. It is thought that 65,000 were made, but as far as is known they did not get to

The German Bergmann 9 mm MP18 sub-machine gun. Arguably one of the most influential weapons of modern times, the Hugo Schmeisser-designed MP 18 was a blowback operated weapon, with a cyclic rate of about 400 rounds per minute. Seen from above one can readily identify the Tatarek and Von Benko 32-round 'snail' or drum magazine on one side and the cocking handle on the other. Despite early problems with this magazine (later replaced with a straight box) the concept was an outstanding technical and tactical success. Its usefulness was one of the factors which led a subsequent generation of allied troops to refer to German SMGs indiscriminately as 'Schmeissers', whoever designed them. (MOD Pattern Room) see combat use. Nonetheless the Pedersen did point the way, both in terms of 'modular' weapons which could be converted from one role to another, and as being a small step in the direction of the assault rifle.

If trench warfare encouraged the invention of the sub-machine gun and the automatic rifle, it gave a completely new lease of life to the grenade. By 1900 efficient rifles and the tactics of the period had made grenades obsolete for all but sieges and town fighting. The Russo-Japanese War of 1904-1905 suddenly showed the potential of grenades in a situation where the enemy was close by, but protected, so he thought, by invisibility in trenches or behind a wall of earth. Lacking sufficient issue grenades the Japanese in particular were soon converting

old shell cases and otherwise improvising bombs. The Germans learnt this lesson better than most, introducing in 1913 a small disc-like grenade which exploded on impact, and a larger 'ball' grenade with a segmented outer case, and a time fuse which was ignited by a pull on a wire. The French similarly used a ball grenade, though with a smooth outer shell, which again was lit by a friction pull.

At the outbreak of war in 1914 Britain had only one type of grenade, and this was on issue to engineers only. It was an elaborate and expensive construction known as the 'Grenade No. 1', with a brass head, wooden handle, and a streamer to make it land nose first. By Christmas it was realised that the small numbers of grenades available were totally inadequate for the task in hand. All armies were clamouring for huge supplies, and in the meantime were reduced to such expedients as filling jam tins with explosives, tying gun cotton to wooden handles, and employing troops behind the front to manufacture crude emergency patterns of cast iron and sheet steel. This multitude of weapons were of variable quality and reliability: one of the worst was the aptly numbered British '13', or 'Pitcher' grenade, which, with its slightly heavier brother 'No. 14', had soon gained an

Italian troops with a 9mm double-barreled Vilar Perosa Model 1915 machine gun. As is seen here the Vilar Perosa was used initially like any other machine gun, despite its short range, and was sometimes fitted with a shield. Only later was it deployed more flexibly in a role approximating to that of a sub-machine gun. It was made both by Fiat in Italy, and also by General Electric in Canada. Stripped of the shield the gun weighed 6.5 kg, and was usually equipped with two 25-round magazines. The cyclic rate of fire was extremely high, and so the Vilar Perosa was best fired in very short bursts. Notice the large spares box in this view.

unenviable reputation. Even an official history went so far to admit that accidents with them were so numerous that they won for bombers the name of 'The Suicide Club'. One such accident with a Pitcher grenade was reported by Brigadier General H. C. Lowther in August 1915:

'. . . about 3pm Corporal Holden of the 1st Battalion Coldstream Guards, who was the only man in the Battalion trained in throwing the Pitcher bomb threw three of these bombs. Two failed to explode. The caps of all these bombs have been difficult to remove. Corporal Holden then took up a fourth bomb and the cap of this was even stiffer than the remainder had been. Just as he succeeded in getting the cap off and the string came away, the bomb exploded in his hand killing him outright.'

It was only during the course of 1915 that the problems of design and mass production were slowly sorted out. Even then British troops fought the battle of Loos largely with second-rate bombs like the 'No. 15' ball grenade; not as dangerous as the '13', but prone to damp and often failing to explode. Probably the most important grenade to be introduced in 1915 was the German 'Stielhandgrenate', or stick hand grenade, which was to become a hallmark of the German soldier over the next 30 years. Though there was a 'percussion' or explode on impact model, most were time-fused grenades lit by pulling a cord which ran through the wooden handle of the bomb. It was a highly suitable weapon for offensive use because its thin metal casing produced a rather localised blast effect rather than a mass of longer range fragments, which in the open would have been as damaging to the thrower as to the receiver. Early stick hand grenades can be distinguished by their rounded handle ends and visible cord, later models had the cord recessed in the handle end and concealed under a metal screw cap.

The 'Mills' bomb, introduced to the British Army in 1915 as the 'No. 5' was a very different device, for its cast iron body burst into hundreds of lethal fragments, and the thrower was therefore well advised to lie down or put his head beneath a parapet. Nonetheless the Mills bomb, which had been developed by Briton William Mills from an original Belgian idea, was probably the most reliable and popular bomb of the war. When ready to throw, the user pulled out a pin, but the striker was not actually initiated until a long spring-loaded lever was released. When the striker came down the time fuse was lit, and the fuse in its turn set off a detonator which exploded the main charge. By the end of the war it had become standard practice for all British troops to be issued with two Mills bombs when there was likelihood of action, in addition to the bomb 'waistcoats' and

A sentry of 127th German Infantry Regiment uses a periscope at Hill 60, Ypres, 1916. The stick grenade he holds is properly described as the Stielhandgranate BZ: the stencilled legend on its cylinder, 'Vor Gebrauch Sprengkapsel Einsetzen', may be translated as 'Before use insert the detonator'. To activate the bomb the grenadier gave a smart tug on a cord which ran through the wooden handle; he usually then had five and a half seconds to throw it before the explosion. The steel helmet worn here is the Model 1916.

specialised carriers containing larger numbers of grenades which were issued to nominated 'bombers'. Britain also supplied Mills bombs to her allies, especially the Belgians and Russians.

Grenades were also developed to be projected from rifles. The idea was probably first proposed by Frederick Marten Hale of Bromley in Kent before the war, but his efforts to sell his bizarre weapon fell on stony ground, except, ironically with some South American countries and the German War Ministry. Therefore whilst Britain started the war with only a couple of boxes of rifle bombs for experimental purposes the Germans were already mass producing a version of their own known as the 'Model 1913'. For best results the rifle was placed in a stand and the rifle fired by means of a lanyard. Britain belatedly began to make her own variations on the Hale grenade, but best success came when the trusty Mills bomb was modified for discharge from a rifle, either with a rod, or a cup discharger. These modifications were known respectively as the 'No. 23' and 'No. 36' both of which could also be hand thrown. The commonality of pattern so far as grenade bodies and mechanisms were concerned also helped to simplify production and training.

During 1916 and 1917 the French and Germans both developed purpose designed, cup discharged, rifle grenades. These were respectively the 'VB' and the 'Werfgranate M1917', and both were remarkable in that they used a bulleted round rather than a blank cartridge to project them. A channel ran through the centre of the bomb, and as the bullet passed through, the explosive power of the

Austro-Hungarian 'storm' or assault troops, c.1917. The soldiers' main weapon, slung across their backs, is the 'Stutzen' or short version of the Steyr Model 1895 service rifle, an 8mm weapon with a five-round magazine. Alongside the bayonet of the lead man is worn a 'Nahrkampfmesser' or close combat knife. The Austro-Hungarian high explosive grenade shown here differs from its German counterpart in having a proportionately longer and narrower head; these assault troops keep supplies in bags hung around the neck.

German rifle grenadiers prepare to fire 1914 Pattern rifle grenades from their G98 service rifles. The 1914 rifle bomb was a 'percussion', or explode on impact model weighing about 2lbs (1kg). It was loaded by sliding the long rod into the rifle barrel and feeding a blank cartridge into the breech of the gun. Squeezing the trigger fired the blank cartridge and launched the projectile. Accuracy when hand held was low, and recoil forces were considerable, so a launching stand was often used. By the middle of the war the rifle grenade had graduated from mere harrassment value to a useful assault weapon.

A German assault detachment armed with the Kleif Model 1916 flamethrower. In this type the back pack cylinder was divided internally into a sphere of pressurised gas, and a reservoir for the 4.8gal (22 litres) of incendiary liquid. Turning on the pressure by means of a stop cock, and operating the trigger, produced short range 'squirts' of flame.

cartridge was trapped to throw the bomb from the discharger. The passage of the bullet also ignited the grenade fuse. There were also a few grenades which were capable of spreading gas, and there were also special bombs developed for signalling, for throwing from catapults and for practice purposes.

Another trench warfare weapon of dreadful novelty was the flamethrower. The most expert exponents were the Germans, who first used them at Malancourt in February 1915. Although 'Greek fire' and flame weapons go back to the dawn of history, the Germans may also claim the invention of the modern military flamethrower, following the 1901 patent of Berliner Richard Fiedler. His first efforts were clumsy and intended primarily for fortress use, but by 1910 he had registered a new model with a back pack reservoir 'producing a long jet of flame, for military purposes'. In the event three main types were used during the war, the 'Fiedler Model 1912', the 'Kleif Model 1916', and the 'Wix Model 1917'. The usual application was to allot two-man flamethrower teams to flamethrower sections which were assigned in turn to assault units. One man held the projector pipe and the other carried the reservoir, and it could even be used on the move. It was not impossible for one man to use the whole kit, and subsequent developments often assumed one man use, despite the factors of weight and fatigue. Flamethrowers were always at their best in close assault, street fighting, or trench warfare, since in these circumstances their relatively short range was not a significant disadvantage, and the elements of surprise and terror were best preserved.

As far as armour was concerned a few of Europe's cavalrymen had gone to war in 1914 with breast plates and helmets, but these were largely ornamental items incapable of stopping a bullet or much shrapnel. Yet from the time that men took to the trenches it was apparent that certain types of injury were causing a disproportionately high percentage of casualties. Prominent amongst these were wounds occasioned by comparatively low velocity fragments of shells and grenades, and bullet wounds to head and shoulders. As early as spring 1915 French troops were putting steel skull caps under their helmets, and the German Army Group Gaede, in the Voges sector, was making and issuing its own metal and leather helmet with a long nose guard. An official issue universal German steel helmet was proposed by Doctor August Bier in August 1915. After much testing the result was the M1916 steel helmet, the first 30,000 of which were issued at the end of January that year. The new German headgear was a deep stamping, with a brow visor and skirt for the neck, available in six sizes, and padded internally with a band and three cushions. The most novel features were the large lugs on either temple, which were hollow to provide ventilation, and also enabled a heavy brow plate or 'stirnpanzer' to be hung on the helmet. The brow plate proved somewhat heavy, as it was able to resist a direct hit from a rifle bullet from fifty metres and upward, but the steel helmet itself was a great success and the old leather 'pickelhaube' or spiked helmet was discontinued in 1917.

Britain began to produce very tough but shallow looking steel helmets at about the same time, and furthermore the US used British type helmets on entry into the war. The 'Brody' or 'shrapnel' helmet was a one piece shell of manganese steel, with a relatively large brim, not unlike an upturned soup plate. France soon adopted a helmet known as the 'Casqué Adrian Modele 1915', a stylish multi-piece construction, painted blue and with a badge to the front which distinguished infantry, artillery, chasseurs, engineers and colonial troops. This helmet was not as strong as either the German or British examples, but a piece of thin corrugated metal inside, together with a leather band, provided some impact absorption. The Belgians, Russians, Serbs and Italians all adopted helmets in the French style, although often with their own national badges, and other differences of detail. The Portuguese who joined in the war on the allied side had distinctively different head protection, having a helmet similar in general outline to the British and American, but with a corrugated surface. The helmets of all nationalities were often provided with camouflaged covers, sometimes officially issued, or otherwise cut from pieces of sandbag.

Generally all these helmets were incapable of withstanding direct hits from rifle bullets, but nonetheless they saved many lives and injuries because many of the strikes were from low velocity fragments of munitions or debris thrown around.

This picture purports to be of British troops examining a German prisoner for intelligence information, although it has rather a staged look about it. It does show, however, one of the few uses for the bayonet, ie. intimidating a prisoner, and also offers a good comparison of the shape and pattern of the respective nation's steel helmets.

British designers tacitly admitted this in calling their steel hat a 'shrapnel' helmet, and shaping it so as to give maximum protection from explosions above, or to a man lying prone with his head down in the direction of blast. Experiment continued throughout the war, not only with the intention of increasing protection, but of producing helmets which would aid national recognition without spoiling camouflage effects. There were also many attempts to produce practical eye protection, which would allow the wearer to see clearly, and which would shield the eye, but not break up if hit and cause further damage. Amongst American experiments were a 'No 6' tilting dome helmet, the whole of which was pushed forward and down when under fire to cover the face, and the 'No. 8' which was equipped with a hinged visor, very similar to that of a fifteenth century knight. Although tank crews were widely issued with face masks against 'bullet splash' coming in at vision ports, and the Belgians and Italians made limited issue of full face protection for trench assault, these masks were not a great success.

Body armour also became quite widespread during the Great War. From May 1917 the German Army issued almost half a million steel breast plates, which hooked over the shoulders and had three smaller plates hanging below on

webbing straps to protect the lower abdomen. Made in two sizes the 'Sappenpanzer' or trench armour weighed over 22lb (10kg), and was not therefore suitable for the assault. It was often worn by sentries or machine gunners, who might require to be exposed but who needed only limited mobility. The French General Adrian similarly devised a breast and an abdominal plate, but it seems that only the latter was issued.

Perhaps the most varied selection of official and commercial armours was worn by the British. Some, like the 'Chemico Body Shield' were only of fabrics, others used one or more metal plates. One of the earliest multi-plate designs was the 'Dayfield Body Shield', over 20,000 of which were in use by 1917. Amongst the single plate models were the 'Best Body Shield', 'Portobank' and 'Star'. One of the most effective was the government issued 'EOB' model, which could resist most pistol bullets and rifles at longer ranges. Some of the British armours resembled the medieval 'brigandine', having a multitude of small plates sewn into or onto a waistcoat. These were light, but they tended to be relatively useless against all but the slowest missiles.

Trench mortars and catapults were of considerable importance in trench warfare, though only the lightest varieties were freely man portable. The main value of these weapons was their high angle of trajectory, which allowed fire out of one trench or weapons pit into another at medium ranges. They thus helped to fill a gap between the hand-thrown grenade and the minimum practical range for true artillery. Some catapults like the British 'Gamage' and 'West

An Austro-Hungarian infantryman using a dual purpose portable trench shield and 'sniper's loop', c.1916. With long periods of virtually static warfare portable shields as well as body armour were viewed as practical propositions by all nationalities, and steel loop holes were issued in large numbers.

The same shield in the deployed position. These devices were best used well camouflaged by snipers since they tended to attract enemy fire once identified. Sniper's loops were notoriously vulnerable to high velocity big game rifles and to armour piercing ammunition. The rifle shown is the 8mm, five shot, straight pull bolt, Steyr Repetier-Gewehr Model 1895, an Austrian general issue weapon which was also used by Bulgaria.

This armour was sometimes worn by French assault sappers in the early years of the century. Two large steel plates are attached to the front and rear of a leather jerkin, and there are leather shoulder straps to hold them in place. The deep helmet has a sloping rim to provide neck and face protection.

A German sentry in full trench armour, c.1918. Weighing about 22lb (10kg) the 'Infanterie-Panzer', or infantry armour, came in two sizes and was composed of four plates. It is thought that 500,000 sets were made during the war, and although too heavy for the assault proved popular with machine gunners and sentries. The steel helmet is fitted with the rather less frequently encountered 'Stirnpanzer' or brow plate, which fits over the distinctive side lugs of the helmet. The rifle is the general issue G98 Mauser.

British experimental helmet and splinter goggles worn with a 'brigandine' or scale-style defence under the service dress. The armour consists of many small metal plates linked by rings on a fabric backing, and covers from neck to crotch. Although defences of this type were reasonably common, and were revived later in the century to resist knife attack, they are considerably less resistant to missiles than solid plates.

The same helmet also seen a with a pair of splinter goggles. The goggles are made of ballistic steel with very narrow vision slits, and have a median hinge to allow different fittings. Eye injuries were especially dangerous in the trenches, but eye defences never became a general issue because of problems with vision and the difficulty of making goggles strong, light, and yet not liable to break up and make wounds worse.

Spring Gun' had the advantage of being quiet and giving little warning of the arrival of the bomb. Both were light enough to be carried around by their crew, the West being borne like a stretcher by means of metal bars which extended from the base. An interesting French variation on the theme was the Brandt Pneumatic mortar (Models 1915 and 1916). Working on compressed air, this was able to shoot anything up to 18 rounds per minute. A four-man team was capable of carrying the gun, tripod and box of accessories and ammunition.

Probably the most practical of the species were the light trench mortars like the British 'Stokes'. This was a simple tube into which the bomb was dropped tail first. A striker activated a cartridge in the tail of the bomb and this threw it several hundred yards to explode in the enemy lines. It was also reasonably manoeuvrable being broken down into loads for carriage by the crew. Like the allies the Germans had numerous variations on the theme, including, at the lighter end of the scale the 'Granatenwerfer' models 1915 and 1916, which threw a finned bomb from a spigot mounting on a base plate, and several different light 'Minenwerfer' or bomb throwers. The best known of these were the short bar-relled 91mm 'Lanz' mortar, and the 76mm 'Leichte Minenwerfer (neuer art)', of 1916. This last was mounted on a base plate and capable of firing high explosive, gas and message carrying shells to a range of 1,420ft (1,300m). Although it

One of the many patterns of trench mortar in action with the French army, c.1916. This muzzle loading projector features a seat on the frame for the firer, who activates the mechanism by means of a rifle style trigger. Trench mortars provided high angle, intermediate range fire, probing beyond the distances possible with grenades.

A British 3-inch Stokes mortar being loaded. Entering production in late 1915, and dogged by faulty ammunition in early 1916, the Stokes got off to a poor start, but eventually proved its worth to become the British Army's standard light mortar. Soon every infantry brigade had its own Light Trench Mortar battery and Stokes bombs were being expended at a rate of about 50,000 a week. The Stokes was one of the few models of mortar which was light enough to carry foward over broken ground, and later became a model for most subsequent infantry mortars.

Austro-Hungarian troops with a 91mm 'Lanz' type smoothbore trench mortar, or 'Minenwerfer'. Also used by the Germans the Lanz was a useful addition to the trench arsenal, but due to the introduction of newer models had become virtually obsolete by the end of 1916.

weighed 313lb (142kg) ready to fire, it had at least pretensions of portability, being mounted on a pair of wheels for transport, and dragged with straps by the crew.

No look at First World War arms and armour should exclude the fearsome arms of close combat, the bayonet, club, and knife. All nationalities possessed bayonets for their service rifles, and in most countries considerable store was set by the morale effect of 'cold steel' on the enemy. Most bayonets were long for maximum reach in bayonet fighting which was an established part of drill, and some, like the broadbladed German 'Seitengewehr 98/05' or 'butcher bayonet' may have been deliberately calculated to strike fear into the heart of the enemy. One type of bayonet, which seems in hindsight to have been something of a miscalculation, was the saw-backed type. In the nineteenth century swords with saw-backs had been issued to pioneers with the intention of giving them a dual purpose arm, and the Germans continued this tradition in the new century with similar bayonets. Allied propaganda portrayed these saw-backs as calculated purposefully to cause the most appalling injury, and those captured with them were sometimes on the receiving end of rough treatment as a result. Many saw-backs therefore had the offending teeth ground off to avoid the charges of atrocity.

In the event bayonets of any sort proved pretty ineffectual and only the tiniest percentage of wounds were caused by them. In one table of statistics submitted by the British medical authorities in France in January 1916, and detailing well in excess of a thousand individuals, bayonets failed to appear as a cause at all, whilst artillery, small arms bullets, and grenades, in that order, appear to have accounted for most, if not all, casualties. Winteringham and Blashford-Snell have it that in the Russo-Japanese war of 1904-1905 the total percentage of wounds by edged weapons was 2.5%,

French Chasseur Alpin, or mountain rifleman, armed with his standard 8mm Fusil d'Infanterie Modèle 86/93', commonly known as the 'Lebel' rifle. He has the distinctive long cruciform bayonet fitted, which would give him a long reach in hand-to-hand combat. In practice, the bayonet was used very rarely for its intended purpose, and few casualties were caused by it.

whilst in 1914-1918 a mere 1.02% of British casualties were recorded as 'accidents and miscellaneous causes', and in this fraction lurked the few who had been bayoneted.

Where bayonets, or at least cut down bayonets and edged weapons might have a role, was in trench raiding. At night, in enemy lines, silence was critical, and a blade might prove useful to cower an opponent into submission, even if not actually used to silence him. At the top end of the scale in terms of overt ferocity was the Gurkha 'Kukri', the traditional heavy down-turned knife of Nepal, which

Gurkha troops in British service press home an attack during a training exercise. As well as fixed bayonets, they are carrying the famed curved knife or 'Kukri', which has become the trademark of these soldiers from Nepal.

had been used by troops in British service since the early nineteenth century. As one officer of the Royal Fusiliers remembered:

'One of my first recollections is a raid at Neuve Chapelle. I was supporting the attack with my machine guns and I'll never forget seeing a Gurkha coming across in front from the German lines, holding something in his hands – and when I looked it was the face of a German! It wasn't his neck or head, just the face cut vertically down . . . '

Other nationalities could improvise almost as vicious weapons from the detritus of the battlefield. A cut-down rifle bayonet could make a passable dagger, while the French Lebel bayonet made a good stiletto. Picket posts for securing barbed wire could similarly be reshaped into a blade, these being popularly known as 'Nails' or 'French Nails'. Entrenching tools of all types could have an edge put on them for use in close combat.

Before long many companies were making specialised trench knives, either for official issue, or for private purchase by the troops. The typical German

'Nahrkampfmesser' or trench dagger had a blade of about 6in (150mm) and a wooden or horn handle, rough in texture to provide a good grip, or cut with diagonal grooves. French and Belgian companies often made better examples of the improvised stiletto, but there was also a French pattern called 'Le Vengeur' with a slightly broader blade, intended, so it was said, to help avenge the defeats of 1870.

The best known British manufacturer of trench knives was Robbins of Dudley, which produced stilettos, 'knuckle knives', and 'push daggers'. Push daggers had the blade set at right angles to the hilt so that the blow was administered with either a pushing or punching motion; 'knuckle knives' incorporated a knuckle duster, or heavy knuckle guard, allowing the user to punch or slash as well as stab. Robbins produced one dagger with a guard just long enough to accommodate three fingers, the little finger being curled around the pommel. John Watts of Sheffield and Charles Clements of London were similarly known as producers of knuckle knives. The US forces also appear to have been particularly keen on knuckle knives, producing an official pattern M1917 knife with a stiletto blade. Right at the end of the war, on 17 October 1918, Major James McNary of the supply section of the US Ordnance patented a version of the knuckle knife with individual finger stalls, and a hilt 'readily detachable from the blade'. Apart from a dagger blade the McNary knife also boasted studs over the knuckle bar and a sharply pointed pommel, thus maximising the different ways it could be wielded.

Two other bladed oddities of trench warfare are also worthy of note, though they saw relatively little use. The most spectacular of these was the 'Welch knife' or 'Joubert' trench dagger. This was patented by F. Joubert in August 1916, and was more like a leaf-shaped Roman 'Gladius' than a handy knife. It was equipped with a folding guard, a cord to run around the wrist, and a pommel which was calculated to be 'a chisel-like weapon of offence'. Though it is probable that a few were bought privately most were concentrated in the hands of a single battalion of the Royal Welch Fusiliers, who had them purchased for them by their commanding officer Lord Howard de Walden. It is possible, though not proven, that the Welch knife was a model for the 'Smatchet' in World War Two. Just as extraordinary was the 'Pritchard', or 'Greener-Pritchard' bayonet. Patented in November 1916 by Lieutenant Arthur Pritchard of the Royal Berkshire Regiment, and made by Greener of Birmingham, this device was a dagger which attached to a Webley revolver, enabling the user to stab or shoot at will. Only a few hundred appear to have been made during the war, but a good number have been made up since, making this rare item problematic for the collector.

Clubs in their many and varied forms were also in use in the trenches, and were especially suited to raiding. Perhaps the most common variety was a wooden handle, shaped like a baseball bat, which had been studded with boot nails, or spikes, or weighted with a lead insert. Examples of this general type have been documented from Austria, Britain, Germany, Italy, and elsewhere: additionally a good number of German examples have been encountered which incorporate a heavy spring and a nut-like endpiece, intended, it is supposed, to make maximum advantage of the flexible 'flail' properties of the spring. A design apparently popular with the French was a simple stick, around which had been wrapped a small bar of lead, to make a thin but very heavy 'knobkerrie'. A number of examples of this type are displayed in the Cloth Hall, at Ypres, Belgium. There were also many extemporised expedients, amongst them pieces of piping, coshes, weighted sandbags and, if one source is to be believed, hanging straps purloined from London Underground trains.

CHAPTER 2

THIRD REICH-ALLIES AND ENEMIES 1919-1945

THE CENTRAL POWERS COLLAPSED IN 1918, not so much because the German Army had been totally defeated on the battlefield but because blockade had starved her factories of materials and her people of food. Even so it is doubtful, with the disintegration of Austria-Hungary and mutinies in progress, whether fighting could have continued for much longer as the allied breakthrough began. The 'Great War' brought several wars in its wake; the attempt of the western powers to defeat the Russian Revolution in 1919, the Russian Civil War, a Polish war of liberation, and a number of lesser conflicts. Nevertheless mass demobilisation was quick, many of the lessons of trench warfare, and the open war of 1918, were unlearned, and the rate of arms development slowed. British thoughts turned back to the Empire and the Northwest Frontier, and the Americans were amongst the first out of Europe. Pace of development in small arms would continue to be slow until the second half of the 1930s when Hitler's reoccupation of the Rhineland, annexation of Austria, and the Munich crisis of 1938 would steadily convince even the appeasers that an army equipped with modern weapons was a necessity rather than a luxury. Certain ideas, tactical as much as mechanical, would get early trials in the Spanish Civil War, Manchuria, and Abyssinia. Even then a good number of arms which had seen service in 1914-1918 would emerge again in 1939, and many armies would seem ill prepared for the holocaust to come.

The greatest advances between the wars were made in the area of light automatic and semi-automatic weapons, especially sub-machine guns, support weapons, and automatic rifles. Most famous was the Thompson sub-machine gun, the original 'Tommy gun' or 'Chicago Piano'. Conceived in 1919, and first sold to the public in 1921, it really had no competition. Named after General John

German soldiers with an MG 34 in North Africa. The MG 34 was the first true general purpose machine gun, designed to be used in light and sustained fire roles. This example is mounted on the sustained fire tripod, although its bipod is folded under the barrel.

Spanish Civil War militia armed with a motley collection of weapons including shotguns, a Smith and Wesson type revolver, and a 7mm Model 1916 'Short' Mauser rifle. Made in large numbers during the Civil War the Model 1916 rifle had a five-round magazine and weighed 8.4lb (3.8kg). Many would later be converted to 7.62mm NATO ammunition.

US Marines advancing c.1944 with, left, the M1A1 Thompson sub-machine gun, and right, the Browning Automatic Rifle. It is interesting that when the designers of the Thompson began their work during World War One they set out to produce an automatic rifle using full size cartridges. Extraction and feed were however found to be more practical with a cartridge with a small surface area, and so the 'Tommy gun' was born. The M1A1 was a simplified version produced during World War Two, and was most obviously different in that it lacked the barrel cooling fins of the original and had a plain fore end. The internal mechanism was also simplified.

T. Thompson it was beautifully engineered, steady and reliable. It fired the powerful American .45in pistol cartridge, and at 10.75lb (4.9kg), was a heavy, solid piece. One unusual design feature which most later sub-machine guns lacked was a delay device which held the bolt closed for a fraction of a second whilst the cartridge was fired. Later experimentation found that removing the component which produced the delay, the so called 'H' piece, had no ill effects but increased the rate of fire. In its early years the Thompson's reputation was based on its viability as a police weapon, and its terrifying use in the hands of organised criminals. US forces first adopted it in 1928 when it was used by the Marines in Nicaragua, and by the Coast Guard in their work against illegally imported liquor. The model first taken up by the military was the M1928A1, capable of mounting the familiar 50-shot drum, or 20- or 30-round box magazines.

Another automatic weapon which was already in service with US forces was the .30in 'Browning Automatic Rifle' or 'BAR', first issues of which had actually been made just before the end of the Great War. It had first been intended as a direct support weapon, to be carried by attacking troops across 'No Man's Land'. It first saw action on 12 September 1918 in the hands of the US 79th Infantry Division, and was very well received. By the end of the war, two months later, 50,000 had been made. This was a very advanced design for the time, even though it was too heavy for a rifle but too light to make a good machine gun. The BAR was a milestone in weapons development, pointing the way forward, both to the assault rifle, and to light machine guns like the Bren. One was issued per squad in World War Two, and when taken together with the Garand rifle and various sub-machine guns it meant that US infantry were able to deploy heavier firepower than most sub-units of other nations.

Several slightly varying models of BAR were produced; the M1918, M1918A1 and M1922 were capable of selective fire, whilst the M1918A2 was automatic only but with slow and fast rates of fire. The usual magazine for all these models was a 20-round box, and the best shooting was obtained prone, using the bipod with which all but the earliest models were fitted. The weapon was made in America by Colt, Winchester, and Marlin and also in Belgium. The BAR would eventually see very widespread use with other countries, and in 1940 it found its way into the hands of the British Home Guard. Their training manual summed it up in the following terms:

'The chief characteristic of this weapon is its high rate of fire and accuracy when fired as a single shot weapon. The volume of fire can be considerably increased by firing in bursts, but the accuracy of the fire will suffer.'

The Garand or M1 rifle was perhaps the most important weapon developed between the wars by any nation, though certainly not the most glamorous. John Cantius Garand was born in January 1888 in Quebec, Canada, but when his mother died the family moved to Connecticut. He worked in several engineering concerns and developed a liking for shooting before arriving in New York, where

American soldiers with a civilian in the Pacific Theatre. They are armed with the M1 Garand, the first mass issue, military semi-automatic longarm. The Garand had an eight-shot magazine loaded by a clip, and fired the same .30-06 cartridge as the earlier M1903 Springfield. Notice the use of fixed M1 bayonets with ten inch (254mm) blades, which succeeded the old 1905 type long bayonet.

he experimented with machine gun designs, and was eventually hired to work at Springfield Armory. Here, after many prototypes, was designed the eponymously named rifle. The gun itself was the first semi-automatic rifle to be taken as standard by the forces of a major power. It was adopted by the US in 1936, and by 1941 when America entered the war it equipped most of the regular army. The Garand itself had an eight-round magazine and was loaded with a clip. The rifle could not be reloaded until all the shots were fired and the empty clip dropped out. This was a minor drawback, but the Garand was powerful and accurate and could lay down impressive fire once a squad was in action.

The US Garand, top; and the M1 Carbine. The semi-automatic Garand was highly influential in design terms, and was arguably well ahead of competing Soviet models before World War Two. The M1 carbine, with its short Winchester .30in cartridge, proved its worth as an alternative to the pistol in the hands of rear echelon troops. An alternative model with folding skeleton stock was also issued.

Garands were made during World War Two by the Springfield Armory and Winchester, joined later by Harrington and Richardson, and also by the International Harvester Corporation. Production during the war is believed to have exceeded three million, with another million or so produced after 1945. Variations included sniper rifles and many different experimental modifications. A copy of the Garand, the BM-59, was produced in Italy after the war and also supplied to Denmark and Indonesia. The Garand was fitted with several slightly different models of grenade launcher; when the first, or M7 model, was fitted to the Garand the rifle was only capable of single shot operation, a defect which was rectified on later types.

Britain's most significant interwar production was the Bren gun. The development team was looking for something that was a little lighter and more durable than the Lewis and in the 1930s began comparative trials with several different weapons. Front runners amongst these were the Vickers-Berthier, and the Browning. A rank outsider was a Czechoslovak gun, the ZB 26, first noticed by

The Czechoslovak ZB 26 7.92mm light machine gun. Based on an interwar design by Vaclav Holek and produced by the Ceskoslovenska Zbrojovka company at Brno, the ZB 26, and its successors the ZB 27 and ZB 30, were well made and ultimately most influential weapons. The ZB 26 shown here is tripod-mounted for sustained fire, although it was often seen on a bipod for squad use. It has a detachable 20-round box magazine, is gas operated, and is capable of a cyclic rate of around 500 rounds per minute. As well as providing inspiration for the British Bren, ZB light machine guns were taken into service by German forces, especially the Waffen SS. Copies were also made in China, Iran, and Rumania.

the military attaché in Prague. The Czech gun passed all tests with ease, so a new prototype, the ZB 33 was made in British .303in calibre, and was eventually selected for service.

Production in Britain began in December 1937, and by the outbreak of war 400 per week were being made. The name 'Bren' came from adding the first two letters of Brno in Czechoslovakia, to the first two letters of Enfield, then site of the Royal Small Arms Factory. The advantages of the Bren were its simplicity, portability, changeable barrel, accuracy, and easy to handle 30-round box magazines. Some said that the Bren was 'too accurate', putting many rounds into tiny groups,

and preferred to use a slightly worn barrel to achieve 'spread'. Military instructors however recommended that 'bursts' be kept short, at no more than five rounds at a time, and aim adjusted as necessary. The remarkable accuracy of the Bren was useful in long range work, for which a tripod was provided, and in engaging difficult targets. With swift magazine changes the Bren was capable of 120 aimed rounds a minute, but it was recommended that the barrel be changed after ten magazines if sustained fire were to be maintained.

The Bren was officially issued one per section during World War Two, so that by 1943, according to official sources, every infantry battalion was provided with 50, the extras being for the carrier platoon and battalion headquarters. Additionally four twin Brens were provided for the anti-aircraft role. The weapon proved so popular and useful that this generous provision was sometimes exceeded. Magazines were carried in the soldier's pouches and in metal boxes of twelve, and could be topped up from the riflemen's supply of ammunition.

Though hampered by the provisions of the Treaty of Versailles, the Germans made considerable advances in the field of light automatic weapons. The MP 18 sub-machine gun was redeveloped in the 1920s by Hugo Schmeisser and the new model, the MP 28, now boasted selective as well as automatic fire. Further models, the MP 34 and MP 35 were independently developed by Theodor Bergmann, and were ultimately used by the German police and Waffen-SS. Another German

A Bren light machine gun in action at Monte Cassino. Few weapons have inspired as many acclamations as the Bren, which as a bipod-mounted squad weapon was to be a cornerstone of British infantry tactics in World War Two. Apart from accuracy and reliability its virtues included easy change barrels and box magazines. The Bren team usually worked as a pair, the gunner being supported by a rifleman. It was common for the infantry section to carry several magazines, and these could be refilled with rifle ammunition if required. Initially produced in the 1930s as .303in weapon, the Bren was later converted to 7.62mm. Made in Canada and Australia as well as Britain it was still in use in some parts of the world in 1990; and perhaps the most unusual application was in the hands of the Chinese who had a quantity in 7.92mm.

French volunteers for the Wehrmacht armed with the 9mm MP 40, and a Kar 98k rifle. The 9mm MP 40 was a simplified version of the MP 38, probably the first 'modern' sub-machine gun. Contrary to popular mythology Hugo Schmeisser had little or nothing to do with the design of the MP 38, which was conceived at the Erfurt Maschinen works, popularly known as 'Erma'. This successful design incorporated several interesting features including the use of moulded phenolic resins, which were the precursors of the plastics used in later grips and butts.

interwar sub-machine gun, the Vollmer, designed by Heinrich Vollmer and made at the Erma works, was exported to France, Mexico and South America and was also used in limited numbers in the Spanish Civil War. The Erma EMP similarly was exported to Yugoslavia and used in Spain.

Infinitely better known than any of these was the Erma MP 38, which would subsequently become Wehrmacht general issue. Designed as a result of study of the Spanish Civil War, the MP 38 was a 9mm weapon with a 32-round box magazine, a folding skeleton stock, and no woodwork. In 1940 the gun was simplified to produce the MP 40, which saved on time and materials by using metal stampings and welds whenever possible. To minimise disruption caused by bombing, production of components was subcontracted out to many smaller factories, and parts were only brought together for final assembly.

About one million MP 40s were made, with contractors involved including Steyr and Heanel as well as Erma. Also occasionally encountered are the models MP 38/40, and MP 40/2 which have minor improvements over the basic guns; the MP 38/40 included a bolt lock to improve the safety of the basic MP 38, and the MP 40/2 was an experimental type which featured a dual magazine housing. At least one source suggests that the MP 38 and MP 40 were best used in short bursts, and that jams could occur if the guns were used extensively for 'hosepiping'. Nonetheless general function, reliability, and accuracy were all very good, or excellent, and the MP 40 received a glowing report when tested by the US Army at Aberdeen Proving ground.

In the field of support weapons the main new German development was the MG 34. This gun was something of a hybrid in that it seems to have taken as its start point the Swiss Solothurn MG 30, which was later improved by Mauser. There were however distinct differences between the MG 34 and the Swiss gun; most importantly the MG 34 did not have the unlocking mechanism of the Solothurn which had first been patented by Louis Stange in 1929. It is also arguable whether the neat 'rocker trigger' which gave single shots in one section of its length and automatic fire in the other was simply a copy of the Swiss machine gun, as the same arrangement had been used long before on the MG 13.

The MG 34 in squad light machine gun role. By quickly changing the top cover it could be made to feed from either a 250-shot belt or a pair of saddle drums holding 75 rounds. Light and effective, it was made to such fine tolerances that it could not be produced quickly, and was sometimes vulnerable to dirt or fouling. Nevertheless it set the pattern for a whole class of machine gun and served the German forces right through the war. Compare this picture with that on page 46.

What can certainly be claimed of the MG 34, was that it was the first large scale issue of a 'general purpose' machine gun. It was introduced into the services in 1936, and with the benefit of various mounts and accessories could fulfil almost any role. For the squad-level light machine gun role, the MG 34 had a shoulder stock and folding bipod, and could be used either with belts or saddle drums. For sustained fire in the medium machine gun role, it could be mounted on a cradle-type tripod called the 'Maschinengewehr-Lafette 34'. Here it would be belt fed only, a typical belt load being three or four rounds of ordinary ball ammunition, followed by a round of tracer to aid observation. The anti-aircraft mount was a light tripod known as the Dreifuss 34, and there were a good selection of pintle, multiple and vehicle mounts.

The weapon was very well made, perhaps too well made for modern war and mass production. During World War Two the Savage Arms Corporation of America was supplied with a sample to determine if it should be copied for the US Army. They replied that whilst the MG 34 was a very good gun it would take an inordinate amount of machine tools to replicate. Until supplemented by the MG

The Degtyarev DP 7.62mm light machine gun carried by Republican troops during the Spanish Civil War. Designed in the 1920s, with production starting at the Tula arsenal in 1933, the DP was simple to make, but the large drum was vulnerable to damage, and the gun was more prone to overheating and stoppages than most. Gradually the faults were ironed out, aided by the introduction, in 1940, of a barrel which was easier to change. A more thorough overhaul in 1944 resulted in the DPM or DP 'modified'. Both the DP and DPM featured an unusual bolt locking mechanism in which plates emerged from the sides of the bolt and engaged into recesses in the receiver.

42 the MG 34 was the main German support weapon, and a single infantry division in 1943 required well over 600. Whatever the mechanical technicalities the weapon proved that it was quite possible to have a 'general purpose' machine gun, and that infantry squads could deal with trailing belts for their light as well as heavy machine guns.

In the interwar years, the Russians also made new essays in the field of light automatic weapons, some of which were tested in Spain. Amongst these were a number of Degtyarev designs, most important of which was the DP 1928 light machine gun. The DP stood for 'Degtyarev Pekhotny' or 'Degtyarev Infantry'. This gun is perhaps best distinguished by its large flat pan-shaped magazine which contained 47 rounds. It proved very robust, and despite the difficulties of using rimmed 7.62mm ammunition in a fully automatic light machine gun, would remain a standard issue in the Soviet Union until the 1950s, and would be seen for long after in Eastern Europe and Asia.

The Japanese also developed light machine guns between the wars, the first of which was the rather unusual 11 Nen Shiki Kikanju of 1922. This was based on the French Hotchkiss but had a strange angular butt and was fitted with a hopper feed on the side of the mechanism. Into this could be put ordinary clips of Arisaka rifle ammunition. The rounds were oiled and stripped from their clips as they went into the breech. Though rather less than perfect this gun would remain in use until 1945. The 96 Shiki Kikanju of 1936 was really an attempt to improve on the 11 Nen Shiki Kikanju, and succeeded in several particulars. For example the hopper was replaced with a more conventional box magazine, a carrying handle was added, and the butt was modified to a straighter shape with a pistol grip. Sometimes the gun was also found with a telescopic sight.

Finally, in 1939, the 99 Shiki Kikanju was introduced. This was as a result of the decision to adopt a 7.7mm rimless round, and the new Japanese light machine gun showed some of the better features of the Type 96 as well as some borrowed from the Czech ZB 26. Although a great improvement, with a much better feed system and more powerful ammunition, the Type 99 was never to entirely replace the earlier guns. Demand was so high that production could never keep up and all three Japanese light machine guns were in simultaneous use throughout the war.

If significant advances were made in the light automatic field, other areas showed less promising development. Nations other than the United States stuck to virtually the same bolt action rifles they had used in the Great War. The changes that were made were hardly startling: the German 98k service rifle, introduced

A German 7.92mm Kar 98k carbine, the standard rifle of the war. This is a late-war 'Kriegsmodell' with a simplified fore end and a stock made from laminated wood.

in 1935, was really no more than a shortened and slightly more elegant version of the original Model 1898 Mauser, which itself continued in service with second line formations. The Italians changed calibre, upping from 6.5mm to 7.35mm, this largely as a result of their experiences in Abyssina, where the smaller bullet had proved not to have enough stopping power. The Soviets carried on with their Moisin-Nagant rifles, the British with the Lee-Enfield, and the Japanese with various models of Arisaka. These would see minor modifications during the war, including the introduction of several short or carbine versions, and models designed for simplified production, but the basics of the mechanisms would remain the same. Thus it was for example that the British 'No. 5' rifle, or 'Jungle Carbine' was little more than a shortened version of the 'No. 4' rifle, which was itself an improved and simplified SMLE. The Soviet 'Karabin' models 1938, and 1944, were essentially similar, except in length and detail, to the model 1910 and model 1930 rifles. The Japanese took the further step of introducing between 1941 and 1943, two models of 'parachutists' rifle. These could be broken down into two parts for jumping or concealment, but were otherwise similar to the 7.7mm Arisaka rifle of 1939.

In the pistol field there were some innovations, principally because the automatic was gaining ground on the revolver. Strangely, Britain adopted a new

A German soldier advancing with the standard issue 7.92mm Kar 98k carbine. Introduced in 1935 the Kar 98k was a shortened and slightly improved version of the old G98 service rifle. The Kar 98k was 43.7in (1.11m) long and weighed 8.6lb (3.9kg), against the original arm's 49.4in (1.25m) length and 9.23lb (4.14kg) weight, but the five-round integral magazine and the basics of the Mauser action remained unaltered.

An array of three bolt action rifles. Top is the Soviet 7.62 mm Moisin Nagant Karabin obr 1938g, or model 1938 carbine. Russian forces had been using similar bolt action weapons since the 1890s, and numerous variants in differing lengths were still in service during the war. (MOD Pattern Room). Middle is the British Rifle No. 4 Mk. I, which was a simplified and improved version of the SMLE Mk. III, and bottom is the British Rifle No. 5 Mk 1. Colloquially known as the 'Jungle Carbine' the 'number five' was developed from the basic Lee Enfield service rifle in 1944 with the intention of producing a shorter, lighter weapon for the war in South East Asia. Although it achieved its primary objectives the price to be paid was a large muzzle flash and a heavy kick from the recoil.

revolver in the 1930s which was very much like a scaled down version of the old Webley. The new gun was the .38in Enfield, or No. 2 Mark 1 pistol which was a little lighter and handier, but still an old fashioned six-shot revolver. Tank crews experienced difficulty with the hammer catching in clothing and equipment in the confined space of their vehicles, so just before the outbreak of war a new version, the Mark 1* was brought out with no hammer spur. This modification, which also applied to the Mark 1**, meant that the revolver could be used 'double action' only, that is it had to be both cocked and fired by means of the trigger. Tank crews were also supplied with a modified holster, with a longer suspension

A British officer at Arnhem in 1944 with the .38in No2 Mark 1* issue revolver. The original No 2 Mark 1 reached the stage of a 'tool room' sample as early as 1927, and was actually approved for service in 1932. It was a conventional six-shot revolver, robust and practical, if both old fashioned and aesthetically unappealing. The Mark 1* version shown here was the most common, and was double action only, having had the hammer spur deleted. Troops were trained to use it as a weapon of last resort, firing quick pairs of shots, if necessary without the use of the sights.

from the belt, and without a full flap. Though the Enfield .38in was made in large numbers there were never quite enough to go round, and other models including Colts and Smith and Wessons from America, and the Webley .38in Mark IV, were widespread. It is interesting that Webley saw their pistol production during World War Two as inferior to their normal standard, and accordingly marked much of their output 'War Finish' perhaps for the benefit of their usually more discerning clientele.

Elsewhere the movement was predominantly from revolvers to automatics. In Russia for example the old Nagant revolver would remain in use, but from 1933 was increasingly supplanted by the new Tokarev semi-automatic eight-round pistol, which had been inspired by an original Browning design. Belgium and Lithuania went directly to Browning for their 'High Power' or Model 1935. The big advantage of this pistol, which was to be remain in service use for more than 50 years, was its two-column 13-round magazine.

The US Colt .45in M1911A1 semi-automatic, showing the major components stripped down. The 'slide' is at the top, over the barrel and barrel bushing; and the seven-round magazine is to the side. Four rounds of the chunky .45in 'Auto Colt Pistol' ammunition are beside the trigger and butt assembly. This amazingly successful semi-automatic was the result of improvements on Browning's original designs, and government trials in 1907 resulted in the implementation of further minor modifications. It was later manufactured not only by Colt but by Ithaca, Remington, Springfield, Singer, the Union Switch company and North American Arms in Canada. Norway and Argentina also produced their own versions under licence.

John Moses Browning would also have other influences on pistols of the Second World War. His first patent for a semi-automatic pistol had appeared as early as 1897, and between then and his death in 1926 he had been granted well over 130 patents. Not only did his Model 1900 and Model 1922 pistols see some use during the war but the Colt Model 1911 was derivative from his basic systems. It can also be cogently argued that the Polish standard service pistol, the Radom, or VIS-35, was also loosely based by its designers Wilneiwczyc and Skrzypinski, on the Browning. Although heavier and larger than the average 9mm the Radom is a surprisingly good gun. After the German invasion of 1939 production continued for the enemy, and the pistol was known in German service as the Pistole 35 (p). Though later guns were of rougher finish they continued to be serviceable weapons.

The Germans, already familiar with automatics, decided to replace their old P08 'Luger' pistols prior to World War Two. The Luger was effective and though it had acquired a near cult status particularly with allied troops it was perceived as

The German 9mm P38 semi-automatic. Designed to replace the Pistole 08 Luger, the Walther-designed P38 was an eight-shot weapon, with double action and a locking breech mechanism. It functioned well, and was made by other contractors including Waffenwerke Brno, Czechoslovakia, and Mauser. Production ceased in 1945, but was restarted in 1957 to re equip the Bundeswehr.

Heavily armed German soldiers on the Russian front. The figure in the background has a Kar 98k rifle; his colleague has not only a P08 semi-automatic, but grenades and a disintegrating metal link belt for a machine gun. The 'Steilhandgranate 39' high explosive stick grenade seen here functioned much like its Great War predecessor, having a screw cap to remove and a cord to pull initiating the fuse, but did not have a belt hook. There was also a marginally lighter 'Steilhandgranate 24' model. Notice also the leather P08 'Luger' holster, with flap top and external compartment for a cleaning rod.

too complex in design and manufacture for a modern mass army. The chosen successor was the Walther P38 self-loading pistol; this was another elegant weapon distinguished by its double action mechanism. Most semi-automatics of the era required cocking prior to firing, but the P 38 cocked itself as the trigger was pulled for the first shot from the eight-round magazine.

The P 38 was also taken into service by the Swedish army in 1939, and was known by the Swedes as the 'Model 39'. Although production of the P 38 was well under way by the outbreak of war, massive expansion of the army precluded issue of the new weapon to all who required pistols. A single infantry division needed 1,100 such weapons, and so the Luger remained in production until the end of 1942. As the war progressed those in charge of pistol procurement never succeeded in achieving uniformity: huge numbers of weapons were lost on the Eastern Front and the army continued to expand until very late in the war. The Luftwaffe, paramilitary organisations, and the Volksturm, or Home Guard all required considerable supplies. The result was that although the P 38 and Luger predominated, many other types saw service. Most famous amongst these was probably the Walther PP, which had been developed for police use in 1929, and its little brother the Walther PPK. The Walthers were only the tip of the iceberg; other German types used included various models of Mauser, the Beholla (made by Becker and Hollander), the Sauer Behorden, and the Dreyse, all of which were semi-automatics. There was also a legion of foreign guns taken into service, including not only Polish Radoms, but Czechoslovak VZ 27 and VZ 38s, Belgian Brownings, and even a few Norwegian, Spanish and Italian pistols.

The Japanese also moved decisively in favour of semi-automatic pistols prior to World War Two, relegating their old 'Meiji 26' revolver of 1893 to reserve and home defence units. The new pistol was the 'Nambu', more properly described as the 'Taisho 04' which was first introduced in 1915. The gun has a rough similarity in outline to the Luger and the Italian Glisenti. The Nambu was effective enough and had an

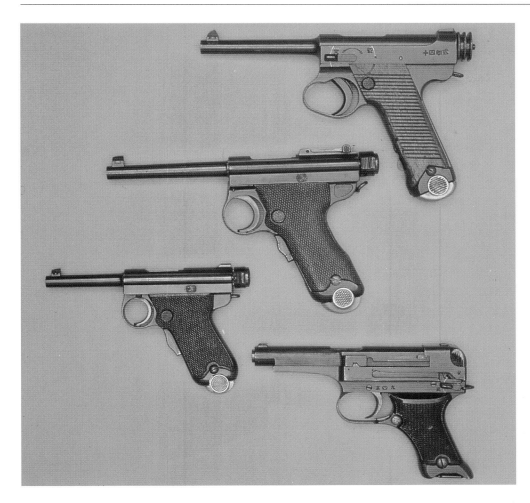

The major Japanese semi-automatic pistols in use in World War Two. Top is the 8mm 'Nambu' Taisho 14th year pistol; an eight-shot weapon introduced in 1925 and which equipped much of the army. The example shown here has the so called 'Manchurian', or 'winter trigger', allowing gloved use. Below this is its predecessor, the 8mm, 4th year pistol, of 1915, at least a small number of which were also used by Siam (Thailand). The small pistol is commonly known as the 'Baby Nambu', a miniature version of the 4th year pistol, chambering a 7mm round, and used by some officers. At the bottom is the awful 8mmType 94 . This six-round gun had numerous inadequacies, the worst of which was a tendency to fire by accident if handled roughly. Other problems included a tiny grip and a low muzzle velocity. Its reputation was not aided by declining standards of manufacture in 1944 and 1945.

eight-round magazine, but suffered somewhat from its unique bottle-necked 8mm cartridge and a weak striker spring. A new model of the gun was introduced in 1925, and is known as the 'Taisho 14'. This was slightly simplified and had a plainer butt and grip and a repositioned safety catch. The Nambu can be found with two different sizes of trigger guard, the idea being that the larger aperture could accommodate a gloved hand in cold weather.

In 1934 the Japanese introduced a new pistol which was probably intended to supersede the Nambu. This Type 94 was, in the words of one leading authority, 'a prominent contender for the title of worst military pistol ever issued'. Having handled the thing the current writer can do nothing but agree. A light,

The Italian Beretta 9mm Modello 1934 semi-automatic pistol. The original Pietro Beretta established his arms business in the seventeenth century, and it is arguable that this neat, well finished, seven-shot handgun represented one of the high points in its achievement. Also available in 7.65mm, the 1934 type pistol built on experience gained with the Tullio Maregoni-designed Modello 1915. The Modello 1934 equipped much of the Italian forces; those stamped 'RE' being army property; those marked 'RM' navy, and 'RA' and 'AM' being airforce marks.

compact 6-shot 8mm automatic was fine in theory but the execution left much to be desired. The grip was tiny, even for the average Japanese, and the sear which releases the striker was exposed through the left hand side of the frame. This alarming feature made it possible to accidentally fire the gun without touching the trigger.

If the Japanese were poorly served, the Italians had managed, by 1934, to produce a thoroughly serviceable, if rather light, military semi-automatic, known as the Beretta 'Pistola Automatica M1934'. The Beretta may not be the world's most powerful gun, but it is one than can be comfortably carried all day in a holster. The Beretta replaced both the Model M1889 'Bodeo' revolver and

the Glisenti semi-automatic, although some of both these models remained in use during World War Two. Well finished and comfortable to handle, the Beretta used a 9mm short cartridge held in a seven-round box magazine.

As the war progressed, automation and simplification were the keynotes, both in design and manufacture. Most armies went for an increasing proportion of automatic and semi-automatic weapons, and for simpler ways to produce them. One of the first countries to feel this pressure was Britain, which had a long tradition of good, if conservative design, coupled with high standards of finish and quality control. The most amazing omission on the part of Britain at the start of World War Two was the lack of a sub-machine gun (SMG). Along with France and Sweden, Britain hastily placed orders for the American Thompson. This was powerful and reliable, but was expensive, had to be imported past the U Boat, and used a cartridge non-standard in European armies.

Clearly this situation was intolerable, but it was not until 1941 that British sub-machine guns would be in production. The two rival designs were the Lanchester, made by Sterling Armaments, and the better known Sten. Both were

The original model British 9mm, Sten Machine Carbine Mark 1. Distinguished by its woodwork and large flash hider the Mark 1 Sten was the most elaborate, and is now one of the rarest, versions of the weapon. Large numbers of the Mark 1 were to be produced for the government from March 1941 onward, with the aid of Singer and Lines Brothers companies. In the event the simplified Mark 2 was developed before the end of the year and this version was made in the largest numbers. (MOD Pattern Room)

9mm weapons, but here all similarity ended. The Lanchester was painstakingly made, with plenty of brass work and wood, and was basically a copy of the Bergmann MP 28. The Sten was very cheap and resembled a welding or plumbing tool. Surprisingly it was the Sten which was a runaway success whilst the Lanchester was used only by the Royal Navy. The Sten took its name from its designers, Shepherd and Turpin, and the Enfield Small Arms factory. During the war it went through six major types, and parts were produced all over the country by firms as diverse as Meccano, Albion Motors, BSA, the British Vacuum Cleaner Company and Hercules Cycles. It also received the rare tribute of being copied by the Germans. The Sten's virtues were simplicity, ease of manufacture and low cost. It was also easy to dismantle and assemble, and could be stripped in a matter of seconds, even by a novice. As well as being used by the army, thousands were dropped to partisans and resistance fighters in occupied Europe. Indeed so many were taken to France that some of the pro Nazi 'Milice' were seen armed with Sten guns.

The first version of the Sten had a folding wooden handgrip, and is now relatively rare compared to most of the later models. The major working parts were a sliding breech block, a large spring, the barrel, trigger, and a 32-round box magazine. It weighed only just over 7lb (3kg). It was not particularly accurate, but provided an impressive stream of fire at close range. The Marks II and III were simpler still, with no grip and usually a crude steel tube and flat endplate forming the butt. The Mark IV was an experimental model, shortened and with a folding stock, and the Mark V was an elaborate version with pistol grip and wooden stock. Also worthy of note were the Mark 2(S) and the Mark VI, which were silenced versions for special forces. Total production of all models was about

4,200,000 and although there were some problems with the fragile magazine lips, and the occasional accidental discharge, the Sten turned out to be an effective solution to Britain's sub-machine gun problem.

Ironically most of the pressures which had influenced the British to produce a replacement for the Thompson also applied to the US Army after they entered the war. The first new American SMGs were the Reising, made by Harrington and Richardson, and the Marlin-made M42. Both were relatively complicated designs, and in the main only saw service with the Marine Corps and the Office of Strategic Services respectively. They were quickly replaced by a much simpler design, known officially as the M3, but more commonly referred to as the 'grease gun'. The M3 was passed for service in 1942, and would remain a mainstay of the army until 1960. Like the Sten this weapon was cheap, had absolutely no unnecessary frills, and was easy to manufacture. It made extensive use of pressed stampings and spot welding, and had a simple extendable wire stock. It usually chambered the powerful .45in cartridge, which fed from a 30-round box magazine, but some

French resistance fighters with a Sten Mark II. Made in huge numbers in Britain and Canada between 1941 and 1943, the Mark II was the most common Sten, and is found with both the skeleton type stock seen here, and an even simpler straight tubular stock. Many Stens were dropped by parachute to European partisans, so many in fact that the French pro-Nazi 'Milice' was also able to arm some of its men with captured Stens.

The US .45in M3 'Grease gun'. This, the first version of the M3, was passed for service in December 1942, a year after American entry into the war. Extremely straightforward in operation it weighed 8.82lb (4kg), and was equipped with a 30-round magazine. A further simplification in 1944 deleted the cocking handle, and produced the M3A1. About 700,000 were made by General Motors, and it was copied elsewhere. A small number of silenced weapons were also made for special forces use.

were converted to fire 9mm. Cyclic rate of fire was slow for an SMG, but this had advantages in that it was easier to hold on target during burst fire, and that it was also possible to fire just one or two rounds with a fleeting trigger pressure. Minor improvements produced the M3A1 in 1944. Like the Sten, its weak point was its magazine and feed system, but the M3 was a cheap, simple and effective enough weapon.

That the M3 never quite achieved the universality of the Sten is probably because another American weapon, fulfilling a similar niche, became so popular. This gun was the M1 carbine. As early as 1938 it had been thought that there might be a requirement for a light, easy to carry weapon which vehicle drivers, signallers and the like could use, and which was more effective than a pistol. After some experimentation, particularly with ammunition, the Ordnance Department laid down the required specification in 1940. The new gun was to be semi-automatic, not to exceed 5lb (2.2kg), have a box magazine to take the special Winchester .30in cartridge, and be effective to 300yd (275m).

On 16 June 1941 several designers had their efforts tested at Aberdeen

US soldiers flush out a Japanese sniper in the Pacific Theatre. They have an interesting mix of weapons, including M1 Carbines, a Thompson SMG, an M1 Garand rifle, and what appears to be a shotgun carried by the lead man.

(Opposite page) Serried ranks of Soviet troops armed with the ubiquitous 7.62mm PPSh 41 sub-machine gun: several parade with their fingers on the trigger! This cheap, simple weapon was so useful that the Red Army formed whole battalions equipped with it.

Proving Ground. A Springfield Armory design had already been disbarred on grounds of weight, and none of the others satisfied all the requirements in their present form. Further tests were set for the autumn, and these were won outright by the Winchester entry. The heart of the new weapon was the so-called 'gas tappet' system, designed by David M. Williams. In effect this was a piston activated by a rush of gas through a port in the barrel, which drove back the operating slide and reloaded the weapon. Though the 'tappet' was Williams' idea the rest of the gun was designed by other Winchester employees. In November 1941 orders were placed for 350,000 carbines, now to be known as the M1. This was only a beginning, for eventually ten major contractors would between them make between 5 and 6 million guns, which were used by infantrymen, paratroopers, officers, military policemen and others, as well as by the original intended recipients. Its low weight and handy size made it popular in situations where a full-sized rifle would have been a cumbersome encumbrance, and after the war it would be widely distributed to Americas friends and allies.

Few countries embraced the SMG as wholeheartedly as did the Soviet Union during World War Two. During the 1930s they had perfected their 'PPD' design

(PPD meaning 'Pistolet Pulyemet Degtyarev', or Degtyarev's machine pistol). The first model was the PPD-34/38, which was issued only in small numbers, but in 1940 this was supplemented by the PPD-40. This, like its predecessor, fired 7.62mm pistol-type cartridges from a 71-shot drum magazine. Both weapons were apparently influenced by the German MP 28 and the Finnish Suomi sub-machine guns.

In 1941 the Soviet Union was attacked by Germany, and Operation Barbarossa swept the Panzer divisions to within a few miles of Moscow. The demand for arms of all sorts to replace the losses of the Red Army was huge, and it was at this point that the now world famous 'PPSh-1941G' SMG made its debut. Designed by Georgi Shpagin this weapon was crudely finished and stripped of all inessentials, and although it retained a wooden stock, was mainly of metal stampings. It was easy to dismantle and could accept either a 35-round box magazine or a 71-shot drum. Some early models could fire single shots but most were fully automatic only. One source has it that at the height of the 'Great Patriotic War' PPSh barrels were actually made from lengths of old rifle barrel; such expediencies, and fully automatic fire in the hands of semi-trained troops, made for little in the way of accuracy. Since about 5 million of these guns were manufactured, however, Shpagin's design made a valuable contribution to the rearming and rebuilding of the Soviet Army. Eventually so many PPSh-1941G fell into German hands that it was considered worth their while to convert some of them to 9mm parabellum.

In 1942 the Soviets added yet another type of SMG to their arsenal. The PPS-42 was designed in Leningrad by Alexei Sudarev to overcome a shortage of weapons during the great siege. The PPS-42 and its modified successor, the PPS-43, were crude and simple in the extreme, making maximum use of sheet steel stampings, rivets and spot welds: nonetheless they functioned, and, besides playing a part in the holding of Leningrad, were a model for other SMGs like the Finnish M44 and Spanish DUX. Total production is believed to have been in

The Finnish 9mm Konepistooli M44 sub-machine gun, made by Oy Tikkakoski AB of Sakara. A copy of the Sudarev-designed Soviet PPS, the Finnish M44 was simply made and capable of fully automatic fire only. It could use 36- or 50-round box magazines, or even a 71-round drum. It is interesting to note that after the war Willi Daugs, the manager of Tikkakoski, fled to Spain. With him went the plans for the M44, and thus was born the Spanish DUX 53. (MOD Pattern Room)

excess of 1million units. After the war the PPS was supplied to other East European countries, and large numbers also went to North Korea.

One country which never really mastered the sub-machine gun was Japan. This is all the more surprising as the SMG is an ideal weapon for jungle warfare and close assault, two areas in which the Japanese gained considerable expertise. In the interwar period Japan imported a few Swiss Bergmann-type weapons which went to the navy, and also did some experimental design work. However only one gun was manufactured during the war, the 8mm Type 100 of 1939. There was a revised version in 1944 and a specialised parachutists' variant, but it is doubtful whether total production of all Type 100 models exceeded 25,000. When one considers that the United States made more than 3 million sub-machine guns during the war, Britain made more than 4 million, and Russia made more than 6 million, it is very difficult to see how the Type 100 could have made any measurable impact on combat at all. The gun itself weighed about 7.7lb (3.5kg), had a wooden stock, and fed from a 30-round box magazine which entered the housing on the left.

Most powers continued to use machine guns which had served them in the Great War. Even where these had technically been supplanted by newer types, old models often continued to be used by home defence, and second line units. Thus it was for example that the MG 08 was still seen in the German forces, right through to 1945, and Lewis guns were still used, not only by the British, but also by the Dutch.

The United States also soldiered on with improved models of World War One designs, The standard medium machine gun was the Browning M1919, an air-cooled modification of the earlier water-cooled M1917. Firing the standard .30in rifle cartridge, this belt-fed weapon was tough, reliable and effective, and served as a tripod-mounted

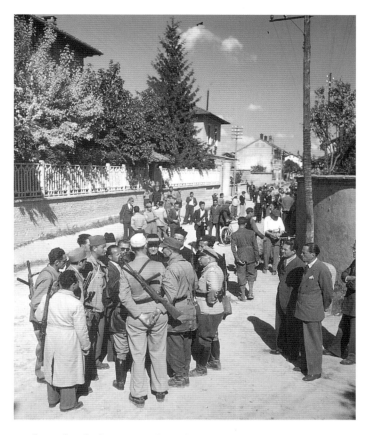

A rather motley gathering of Italian partisans. Amongst their weaponry are 9mm Model 1938 Beretta sub-machine guns, and 7.35mm Mannlicher-Carcano rifles.

Bulgarian troops dig in covered by a Maxim machine gun on a Schwarzlose tripod. Many World War One machine guns, though theoretically obsolete in 1939, turned up in the hands of second line troops or minor powers during World War Two. The Austrian Schwarzlose was seen in Czechoslovakia and Italy, while German Maxims were also in the hands of German home defence units, and in use in Belgium, Poland and Yugoslavia.

infantry weapon, as a light anti-aircraft gun, and as a vehicle-mounted machine gun. It became the standard US medium gun of the war, and remained in service for many years afterwards. A bipod-mounted light machine gun variant was also produced, but was not a great success. Another mainstay was the M2 heavy machine gun, again developed from a World War One design. This Browning gun looks rather like the big brother of the M1919, and was originally designed as an anti-tank and anti-aircraft weapon. It fired a large, powerful .5in cartridge, which was effective out to more than 2,000yd (1,830m) and could be used against personnel, aircraft, vehicles and light armour. It was used on a tripod mount, and many were also seen on tanks, armoured half-tracks and other vehicles.

There was no true general-issue light machine gun in US Army service, although the BAR was widely distributed and almost fulfilled this role. An experimental weapon was the Johnson M1941, but this turned out to be unreliable and fragile, and only saw limited service.

The Japanese continued to use various home produced machine guns based on the old French Hotchkiss design, which was air cooled and fed with ammu-

British parachutists firing a late model, smooth-jacketed .303in, Vickers Mark 1 machine gun. This picture reveals details such as the water pipe leading to the condenser can, the flip up sight, and canvas barrel cover. The soldiers' headgear is the plain steel, third version, of the airborne forces helmet, heavily camouflaged.

The Browning .30in Model 1919 machine gun. Although more modern in appearance the air-cooled Browning Model 1919 was technically very similar to the water cooled Model 1917, having a barrel extension and bolt which move back by gas pressure before unlocking. In World War Two and Korea it was a standard issue US Army company level weapon on the M2 tripod. Effective in this fire support role it was also widely used outside the US by many countries including several from NATO, and by Iran, Vietnam, Haiti, Liberia, Mexico, South Korea and Israel. (MOD Pattern Room)

The Browning .50in calibre, M2 machine gun in a concealed position. Conceived at the end of World War One as an anti-tank weapon, the Browning heavy machine gun was made obsolete before deployment in this role by the increasing thickness of tank armour. Nevertheless the project was persisted with, and happily so, since the M2 made an excellent long range fire support weapon. Notice the M1-type helmets of the crew, worn with and without the camouflage net.

nition strips rather than belts. Their medium model which saw most action in World War Two was the Type 92. This was remarkable for although generally reliable it had an antiquated cartridge oiler system, in which oil fed from a reservoir to a brush which anointed the ammunition on its way into the breech. This was intended to aid both feed and extraction. Another interesting feature of the Type 92 was the method of carriage, for each foot of its tripod was fitted with a bayonet type socket into which a pole could be inserted. Two, or preferably three, men could now stretcher the gun between them; the man at the breech got the worst of the arrangement with a form of yoke device to shoulder his portion of the burden.

US Marines with a captured Japanese 7.7mm Type 92 machine gun on Iwo Jima. The 'Number Two' feeds 30-round strips into the gun mechanism from the left, where the rounds are oiled by a brush mounted under a reservoir, before being fired. The gun and tripod weighed 122lb (55.3kg), and the weapon had the relatively low cyclic rate of 450 rounds a minute. Hearing it through the trees the Allied troops sardonically christened it 'the Woodpecker'. The Type 92 is generally similar in appearance to the earlier 'Taisho 3' Japanese machine gun, which was also Hotchkiss inspired ,though this weapon was in 6.5mm and can be distinguished by its 'spade' style grips.

A comparison of the German 7.92mm MG 42 machine gun (top), with the British .303in Bren. Both excellent in their own ways, the two weapons were radically different machine guns, technically and tactically. The Bren was first and foremost a squad light support gun, highly accurate, with self-contained magazines, and with a relatively slow rate of fire. The equally compact MG 42 was about 10% heavier and was not perhaps so handy in a bipod-mounted role: it was however much better as a general purpose gun, and its 1,200 rounds per minute cyclic rate would result in a fearsome saturation of the target.

Whilst many of the machine guns used in World War Two were not new, there were some actually designed and produced during the war which were to have a lasting impact. Most remarkable of these was the German MG 42. This weapon was intended to make use of modern production techniques in an attempt to make a simpler, more rugged replacement for the MG 34. In this design, barrel, bolt and barrel extension all recoiled together and were only disengaged as cam tracks in the gun body engaged with a pair of rollers on the bolt. The further movement of the bolt also operated pawls which fed the disintegrating link ammunition belt, and the theoretical rate of fire obtainable was an astonishing 1,200 rounds per minute. Those who heard it in use described the sound like loud tearing cloth, and this fearsome rate of fire could have a powerful effect on the morale of allied troops faced with having to advance into German defensive positions. The MG 42 was made by a number of manufacturers, including Mauser and Gustoff, and between 1942 and the end of the war production exceeded three quarters of a million. The gun weighed only some 25lb (11.5kg) and was used both in a 'light' squad role on a bipod, and in a sustained or 'heavy' role from a tripod. It proved itself both versatile and more reliable than the old MG 34, and like the earlier weapon the MG 42 was also fitted on anti-aircraft

and vehicle mounts. In 1957 manufacture was restarted with the weapon rechris-tened the MG 1 and rechambered for NATO 7.62mm ammunition. There were various sub models and variations of MG 1 types, perhaps the most important of which was that certain models could be made to fire at slower rates.

The Russians also produced a new machine gun during the war, the Gurynov SG 43, which was intended to replace the Model 1910 Maxim. This was never actually achieved, since the demand for machine weapons of all sorts was so huge, and the old Maxims were seen in the line right up to Berlin. Nevertheless the air cooled SG 43, although heavier than the German equivalents, was a success and was much more manageable than the watercooled Maxim or the massive 12.7mm 'DShK'. The SG 43 was simple, apart from its feed system, and was very robust. It could also be mounted on vehicles, or trundled around on its characteristi-cally Russian Solokov wheeled carriage. Post World War Two the Gurynov SG 43 became the standard Soviet medium machine gun, and a similar gun was made by the Chinese in the 1950s.

A particularly significant wartime development was the increasing number of semi-automatic rifles, and even more important, the birth of the 'assault rifle'. Germany and Russia made the greatest advances, but although there had been early experiments it was not until the appearance of the US Garand, and the out-break of war, that there was a real sense of urgency in this work. In 1940 the Germans began a programme to find a semi-automatic rifle, and designs were

An Italian Breda 6.5mm Model 1930 light machine gun. The Breda had a 20-round permanently attached box magazine, but though reasonably manageable at 22lb (10kg) was mechanically weak, and gave only a low rate of fire. Other disadvantages included a cartridge oiler and the lack of anything to carry the gun by. Despite these drawbacks it was also sold, in 7.92mm form, to Portugal and Lithuania, and was later modified to 7.5mm to create a 'Model 1938'.

The Soviet 7.62mm Goryunov 'SG 43' machine gun. Designed by Peter Maximovitch Goryunov the SG 43 was prepared in the early 1940s and entered service in 1943. Tough and simple, it lacked fancy sights or similar refinement, and was gas operated, feeding from 250-round belts. Notice the shield and the wooden wheeled carriage which could be tipped up, and the gun remounted on the trail, to make an ingenious anti-aircraft mount. (MOD Pattern Room)

prepared by both Mauser and Walther. The Walther gun was deemed the better of the two, and would subsequently be refined into the Gewehr 41. Sometimes this weapon was known as the Gew 41 (W), with the 'W' denoting the maker. The rifle was in standard 7.92mm calibre, with an integral 10-shot box magazine, and though it worked well enough had several drawbacks; it was slow to load, rather muzzle heavy and expensive. Nonetheless several thousand were made and issued, most of which saw service on the Eastern Front.

Even whilst this was going on the hunt had begun for something better. A new design was thus prepared, with a gas cylinder and piston arrangement over the barrel, which was a distinct improvement over the Gewehr 41 and its muzzle cup system. The new semi-automatic rifle appeared in 1943, as the Gewehr 43, and continued in service throughout the war. It was much better than its predecessor and cheaper to produce, but whilst made in large numbers never managed to replace bolt action G98. Indeed the Gew 43 was often seen fitted with a telescopic sight, being used by snipers, and after 1945 it was adopted by the Czechs as their standard sniper weapon.

The Falschirmjäger Gewehr 42, and the Sturmgewehr 44 were two further German automatic rifles which turned out to be much more significant milestones in weapons development. The FG 42 is interesting in that it was intended not only as a specialist parachutist weapon, but that ultimately it was supposed to replace rifles and light machine guns in such units. This never actually happened, but nevertheless the design had great potential and versatility. Developed by Rheinmetall in accordance to a specification from the Reichsluftfahrtministerium, the first model appeared in small numbers in 1942. This was unsatisfactory and so further work was undertaken, with the main production model appearing in 1944. Amazingly the FG 42 was capable of both selective and fully automatic fire, yet used a full power 7.92mm rifle cartridge while weighing only 9.9lb (4.5kg). It had a folding bipod, and was fed from a side-mounted 20-round magazine. When firing bursts the cyclic rate of fire was about 750 rounds per minute, and while this made it difficult to fire accurately at distant targets, it was an extremely handy support for raiders and lightly equipped troops. This was amply demonstrated when it was carried during the rescue of Mussolini by Otto Skorzeny and his parachutists. Perhaps fortunately for the allies the FG 42 was never made or issued in very large numbers.

The Sturmgewehr 44 was the true forerunner of the modern assault rifle. The real breakthrough for this class of weapon was the acceptance that a cartridge smaller and less powerful than the standard rifle cartridge would be adequate, and more practical, for a hand-held weapon which was expected to fire bursts. Such a short-cased or 'Kurz' 7.92mm cartridge was under development by Polte of Magdeburg in 1940, and soon after this Louis Schmeisser was producing prototype arms to fire it. By 1942 Haenel Waffen und Fahrradfabrik was producing the Mkb 42 (H) in small numbers, a short rifle, which, after further minor modifications, would be rechristened the MP 43, and eventually the MP 44. The MP 44 weighed 11.25lb (5.1kg), was under 3ft (1m) long, and was equipped with a 30-round detachable box magazine. The alternative title of 'Sturmgewehr' translates literally to 'assault rifle' and has been said to be Hitler's own idea. In any case the gun functioned remarkably well, was capable of being fitted with both an optical sight and a grenade launcher, and could well be claimed as an important stage in the development of twentieth century arms.

One strange fitting associated with the MP 44 has excited much interest and speculation; this device is the Krumlauf attachment, a bent piece of tube which

The remarkable FG 42 automatic rifle, being used by a German paratrooper. The 7.92mm FG 42 was both fully automatic and semi-automatic in operation, and, whilst it used a full size cartridge had many of the advantages of an assault rifle. The improvised rest is a box of stick grenades; a machine pistol MP 38 or MP 40 is also on hand.

The German Sturmgewehr 44. Arguably the spiritual parent of most modern assault rifles the SG 44 used a short 7.92mm cartridge, and had a cyclic rate of 500 rounds per minute. The effective range was only about 500yd (455m), but this was more than adequate for its use as a personal weapon to be used in the forefront of the assault. Selective fire gave it most of the advantages that could be claimed by carbines or sub-machine guns. (MOD Pattern Room)

allowed the assault rifle to be shot round corners. It was probably first invented so that the gun could be tested in cramped conditions on a short indoor range without danger to technicians. In the closing stages of the war it was realised that this might have some utility for tank crews trying to sweep infantry away from their vehicles, or could be handy in street fighting. A very limited number of Krumlauf attachments were used for these purposes.

Although the Russians had toyed with the idea of a semi-automatic rifle as early as 1916, none had been adopted until 1936. The rifle then taken into service was the Simonov, or AVS 36, which had a 15-round detachable box magazine, and though capable of full automatic fire, was unpleasantly heavy in blast and recoil. Although the AVS was the contemporary of the American Garand it was no match in terms of quality, and very soon the designers were back at work attempting to find something better. After two years the Tokarev SVT 38 was in production: this 7.62mm weapon with a 10-round magazine was an improvement, but really too delicate for mass issue. It was therefore sometimes encountered during the war as a sniper rifle. A tougher version appeared in 1940, the SVT 40 but again this never became a general issue and was therefore most frequently seen in the hands of snipers and NCOs.

In 1943 came a real breakthrough with the 'SKS' or Samozaryadnyi Karabin Simonova. Like the Germans, and some say because of awareness of German work, the Russians had now adopted an intermediate cartridge, sized between that usually used by the rifle and pistol. Though an undistinguished design the SKS was simple and workmanlike, and after the war would be widely manufactured throughout the Communist bloc. It was also easy to use and maintain, and was not too heavy at 8.6lb (3.9kg), but was perhaps somewhat hampered by the fact that it only had a ten round magazine.

Another fascinating area of experiment during World War Two was the field of silenced, or more properly, sound moderated small arms for clandestine or special forces use. In most attempts to quieten the report of a firearm the method used was a tube extension to the gun barrel casing, containing a series of baffles. Gas from the explosion of the cartridge would be slowed and dissipated, and the device could be especially effective when used with a relatively low-powered, subsonic round. The British arsenal included several such weapons, perhaps the most sinister looking of which was the Welrod pistol. This was a 12in (305mm) in length, single shot, and used a .32in cartridge with a muzzle velocity of only 700ft/s (213m/s). The gun was very nearly silent but suffered somewhat because the baffles were made of oil-impregnated leather or rubber washers which wore out very quickly. This would have been a significant disadvantage in a weapon intended for general issue, but for specialist clandestine use was not a great drawback. The American equivalent, for OSS use, was a conversion of the commercial .22in Hi Standard pistol. This did not have quite the stopping power of the Welrod, but magazine feed made repeated shots possible. US agents also used a version of the German Walther PPK, which had been captured and modified by the addition of a silencer.

The British Welrod sound moderated pistol. The Welrod took its name from Welwyn where researchers perfected this remarkably quiet pistol. Most were only single shot, but the Mark 2A had a five-round magazine. The Welrod was made in .32in, 7.65mm, and 9mm. The real secret of the gun's quietness was the use of leather or rubber baffles, and these had the odd quality that they caused the gun to hiss for a moment after firing. (MOD Pattern Room)

Perhaps the closest British forces came to a standard silent weapon was the Mark 2 (S) Sten gun, very much like the ordinary SMG but with a substantial sound moderator added. More interesting from a technical point of view, but in very limited use, was the De Lisle carbine. The De Lisle was actually a clever composite; the wood work was taken from a standard Lee Enfield rifle, the barrel from a Thompson and the magazine from a Colt Model 1911 pistol, all combined with an integral silencer. The combination of slow moving but hard hitting .45in bullet, with shoulder stock and magazine, made the De Lisle a formidable weapon. At distances of over 50yd (46m) its noise was difficult to detect, and it could kill at over 200yd (183m).

It could fairly be said that the mortar came of age as an infantry weapon between the last year of the Great War and World War Two. By 1939 mortars were generally divided into three categories; light, medium and heavy. The typical light mortar was easily carried by one man, had a calibre not in excess of 60mm, and a range of under 1,000yd (914m). Medium mortars could usually be broken down into several loads so that they could be carried, if needs be, by a group of men. They tended to be under 90mm in calibre, and with a range of less than 3,000yd (2,740m). Heavy mortars, which were not normally man portable, and therefore beyond the scope of this book, were usually over 100mm in calibre and often classed as artillery. All major powers had a full range of mortar equipment, but it was the Soviets who used the greatest number to greatest effect. Partly this was because the simple tube, open at one end, was perceived as highly cost effective, and partly because they lacked the sophisticated command and control systems to make full use of their artillery in close infantry support. At the lower end of the scale the Soviets preferred mortar calibres were 50 and 82mm, and there were several models of each, produced between 1936 and 1943. The quintessential Soviet mortar was the 82mm 1941 model. This had a circular base plate, made maximum use of steel stampings in its fabrication, and possessed a crude pair of pressed steel wheels which allowed

The US .45in single shot Liberator pistol. The Liberator was arguably the ultimate in firearms kitsch, a 23-part, unfinished looking, smooth barrelled monstrosity, unlikely to be effective beyond a few feet. Disguised as a project to build a flare pistol, and made by General Motors at Anderson, Indiana, the purpose of the Liberator was to be dropped to friendly partisans in occupied territory. Each Liberator cost just $1.72 and came in a small cardboard box complete with a wordless cartoon instruction sheet designed to be universally applicable. Amazingly a used cartridge had to be poked out of the breech with a stick, whilst there was a small storage space in the butt for spare ammunition. Not surprisingly most partisans preferred a Sten gun if they could get one. (MOD Pattern Room)

Free French troops in England after the fall of France. They have a 60mm light mortar and 7.5mm MAS 36 rifles. The five-shot MAS 36 was one of the last bolt action rifles to be adopted, and was loosely based on the Mauser but with a modified locking mechanism. The steel helmets are slightly updated versions of the old Adrian, made with fewer parts.

the crew to move it around without mechanical assistance. Extreme physical exertion made a rate of fire of 20 rounds per minute possible for very short periods. By the end of the war each Soviet division was supposed to have 98 mortars.

The western powers usually applied a more sophisticated approach to mortar design and deployment, but it could be suggested that some effort was wasted in 'over engineering' something which was best deployed as a surprise 'area' weapon.

The US 81mm M1 mortar in action. Based on a French design and first introduced in the 1930s the M1 was capable of 18 rounds per minute for short periods, and could fire high explosive, smoke, and illuminating rounds. Weight in action was 132lb (60kg), but it could be man-carried in sections. Its range was about 3,000yd (2,700m) with a high explosive bomb.

Loading the German 81mm mortar, or Granatwerfer 34. Standard equipment of German rifle battalions, the Granatwerfer 34, like many other mortars, owed much to the Stokes design of World War One. Its range was about 2,500yd (2,270m) with a high explosive bomb weighing 7.5lb (3.4kg). Lack of mechanical transport often meant that the mortar was manhandled onto a special horsedrawn cart.

The Germans for example employed the Granatenwerfer 36 as their standard light mortar, but even before the war had realised that its sighting system was more precise and complex than the nature of the weapon warranted. The Granatenwerfer 36 was also very well finished and could be levelled independently of its base plate. The Granatenwerfer 34 was their standard medium mortar, and this fired very unusual bombs with a two-stage explosion. The intention was to produce a bouncing or 'airburst' effect with the initial detonation blowing the projectile back into the air after landing and a second bang bursting the bomb and producing the shower of lethal fragments.

The British 2in calibre light mortar has also been described as a 'relatively luxurious' weapon in its early days. The first model was equipped with a substantial base plate with spikes to hold it firm in the ground, elevating mechanism and a bubble sight which was levelled like a spirit level. In the words of the 1939 manual:

'The chief characteristics of this weapon are, firstly its ability to make a smoke screen to hide movement, and, secondly its high trajectory, which enables it to engage with HE targets which are immune to small arms fire. The number of bombs which can be carried into action is strictly limited owing to their weight. They should be used sparingly and only as a part of a definite plan.'

High explosive bombs for the '2in' came in packs of six and each bomb weighed about 2lb (.9kg). During the war the mortar was much simplified, and a special short version was supplied to airborne and special forces. This was especially light and handy, and could even be strapped to the back of a parachutist during a jump and then be rapidly brought into action on landing. The 2in would remain in use until the 1980s when it would be replaced with a rather similar 51mm model.

Next up the scale in British service was the 3in mortar. Having lifted one

The British 2in mortar in action. Inspired by a Spanish weapon made by Esperanz of Vicaya, the 2in was designed in the 1930s, and had been delivered in large numbers to the infantry by the outbreak of war. Initially overcomplicated with a levelling device and large base plate, it was soon simplified to a more practical form. It was especially useful for laying smoke screens and could also fire a high explosive bomb to a range of about 500yd (455m). The HE bomb was declared 'practically certain' to be effective against personnel in the open, at up to eight yards (7m) in any direction from the point of impact. By 1945 the total number of 2in mortars produced was almost 40,000 and included a carrier version, and a specially shortened and lightened model for parachutists and commandos. The 2in would remain on hand with British forces until the 1980s.

around a museum, the present writer can confirm that this projector was on the very limits of man portability, with a barrel weighing 44lb (20kg) and a total 'in action' weight of 112lb (51kg). It was often carried into action in a truck or Universal Carrier. The '3in' had a range of 1,600yd (1,460m) in its first version, which was increased to 2,800yds (2,560m) with the Mk2. Efforts to get even greater ranges were not entirely successful and so work began on a replacement in 1945.

The Japanese made extensive use of mortars and had two 50mm models, as well as 81 and 90mm types. Perhaps the best known of these was the light and handy Type 89 50mm model which is also described as a 'grenade discharger' since it could throw grenades as well as bomb-shaped projectiles. The Type 89

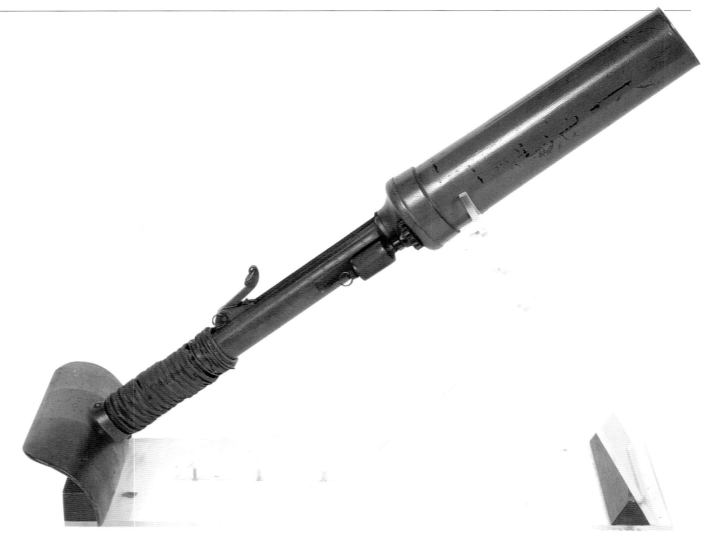

The Japanese Type 89 light mortar, or grenade discharger. The Type 89 or 'Hachiku shiki tekidanto', produced in 1929, was an updated version of the 10th year type. It had a rifled barrel, improved trigger, weighed 10.14lb (4.6kg) and had a maximum range of 715yd (650m). This mortar was sometimes known to allied troops, quite erroneously, as the 'knee mortar'. (MOD Pattern Room)

consisted of a short tube on a spigot with a base plate. Some allied troops believed that the curved base plate was rested on the knee when firing and mistakenly christened it the 'knee' or 'leg' mortar; anyone who did try and use it like this would have been rewarded with a nasty fracture.

The standard small mortars used by the United States were the 60mm M2, and the 81mm M1. Their maximum ranges were 2,000yd (1,830m) and 2,500yd (2,280m) respectively. The 60mm was an exceptionally effective light mortar (compare its range to that of larger weapons) and was able to fire a range of ammunition, including white phosphorus smoke bombs. An interesting feature of the 81mm medium mortar was that when first issued its bombs were of a folding fin pattern. Bombs were dropped into the barrel with the flights folded, but once fired the fins opened up and provided the round with very good aerial stability. This bomb was however declared obsolete in 1940 as prolonged storage was found to impair the ability of the fins to deploy which reduced accuracy.

Grenades remained important in World War Two, especially where there was street fighting or earthworks. For their standard high explosive bomb many countries updated versions of patterns which had been in use at the end of the Great War. Thus it was that the British continued to use their No 36 Mills bomb, and the Germans used the Steilhandgranate 39, a slightly improved version of their First World War stick grenade. The Americans likewise were using the Mark 11A1 grenade, a minor update of the bomb which had been introduced in 1917. Although this had some external similarity to the Mills bomb the mechanism was in fact rather different having a 'Bouchon' or 'Mousetrap' type igniter. Like the Mills the US bomb could be rifle launched.

The two major grenade models used by the Japanese were the Type 91, and the Type 97, which were interesting conceptually if rather unreliable in practice.

US special forces equipment. Along with the parachute packs and small items of equipment are shown explosives, a Thompson with drum magazine, a machete, a Colt Model 1911 pistol behind which is a 'knuckle knife', and four M2A1 fragmentation grenades. These last were standard issue: the delay between activation and explosion was 4.5 seconds, and their effective radius was about 11yd (10m).

British troops street fighting. World War One vintage SMLE rifles and sword bayonets are in evidence as the lead man prepares to throw a 'No 36' Mills bomb. Developed in 1917 from the original 'No 5' Mills, the 'No 36' varied only in matter of detail but was capable of being fired from a cup discharger. The helmets are of the Mark 2 type, differing from the first model only in details of the lining and rim.

A US flamethrower team practice against a bunker. The maximum range of the American man pack flamethrower was about 50yd (45m), for a continuous duration of about eight seconds. Best results were obtained with specially thickened fuels, delivered in brief squirts. The flamethrower was at its most useful in the Pacific campaigns where it could be used to asphyxiate as well as burn the enemy out of their hideouts.

The Type 97, which was introduced in 1937, was hand thrown only, but the Type 91 had a threaded base which allowed it to be fitted with a tail piece or a base plate, for rifle or launcher firing. When hand thrown both the 91 and the 97 were actuated in the same way: first a pin was withdrawn, then the top of the grenade was banged down to initiate the fuse.

Given the technological advances of the twentieth century it is perhaps surprising that the bayonet and other edged weapons should have remained in widespread use during World War Two. If there had been any identifiable trend in bayonet development between the wars it was towards shorter blades, perhaps because it was realised that wounds caused by the bayonet when actually attached to a rifle were few and far between, and that a shorter 'Knife bayonet' might be more readily carried and even used for other purposes. Although the US Garand rifle was at first supplied with a bayonet with a 16in (406mm) blade, a new model with only 10in (254mm) soon followed. The M1 carbine was not always fitted to accept a bayonet, but when it was the blade used was the short 'M4 bayonet-knife', a weapon which could almost equally well be used independently and was virtually identical to the M3 trench knife. The Germans similarly tended to use relatively short bayonets with their new 98k short rifles, and these Seitengewehr or sidearms were also manufactured in less practical forms for parade and dress wear.

One unusual bayonet, some might say aberration, was the short 'spike' bayonet issued for use with the updated British Short Magazine Lee Enfield, or No.

4 rifle. The germ of this idea had its origins in the 1920s when it was realised that sword bayonets were really a clumsy compromise. They were long, to achieve maximum reach in bayonet fighting, while the hilt and blade shapes were intended so that they would also serve as separate weapons or tools. In practice the authorities discouraged the troops from using the bayonet as a tool because of the damage caused. The commandant of the Small Arms Training School therefore suggested that a blade be produced that was a good bayonet pure and simple, whilst the other requirements be met by specialised fighting knives and machetes. Since the most thickly clad enemy the British soldier was likely to encounter was a Russian in winter dress, a stiletto type blade 6in (152mm) long would be per-

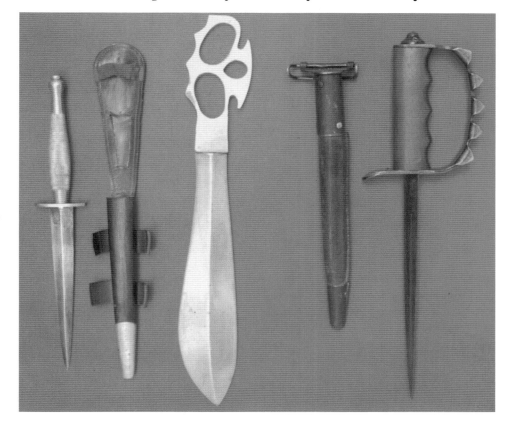

Allied fighting knives. Centre is the British 'Middle East' Commando knife with its distinctive skull-shaped grip which doubled as a knuckle duster. It is flanked by the Fairbairn-Sykes, the scabbard of which has leather tabs allowing it to be sewn to a battle dress, and a US stiletto with a ridged knuckle guard of 1917 or 1918 vintage.

fectly adequate. Much experimentation, including folding blades, lightened rifles and other exotica led finally to the Bayonet No. 4 Mk1 of 1939, and its even more utilitarian and screwdriver-like brother the Mk II, of 1941. Though the concept was sound it was based on a false premise; the soldier did not really need a practical 'pigsticker'. What the troops actually wanted was a general purpose knife which would look suitably ferocious when put on the end of a gun. In terms of being a useful knife or a psychological prop the spike bayonet was a signal failure.

Many fighting knives which had seen use in the trenches were reused from 1939, but there were also many new varieties introduced. Perhaps the single most important of these was the Fairbairn-Sykes or 'F-S' knife, invented by W. E. Fairbairn and E. A. Sykes of the

Shanghai International Police in the winter of 1940, and first produced by Wilkinson Sword in the UK in January 1941. Now famous as the British Commando dagger the 'F-S' was a stiletto type knife with a very sharp 7.5in (190mm) blade. It came in a leather scabbard, usually brown, capable of hanging from a belt or being sewn to the battledress by four tabs. An immediate success, the knife went through several slightly differing patterns, and it is likely that a few hundred thousand were made. The use of the knife and other edged

Two Japanese swords and their scabbards. Although most armies retained swords for ceremonial, the Japanese were perhaps unique in carrying them on active service. The commonest patterns were the army officer's, and the NCO's, 'Shin-gunto', both introduced in 1933, and based on the traditional 'Tachi'. The top one is an Army pattern weapon, while the bottom one was Navy issue.

weapons in close combat were described in Fairbairn's 1943 book 'All-in Fighting'.

The 'F-S' was also influential in the development of special forces knives in other countries, most notably America, where the US Marine Corps new stiletto and the OSS knife showed remarkable similarities. Another fearsome close combat knife of the period was the Smatchet, a very broad-bladed weapon with an iron or brass butt end, which was calculated to have almost as much psychological as physical impact. Both Britain and America produced Smatchet-type weapons. One other British knife which deserves mention is the so called 'Middle East' commando knife, which is a mixture of knife and knuckle duster. There are several variations and post war productions: but most, original or not, have a large brown scabbard which secures the knife by means of a strap and stud. The handle section, which doubles as knuckle duster, is of brass, and the pattern of cut outs bears some resemblance to a skull.

The Germans were a little more conservative in the fighting knife field, relying in the main on variations of the old Nahrkampfmesser, or close combat knife. There was one area in which they made a definite advance just before the war, and this was with 'flight utility' knives, though it could be argued that these were more tools than weapons. Pilots and airborne troops had special requirements for a knife, which were not really common to those of the infantryman or commando, in that they needed something which could be made safe when not required in an aircraft or during a parachute jump, that could cut rigging lines, be used with one hand and also be useful for survival purposes. The 'gravity knife' fulfilled all these requirements very well. At first glance such a knife looks like a very large penknife, but a press with one hand allows the blade to slide out of the handle under gravity, locking securely into place. A similar knife continued in use with German forces after World War Two and it has been copied in Britain and elsewhere.

German forces also made extensive use of daggers with dress uniforms. These were in the main not intended for any combat or practical function, and served as a ceremonial distinction between the Luftwaffe, Kriegsmarine, Wehrmacht, SS, and paramilitary formations. The large scale production of these items between the wars also provided a very useful boost to the Sollingen steel industry. Collecting such pieces has become a field in its own right, but the collector has to be especially wary since they have been widely copied, repaired, or re-engraved, and fetch relatively high prices. Generally speaking the German Navy, Air Force and Army favoured a narrow bladed dirk-style dagger, whilst the SS and SA had the broader bladed type similar to that seen in sixteenth century paintings by the artist Hans Holbein. The SS daggers had blackened wood grips, the SA pieces had brown. A myriad of other groups including the judiciary, fire service, 'water protection' police and Red Cross all had their own distinctive side arms.

Another item on the fringes of tool and weapon was the machete, which saw extensive use in jungle warfare from 1941 to 1945. Some of the best known are the US types made by Collins of Hartford, and the Camillus company of New York. The Camillus folded up and made a particularly handy survival tool for USAAF crews. The British seem to have largely copied the Collins design, but UK-made examples often carry the Martindale of Birmingham Crocodile trademark, and British ordnance stamps.

Personal armour was perhaps at the nadir of its fortunes during World War Two, but nonetheless certain items were widely issued. Without doubt the most important was the humble steel helmet, and in several cases the exact model used by many nations in World War Two was a minor update of that from the Great War. Thus the British shrapnel helmet and the French 'Adrian' differed only in detail from their 1918 counterparts; the main difference with the French helmet

(Opposite page) Japanese troops raise their swords in celebration of victory at Bataan in the Philippines. Many officers eschewed the issue weapons and instead carried ancient family blades which were rehilted for service use. Notice the steel helmets with the chin cord tied rather than buckled, sometimes worn over the field cap, and often with either netting or a cover.

being that the shell was of one piece rather than having a separate peak. Britain made no very significant change, except to chin straps and linings, until 1944, when it was eventually decided that the protective qualities of the old 'soup plate' or tin hat were insufficient and a new deeper helmet began to be introduced. Although many civilian services including the Police and Fire Brigade wore the old Mark 2 shallow hat, there was a slightly more capacious and cheaper steel helmet made for the Air Raid Precautions service and 'fire watchers'. This is easily identified not only by its different outline but by a rather shoddy liner which is attached by means of tie-through perforations in the shell of the helmet.

The Germans kept their distinctive outline with the M1935 helmet, but the new headpiece was slightly smaller and lighter than its predecessor and lacked the

Waffen SS troops wait in ambush c. 1944. On the right is a sniper with a second pattern camouflage cover over his steel helmet, and a scope mounted Kar 98k rifle; between the two figures lies a Panzerfaust. The sub-machine gun is an Italian 9mm Beretta Model 38/42, a type also widely used by the Romanians and Germans. In German service it was designated the Maschinenpistole (Beretta) 38/42 (i).

large side lugs. Internally the differences were more obvious, the old three cushion lining system being replaced with an all round leather 'basket' style liner. Initially the new German helmets all had stylish side 'decals' indicating nationality and/or service, but progressively these were phased out. It is interesting to note that the Chinese also adopted the M1935, and initially at least, actually had their helmets made in Germany. Similar, though not identical headgear was also taken up by Spain and Hungary. After the war vast numbers of left-over German helmets were reused by Norway, Austria, and of all people, the Egyptian Presidential Guard. The M1935 was not the only type of helmet in use by German forces and their allies in World War Two as there were many Great War left-overs, light weight 'parade' helmets and other variations in service. Distinctively different though were the helmets of the parachutists and the civilian air defence corps; the former lacked the peak and deep neck guard, while the latter 'Luftschutz' helmet was of excessively Ruritanian splendour. It sported front and rear peaks, vents, a large wings and Swastika motif to the front, and was finished in midnight blue.

It is a little known fact that the Germans were actually developing a new steel helmet at the end of the war, which at one point was intended for general issue. It had been realised that a helmet with sides less close to the vertical would provide better protection, and that further savings in materials could be made. The so called type 'B' helmet was actually presented at the Fuhrer's headquarters in late 1944, but it was turned down at that stage. This design, or one very close to it, was actually adopted by the East German state after the war.

Many American soldiers started the war with British-style helmets but a decision had actually been taken in June 1941 to phase these out in favour of a new M1 helmet. Millions of these were eventually made and it was to be adopted in several other countries. The M1 was a sensibly designed non-magnetic steel hat, but its main innovation was the fact that it had an entirely separate, and helmet shaped, inner liner. On parades, and out of combat areas, the liner could be worn independently and made a smart protection against the minor knocks of training. Another area of protection in which the United States was particularly inventive was flyer's armour. The M1 and M2 Flyer's Vests were made up of steel

plates inside a canvas cover, not unlike a medieval 'brigantine' in general configuration. Especially useful for gunners in bombers both could be rapidly jettisoned by means of quick release catches. Other accessories included neck and groin protectors, and they were usually worn with the M3 or M4 helmets.

Other nations producing their own steel helmets included the Russians, Japanese, Italians, Poles and Czechs, but for the most part these were all relatively uninspired, if practical, hemispheres of steel with moderately varying side profiles and angles of incidence to the skull. The Japanese helmet was remarkable only in that it lacked a buckle to its chin strap and was tied by cords in a distinctly ersatz-looking manner. The Dutch helmet was one of the few others which was distinctively different, and easily identified at a glance, having a more gently sloping front and rear.

March 1945, and British troops fight in the streets of Kervenheim. The man in front has a No. 4 rifle, while the man behind has a captured MP 40, a much-coveted prize for troops used to the Sten. Note his fore hand low on the magazine, a grip likely to put strain on the feed system and cause a stoppage.

Britain was one of several countries to experiment with body armour for foot soldiers in World War Two, and one of the first lines of enquiry pursued was to fit a metal plate behind the respirator bag, a practical suggestion but one which was quickly abandoned due to the fact that the gas mask was not always worn over the vital organs of the chest. The 'Body Protection Committee' then went on to consider more extensive coverage, including a machine gunner's suit, but eventually put a weight limit for infantry armour at 4lb (1.81kg). A set of three steel plates on a harness known as the MRC body armour was produced in 1941, and about 200,000 sets had been made by 1944 when production ceased. Of those that did get issued the majority went to the RAF, and the concept never really caught on, but in any case the MRC was only capable of stopping low velocity fragments and sub-machine gun rounds. The basic problem seems to have been that if steel had to be made so thick as to protect against modern rifle bullets it became impractical for movement, unless the plates were made uselessly small. Body armour was therefore only in very limited use on the ground during World War Two although certain items were used by specialists including face masks and leg protectors by engineers involved in mine clearance. It would not be until the invention of new ballistic materials that the idea of body armour as a general issue item would again be considered.

The .50in calibre Browning M2 heavy machine gun, on a 'ring' mount above the cab of a half track. Notice that the top cover of the weapon is open as it would be to load, also the box for a belt, and the size of the cartridges.

CHAPTER 3

FROM KOREA TO VIETNAM 1946-1975

AFTER WORLD WAR TWO an 'Iron Curtain' descended across Europe, dividing the communist Eastern Bloc from the West. Two Germanys carried on a separate development, but fear of the atom bomb would effectively prevent a major European war. Conflict would therefore be carried on mainly by proxy, and in new empires held together by ideologies rather than dynasties. There were many small wars, and 'low-intensity' struggles, including those in China, Indonesia, Malaya, Biafra, Angola, Mozambique, and the Middle East, but the two big wars of the three decades following World War Two were in Korea and Vietnam.

On 25 June 1950, following a mortar and artillery barrage, the Korean People's Army crossed the 38th parallel and drove into South Korea, beginning the Korean War. In two months the southern Republic of Korea's troops were driven back to a small enclave around Pusan. The US and UN then sent forces which decisively turned the tide against the North Koreans. By mid-October 1950 it was the North which was on the verge of collapse, and the turn of China to come to the aid of its communist ally. Massive Chinese offensives pushed the war back to Seoul and the 38th parallel, where it settled for another two years, before the armistice of July 1953.

In terms of hand-held weapons, there was little used in Korea which had not been seen in World War Two, although it was the weapons of the former allies which were now turned against one another. During the conflict the communists were especially short of air power, artillery and armour. The terrain was hilly, if not mountainous, and the result was that a high proportion of UN casualties were caused by small arms, machine guns and mortars. The North Korean and Chinese arms were for the most part closely based on Soviet models, manufactured in either Russia or China. Both bolt action and semi-automatic rifles were used, and in the former category were several modelled on the old Russian Moisin Nagant, including the M1891/30, and the M1944 carbine. The M1944 carbine was also manufactured in China, where it was known as the Type 53, and the

An American trooper in Vietnam fires an M60 machine gun from the shoulder - a tiring way to shoot. US tactics demanded a high volume of suppressive firepower, especially if ambushed, and the M60 gunner was an essential component of this.

North Koreans also made use of a considerable number of Japanese Arisaka rifles left over from the occupation in World War Two. Perhaps the most common semi-automatic type was the Soviet designed Simonov, later manufactured in China and North Korea, where it was known respectively as the Type 56 and Type 63.

Pistols and sub-machine guns similarly followed Russian precepts. The Chinese Type 51 pistol, for example, was simply a copy of the Soviet Tokarev TT33. This eight-round, recoil operated, 7.62mm semi-automatic was the standard sidearm in the Eastern bloc for many years, and was not only produced in the Soviet Union and China, but in Hungary, Poland and Yugoslavia. It would eventually be produced in North Korea as the Type 68. Although based on well-known principles pioneered by Browning, and having some mechanical similarity to the Colt Model 1911, it was unusual in that it had no safety catch. Nevertheless it could be made safe to carry by putting the hammer into a 'half cock' position, which also locked the slide.

The Soviet PPSh 41 SMG was just as popular with North Korean troops as it

Chinese troops in a river crossing. The pistol shown foreground is the 7.62mm Type 51, a direct copy of the Soviet Tokarev TTM pistol of 1933. This recoil-operated semi-automatic has an eight-round magazine, weighs 1.83lb (.83kg), and with a muzzle velocity of 1,362ft/s (415m/s) was effective to about 55yd (50m). Similar copies of the Tokarev were made in several Eastern bloc states.

had been with the Russians in World War Two. GIs who faced this weapon in combat christened it the 'burp gun', due to its distinctive rasping sound. Eventually it would be made not only in Russia, China, and North Korea, but in Iran and Hungary as well. Its use was world wide, and it was seen in Vietnam, the Middle East, and in the hands of East German border guards as well as in action in Korea.

The main weapon of the communist infantry in Korea was the machine gun, either placed in bunkers in defence, or pushed well forward in the attack. The Chinese were particularly happy to put their gun crews in positions at close range where they could do most damage, even though this increased their own casualties. A variety of weapons were used, the oldest being the 7.62mm Maxim Model 1910. This venerable piece was a veteran of both World Wars, and indeed went back to the beginnings of the machine gun in Russian service. Prior to 1905 Russia had imported German weapons, but in that year she had commenced making a model of her own at the Tula arsenal. This 1905 Model Maxim, though

A late production example of the Russian 7.62 mm Model 1910 Maxim machine gun which saw widespread use in Korea. Notice the so called 'snow cap' on the barrel jacket, which allowed the gunners to use ice and snow in the cooling jacket in lieu of water. (MOD Pattern Room)

efficient enough, had a heavy brass barrel jacket, and the authorities were soon looking for a cheaper and lighter alternative. The Model 1910 fulfilled this requirement, for whilst it weighed 44lb (20kg) this was still 15.4lb (7kg) lighter than the old model. By the height of production in World War One 1,200 of these machine guns were being made per month. This was negligible compared to the massive numbers made during World War Two, when something in excess of 300,000 were fabricated. Understandably there were considerable stocks of the Model 1910 still available in 1950, and many were passed on to China and North Korea.

The more modern SG 43 machine gun was seen in considerable numbers in Korea, and was also manufactured in China, where it was known as the Type 53. Like the 1910 Maxim this was usually mounted on a Solokov wheeled carriage, and it is interesting to note that it was possible to use this either with or without a small armoured shield. The carriage could also be tipped up and the gun attached to what had been the trail in order to produce an anti-aircraft mount.

On the UN side South Korean troops were

American gunners in Korea fire a .50in calibre M2 heavy machine gun from a raised tripod at communist positions on higher ground. Originally designed as an anti-armour and anti-aircraft weapon, the M2 could provide longer ranged fire than that possible from a .30in calibre gun.

most numerous, but the Americans were a major driving force, and it was predominantly with American weapons that the war was fought. Nonetheless there was a significant British Commonwealth contingent, and countries as diverse as France, the Netherlands, Turkey, Thailand, Ethiopia and Columbia supplied some troops. There was even a Luxembourg detachment of 48 men, who fought alongside the Belgians, in support of the British on the Imjin river.

The performance of American weapons in Korea was analysed even before the end of the war by Brigadier S. L. A. Marshall in his classic 'Infantry Operations and

US snipers in Korea. In the foreground is a scoped Model 1903 Springfield rifle. The telescope itself is an eight-times magnification Unertl, of a type commonly used by the Marine Corps.

Weapons Usage in Korea' of 1952. Much of the work was based on interviews with the troops, and the findings make interesting reading. The M1 Garand for example put up a creditable performance:

> 'The issue rifle has performed adequately in Korea and is regarded by the troops with a liking amounting to affection. This is true of all forces, Army and Marines alike. They have found that it stands up ruggedly against the most extreme tests by terrain, weather, and rough handling. They want the weapon left as it now is, and they have no suggestions as to how it might be changed for the better.'

On the few occasions on which the Garand did fail, the cause was almost always that it had frozen solid in sub-zero temperatures, or that it was very dirty. One significant advantage of the semi-automatic Garand was that it operated quickly enough to bring down effective fire, but not so fast as to exhaust the available ammunition supplies. The old Browning automatic rifle was similarly found to be very useful, despite being more than thirty years old. It was at its best engaging enemy machine guns or snipers, and only weapons which had been badly reconditioned in the intervening decades gave trouble.

The only weapon which really seems to have been unpopular was the .30in carbine, which was interesting as it had not given serious problems in World War Two. The main reason appears to have been that since 1945 the old M1 carbine

A North Korean soldier being searched whilst covered by one of the several models of .30in calibre carbine. Malfunctions of the later carbines with full automatic facility in severe weather undermined soldiers' confidence in this light and handy weapon.

had been 'improved' to include fully-automatic fire, and it was this M2 version which was most troublesome. As Marshall observed:

> 'In subfreezing weather, the carbine operates sluggishly and, depending upon the degree of cold, will require anywhere from 5 to 20 warm up shots before it will fire full automatic. Since being made full automatic, it is hypersensitive. In hot weather, even small amounts of dust and moisture together will cause misfire. In cold weather, it is more sensitive to frost than any other weapon, and it is more difficult to lubricate in such a way that it will remain operative. The magazines are a source of continuing trouble.'

Another complaint was lack of power, the short cartridge being fairly useless at much more than 50yd (46m), and unable to stop a charging Chinese soldier with one round, even at half that distance. One result was that those armed with

The US mortar in action. Korea was natural mortar country: in the words of S.L.A. Marshall, 'Frequently, the situation is such that the 81s and 4.2s set up boldly in the open, wherever the ground is best for emplacing, and fire away in plain sight of the enemy held hill, out of practical range of his bullet firing weapons. It is not unusual to see the 81s, 4.2s, 75 recoilless, and sometimes the AA multiple mount weapons all firing in battery from the same location against one broad target - this in support of the attack during daylight operations.'

carbines tended to fire lengthy but ineffective bursts early in the firefight and exhaust their ammunition. The Garand, BAR and .30in M1919 and .50in M2 machine guns all appear to have been used in a more deliberate manner, and as a result stayed in action longer. It could also have been argued that the carbine was not intended for a protracted medium range firefight, having been designed as immediate close defence for second line troops.

Amongst the ancillary weapons, the grenade, mortar, and recoilless rifle all saw heavy use. The 4.2 inch, 81mm, and 60mm mortars all performed well, and were especially important given the hilly terrain. The main limiting factor to their activity was availability of ammunition. There were some breakages and failures, but these were generally associated with prolonged use in extreme cold. Illuminating rounds were put to good use during night fighting, and on certain occasions mortar 'duels' would arise with enemy positions. The hand grenade was also a mainstay of infantry combat, and as in World War One some troops became so used to it that they would sometimes prefer to throw bombs at a target which would have been easily engaged with the rifle. American troops were on the receiving end of Chinese 'potato masher' grenades, which Marshall states were treated with a 'scorn bordering on contempt'. In general US bombers performed better than their communist adversaries, but this was perhaps more a matter of luck and physique as the training that American troops received in this respect was sometimes deemed inadequate.

Bazookas and recoilless rifles were, of course, primarily intended for engaging vehicles, but in Korea they were often used against personnel and field works. One particular type of target which they were applied to were the bunkers which

the North Korean troops tended to make out of double tiers of thick logs, tied together with cable, and roofed with earth. Hand-held anti-tank weapons proved especially adept because such positions were difficult to locate with artillery at long range, and were often too deeply covered to be destroyed by the plunging fire of mortars. Smaller machine gun nests, and even individual foxholes were also sometimes engaged in the same way.

Amazingly, the bayonet was put to use for its intended purpose in Korea, and there were even some in the American ranks who placed significant reliance upon it. Marshall concluded however that this was often a mixture of bravado and desperation. Analysing an action by 'E' Company 27th Infantry at Hill 180, in which 18 enemy soldiers were killed by the bayonet, he came to the conclusion that in six cases this was because the GI had forgotten to load his rifle or had a misfire, and in four cases he had run out of ammunition altogether. He also pointed out the commanding officer's willingness to charge, the lack of grenades, and the ineffective artillery fire.

British infantry weapons in Korea again differed little from those in use in 1945, although a number of items, including the 3.5in rocket launcher and the .30in machine gun came from the Americans. Mainstays were the bolt-action

A US M7 flamethrower in action on a Korean hillside. The backpack consisted of three tanks, two for fuel and one to provide the necessary pressure. The gun itself had two handgrips, the forward one mounting the trigger, and the jet was lit by means of an ignition cylinder mounted on the nozzle. The 4 US gal (15l) of fuel would last for about eight seconds in continuous use, with a range of about 55yd (50m).

A British Bren team on watch in Korea. Notice the deeper silhouette of the Mark IV steel helmet, which was first issued in 1944.

Lee-Enfield No. 4 Mark 1 rifle, and the latest version of the Sten gun, the Mark 5, superior to earlier versions only in its woodwork. Even so, the Sten proved useful, especially in the close quarter fights which could arise from night patrolling. The Bren was the section support weapon and the Vickers, heavy and cumbersome by modern standards, was the main medium machine gun. Despite the fact that more light automatic arms would have been desirable, most British veterans expressed satisfaction with the performance of their weapons.

One interesting invention to come direct from the Korean conflict to the British arsenal was the 'Raschen Bag'. Frozen or soft and uneven ground caused problems with the base plates of mortars, and these could break or sink in, depending on circumstance, leading to unserviceability or inaccuracy. This was solved by a young engineer captain called Dan Raschen, who invented a segmented, air-filled, padded bag to put around the plate. This spread and dissipated the downward forces, making it possible to bring a mortar into action more quickly on difficult ground and reduce the number of failures. Colonel Raschen, as he later became, told the present writer that the inspiration for the bag was a close look at the inside of a box of cheese portions . . .

Body armour was one of the important developments of Korea. From 1943 the US Army and Navy had been experimenting with a new glass fibre laminate called 'Doron', named after Colonel G.F. Doriot of the Military Planning Division. Doron was actually layers of glass fibre filaments bonded together with resin under pressure. Just an 1/8in (3mm) of Doron would easily prevent the penetration of a .45in pistol bullet, and such was the confidence in the material that one of the researchers, Dr Corey, allowed a Colt to be fired at his Doron-clad arm at 15ft (4.6m) for the purpose of testing. Only a few jackets with Doron protection slid into the pockets had been issued by the end of World War Two.

Work carried out in Korea at the start of that war indicated that an incredible 92% of wounds were caused by fragments, and that many low velocity pieces could be stopped by body armour. A new Doron vest in which the plates were sheathed in layers of nylon was rapidly fabricated. Tests indicated that the new vests, designated M1951, would stop a bullet from a Colt or Thompson at the muzzle, grenade fragments at 3ft (1m), and most of the effects of a mortar round at 10ft (3m). The results of the introduction of the M1951 were impressive and it was claimed that battle casualties were reduced by as much as 30%. During 1952 two further models of armoured vest, the T-52-1 and the T-52-2, were introduced. These were all nylon and had a lining of sponge rubber which held the vest clear of the body and helped to absorb shocks and impacts which could otherwise have led to fractures or bruising.

There were indeed some remarkable survivals by troops wearing body armour; more than one UN soldier was hit at close range by fire from a Chinese 'burp' gun and got away with bruises and shock. Lieutenant George Forty of the 1st Royal Tank Regiment, later curator of the Bovington Tank Corps Museum, also had an extremely lucky escape. When outside his tank and wearing M1951 body armour and a steel helmet he was blown off his feet by a mortar round which

Men of the Royal Australian Regiment in Korea. The rifle in the foreground is the old .303in SMLE, or 'No 1', with the folding leaf sight above the barrel. The bolt is shown here fully retracted so that a fresh charger of five rounds can be loaded from the top. Two such chargers filled the magazine.

landed in a ditch nearby. Although 150 small fragments pierced his arms and legs, he survived, as none had penetrated his flak jacket to find a vital organ. By the end of the war more than 26,000 1952-type jackets alone had been issued, and a new era had been ushered in when body armour was a commonplace amongst front line soldiers, rather than a rarity.

Just over a decade later the Americans would be fighting another Asian

North Vietnamese troops after the First Indochina War. Bolt action Mauser-type rifles have yet to be replaced with anything more modern.

enemy, but this time with less favourable results. The origins of the Vietnam war go right back to before 1941, with the establishment of communist party organisations in South East Asia. Having helped to oust the Japanese in World War Two these groups now turned on their former Imperial masters. In Vietnam the Vietminh succeeded in taking control of the north of the country from the French between 1945 and 1954, in the 'First Indo-China War' which culminated in the bloodbath at Dien-Bien-Phu. After this America became steadily more involved in helping to organise the defences of the south. By 1965 US troops were fighting openly in significant numbers against the Viet Cong and their North Vietnamese allies. Despite heavy bombing raids, napalm, helicopter gunships, defoliants and all manner of electronic wizardry, the Vietnam war was still very much fought with personal weapons; and the men on the ground still took the brunt of the fighting. By 1972 America had lost 46,370 killed, and a third of a million wounded. Even so this was but a fraction of the 200,000 South Vietnamese, and 900,000 North Vietnamese who were killed.

For America, Vietnam was a difficult war to understand and an even more difficult one to win, despite vastly superior economic strength. The communist forces were prepared to accept limitless casualties over an indefinite period, a luxury that public opinion would not allow any US general. The Chinese and Russians assisted the North Vietnamese war effort, pushing supplies painfully

down the Ho Chi Minh trail to the Viet Cong. Attempts to cut this lifeline helped to pull Laos and Cambodia into the war, with disastrous consequences. General William Westmoreland, who had called for an all out 'big unit' war, was replaced by General G. Creighton Abrams, and from 1969 President Nixon engaged in a policy of 'Vietnamisation' of the war. The corrupt regime in the South was no match for the fanatical leaders of the North, and the resultant debacle, with the final defeat of the South in 1975 still rankles badly with the American military, despite subsequent successes. The whole exercise had perhaps been based on two important misconceptions; that the communist world could form a seamless monolithic bloc, and secondly that the countries of the area would fall, 'like dominoes' to the virulent ideology. As hindsight has demonstrated the communist world had several faces, and it is capitalism which has been able to spread like wildfire in Asia and Eastern Europe.

The American soldier began the Vietnam war armed with the M14 rifle, which had been adopted in 1957 after extensive tests against other weapons, including the FNT 48, and the British EM 2, as well as American made experimental designs. Even so the M1 Garand was still in evidence, particularly in the hands of the South Vietnamese Army. The M14 was a 7.62mm NATO calibre weapon which showed several improvements over the Garand. Magazine capacity was increased to 20 rounds, and fully automatic fire was available as well as

French troops in Indochina, armed with the 9mm MAT 49 sub-machine gun. In 1946 France had decided on the adoption of a new SMG to be based around the standard 9mm Parabellum cartridge. Various designs were proposed by the Chatelleraut and St Etienne arsenals, but it was one produced at Tulle which was selected. Its handiness was aided by the telescopic wire butt, and that the magazine housing could be folded forward to lie under the barrel when not in use, as shown here. Common in French territories, many would see use in Vietnam. Notice also the US-type fragmentation grenade and the machete.

An M60 machine gun flanked by two riflemen armed with the 7.62mm M14 self loading rifle. Adopted in 1957 the M14 was standard issue in Vietnam until the appearance of the M16. Using full automatic the M14's cyclic rate of fire was a theoretical 700 rounds a minute, but allowing for magazine changes 60 aimed rounds was about the maximum practical. Although the bullet would take effect at over 3,280yd (3,000m), 'battle range' was more like 550yd (500m), this being the limit of the soldier's accuracy without resting the weapon. Most engagements indeed took place much closer than this.

selective single shots. Allowing for magazine changes it was expected that for short periods the soldier could manage up to 60 rounds per minute. There were two main variants on the basic model, the sniper rifle, since known as the M21, and the M14A1, a slightly heavier version intended for light support. An interesting selection of accessories were made to complement the M14 family of weapons; these included a blank firer, a bipod, a knife bayonet, and an arctic trigger kit which allowed the user to wear mittens. There was also a grenade launcher and sight which could be fitted to the rifle. In US service the M14 was made by four major manufacturers; Springfield Armory; Harrington and Richardson; Thompson-Ramo-Wooldridge; and Winchester. Between them they made about 1.3 million pieces, before production ceased in 1964. Although superseded for front line troops during the late 1960s the M14 would remain in use for many years as the weapon of the Reserve and National Guard, and was also produced in Taiwan. The South Vietnamese Army also used the M14 in large numbers.

The replacement for the M14 was the M16, the so called 'black rifle'. This was at first taken by US forces on an experimental basis, but by 1969 it was general issue, and was quickly becoming the most common shoulder arm in the American arsenal. The M16 was based on a 1950s concept designed by Eugene Stoner of the ArmaLite Company, and was from the outset a purpose-built assault rifle. Early models were produced in the Netherlands, and, differing in detail from the model which was later to be US standard issue, were designated as the AR series of arms. Portugal, Nicaragua, the Sudan and Burma all had samples or small issues of the 7.62mm AR10 at an early stage.

The US M16A1 rifle. The key to the success of the M16 was its 5.56mm cartridge, and an acceptance that it was mainly to be used at close to medium ranges. Exceptionally light at just over 6lb (2.8kg) empty, it was gas operated with a rotating bolt locking mechanism. The firer had a choice of single shots or easily-controllable bursts. Seen here with a 30-round magazine it was also used with a smaller 20-shot box. (MOD Pattern Room)

At about that time the Infantry Board at Fort Bennings laid down a specification for a new weapon to re-equip the troops. This stated a need for a gun which would be as accurate and as lethal as the M1 rifle within 500yd (457m), and able to penetrate a steel helmet at that distance. It was to have a selective fire capability, yet be no heavier than 6lb (2.7kg) when loaded.

One possible solution was to scale down the AR10, and work began first on the cartridge, the result being a light 5.56mm round. This was an important step, as, though it could not have been realised at the time, 5.56mm would ultimately be accepted as a world standard. The scaled down arm was redesignated as the AR15, and the Colt factory signed an agreement to produce it in 1959. In 1961 the US Air Force took delivery of 8,500 weapons, and army orders soon followed. Vietnam undoubtedly speeded up the process for by 1966 not only had the AR15 been accepted, and redesignated M16, but 400,000 had been produced and delivered to the military. The next year the US Government and Colt signed an agreement, in which, for a consideration of $4.5 million, the company allowed the production of the rifle by other contractors.

In many ways the M16 was highly suitable for the war in South East Asia; it was light at 6.3lb (2.86kg), and proved handy and effective. It had a 20- or 30-round magazine and could deliver very impressive firepower, particularly at closer ranges. More than one story has been told of Viet Cong virtually cut in half by fully-automatic bursts. The M16 was not however a miracle weapon, for tactical as well as technological reasons. For one thing the burst fire capacity was arguably overused by conscript troops, who would blast away magazine after magazine at fleeting or non-existent targets. Research conducted by the army suggested however that this

An M16A1 caught in mid burst, with two empty cartridges on their way to the ground from the open ejection port. Apparent are the short 20-round magazine, and the sights which are protected within the carrying handle. Typically this soldier has made his feelings obvious in marker pen on his helmet cover: he is however careful with his aim, US Marine Corps research suggested that a measurable percentage of troops shut their eyes before squeezing the trigger.

was really only a serious problem for the first five minutes of an action. Another point was that the 5.56mm round was criticised as having insufficient range or lethality, but to be fair to the designers and manufacturers the M16 was not originally intended to be a long-range machine gun. It is interesting to relate that until Operation Cedar Falls in January 1967 the vast majority of recorded incidents in which the M16 was used were at 66yd (60m) or less. Thereafter there were more engagements at longer ranges, a factor dictated almost totally by terrain, since after that time there were often fights across open paddy field.

One other area of concern was the fact that the M16 had originally been marketed as a virtually 'maintenance free' weapon. This was patently unrealistic as heavy usage quickly caused fouling and many jams were reported. Minor

Watching the jungle with the M16A1. Dirty and humid conditions soon proved that there was no such thing as a 'no maintenance' weapon. The A1 version saw the addition of the bolt-closing device (seen just above the soldier's hand) which enabled a fouled bolt to be rammed home manually. Notice the zip-fronted M1955 body armour.

modifications, including the addition of a manual bolt assist, and better instructions on cleaning, soon cured this problem. As S.L.A. Marshall reported in the US army's 1967 'Vietnam Primer':

> 'The M16 has proved itself an ideal weapon for jungle warfare. Its high rates of fire, light weight, and easy-to-pack ammunition have made it popular with its carrier. But it cannot take the abuse or receive the neglect its older brother, the M1, could sustain. It must be cleaned and checked out whenever the opportunity affords. Commanders need assign top billing to the maintenance of the weapon to prevent battlefield stoppages. The new field cleaning kit assists the purpose.'

One variation on the basic weapon which appears to have been spawned by experience in Vietnam was the Colt Commando, a shorter, lighter gun, with a telescopic butt, and intended for close quarters work. The original intention had been that this was an emergency or survival gun, but it functioned well enough to become popular with special forces. One other noticeable difference with the Commando was that it had a large flash suppressor; this was needed because shortening the standard barrel produced a good deal more muzzle blast and flash.

Taking aim from a trench with the US M79 grenade launcher. The single shot M79 had a maximum range of 440yd (400m), but for point targets it was seldom accurate at more than about 165yd (150m). Nevertheless it was a handy source of suppressive fire for the infantry squad.

A useful ancillary to rifles was the M79 grenade launcher, sometimes known to the soldiers as 'blooper' or 'thumper', suitable onomatopoeic descriptions of its delivery of a 40mm high explosive grenade. In Vietnam a standard infantry section was often composed of eight riflemen and two grenadiers with M79s. The grenade launcher was a single shot weapon which broke in the middle to facilitate loading like a giant shotgun. For close quarters it could also take a special buckshot or 'flechette' round which had a devastating effect not unlike a small cannon going off. Ammunition for the grenade launcher was carried in the universal ammunition pouch which could accommodate three rounds, and a special bandolier was capable of taking a further six cartridges. Grenadiers armed with the M79 usually carried a pistol as a back up armament. By 1969 a new grenade

The rather strange looking US 40mm M79 grenade launcher. One of its best qualities was its lightness, as, even loaded, it weighed only 6.5lb (2.95kg). With the sights flipped down in the position shown it could engage targets between the 'minimum safety' range of 33yd (30m) and 110yd (100m). They were flipped up for more distant targets. (MOD Pattern Room)

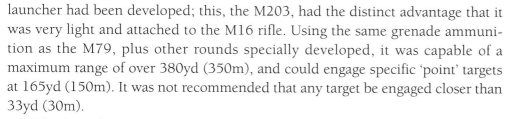

launcher had been developed; this, the M203, had the distinct advantage that it was very light and attached to the M16 rifle. Using the same grenade ammunition as the M79, plus other rounds specially developed, it was capable of a maximum range of over 380yd (350m), and could engage specific 'point' targets at 165yd (150m). It was not recommended that any target be engaged closer than 33yd (30m).

The Australians in Vietnam used some M16s but also some British and home-produced arms. Their standard rifle was the L1A1 7.62mm Self Loading Rifle, and the Lithgow New South Wales-produced item differed only in detail from the Enfield arm. The SLR was a British version of the Belgian FN FAL, a heavy automatic rifle. Its full-sized 7.62mm NATO cartridge was really too powerful to control in burst fire, so the SLR was made to be only capable of semi-automatic single shots. The SLR was heavier than the M16, but more than adequately powerful, its round being capable of cutting through small trees and still killing the enemy behind.

The Australians also used the F1 9mm sub-machine gun. The F1 was interesting if only because its invention had at least an indirect input from its users, the

The M16A1 fitted with the M203 grenade launcher. Developed by the AAI Corporation of Cockeysville, Maryland, the M203 was the replacement for the old M79. As it used the same 40mm rounds general performance was similar, but it had the advantage that the grenadier did not have to change weapons to fire conventional ball cartridges. Aim was by means of a post fore sight and a quadrant rear sight, which clamped to the M16 carrying handle. The M203 was fired by means of a trigger, mounted forward of the rifle magazine. Interesting variations on the standard high explosive grenade included an air burst shell, practice and illuminating rounds. Later the M16 would also be fitted with an M234 non-lethal launcher for crowd control; the so called 'Ring Airfoil System'. (MOD Pattern Room)

Australian troops. In May 1945 a questionnaire had been circulated which solicited 1,500 replies; at least partly inspired by the suggestions returned, the Australian design team came up with an experimental piece they christened the Kokoda. This had some advanced features such as a magazine which came up through the pistol grip, and a telescopic butt, but was excessively prone to over-

Ready for anything. A US machine gunner with the 7.62mm M60, emplaced on the perimeter of 173rd Airborne Brigade's positions prior to the assault on Hill 875, November 1967. The gas-operated M60 with its disintegrating link belts more than proved its worth as a light support gun in Vietnam. Weighing 23lb (10.5kg) it had an effective bipod range of 1,100yd (1,000m), and a tripod range of 1,970yd (1,800m): the gun was not perfect however, and its faults included poor barrel changing and a weak carrying handle.

heating. A good deal more experiment, and some consultations with British designers had led finally in 1962 to the F1, which in the event was much more conservative in concept. It had a 34-shot top mounted magazine, derived perhaps from the old Owen, and it also used a number of components common to the SLR. New Zealanders in Vietnam used many of the same weapons as the Australians but substituted the British Sterling SMG for the F1.

The standard US support weapon was the M60 general purpose machine gun, and the average infantry platoon could usually count two or more in its ranks. Using the feed system of the German MG 42, the M60 had been designed in the late 1950s. It could be deployed in several ways; on a bipod, a tripod, or, rather

strenuously, from a strap around the neck, to fire from the chest or hip! Such heroics were unlikely to be accurate or sustainable for more than a moment or two, but at the right moment could have a psychological impact in encouraging friends or deterring foes. US Army research on Vietnam suggested that M60 gunners were in fact relatively sparing and controlled in their use of fire compared to others. On patrol they would seldom carry more than 1,200 rounds for immediate use, and it was not usually exhausted.

The M60 could make a telling difference on the rare occasions when a mass target presented itself, but was not without its flaws. Most significant of these was the difficulty of changing overheated barrels in a sustained fire role. Whilst one man held the gun steady his partner had to don an asbestos glove to remove the barrel assembly. Loss of the 'Mitten Asbestos M1942' could be very embarrassing. The Australians discovered a novel tactical use for the M60 on jungle patrols by fitting it with a short belt, or a 28-round box magazine. When the enemy was sighted or sprang an ambush it was the machine gunner's duty to empty his weapon in their general direction whilst the

A remarkable demonstration of the fact that the M60 could indeed be a 'light machine gun'. Also visible is the carrying sling and the soldier's body armour. The M60 manual of 1984 would recognise three 'Assault fire' positions: from the shoulder, hip, and underarm; adjustment of fire being by tracer and impact of shot.

rest of the section immediately dived for cover. The Australians also made use of the old Bren gun modified to 7.62mm calibre.

Heavier sustained fire for US forces was provided by weapons of equal, if not greater antiquity, mainly the .30in and .50in Browning machine guns. The .30in M1919 was used as a company and battalion support weapon, and the .50in M2 mainly in firebases; both were often mounted on the M2 light tripod. The M1919 was effectively World War One technology, but its range of 1,000yd (910m) and more, and its cyclic rate of 500 rounds per minute were perfectly adequate for the task of covering beaten zones and making it difficult for the enemy to close on defended localities. Remarkably the BAR was also seen in Vietnam, but usually in the hands of non-American troops such as the CIA-sponsored Civilian Irregular Defence Group (CIDG), which was made up of various minority groups within Vietnam.

One other machine gun which was in American hands was the Stoner Mk 23 Commando 5.56mm, although its use appears to have been limited mainly to

Eugene Stoner designed a family of modular weapons, which included machine guns and rifles, all with interchangeable parts. The only element which made its mark on the battlefield was the XM207 light machine gun, also known as the 'Mark 23 Commando'. This was especially popular with US Navy 'SEAL' teams where lightness was a boon. The 5.56mm weapon had an effective range of about 875yd (800m), and a cyclic rate of 750 rounds per minute. It was usually seen in Vietnam with either a box, or a drum magazine as shown here. The grenade at the man's belt is the standard issue M26A1 fragmentation type, which weighed 1lb (.45kg) and had a smooth steel sheet exterior with a notched fragmentation coil inside.

the Navy SEALS special forces teams. This was an effective light support weapon, which could be fitted with either a box or a drum magazine. It was invented by Eugene Stoner, originally as just one element in the Stoner 63 system, which included an assault rifle, sub-machine gun and heavier machine gun as part of an integrated package. The concept was far sighted, but the vicissitudes of defence procurement made it unlikely that any government would purchase a complete system of this sort. The light machine gun therefore underwent further work and was supplied as a separate element. The Stoner 23 was popular, especially with special forces patrols, because together with 800 rounds of ammunition the total carry weight was only 35lb (15.9kg).

Hand-thrown grenades continued to be a vital part of the US arsenal. The first hand grenade used in Vietnam was the old Mk 2, a classic pineapple-shaped cast iron bomb, with a 4.5 second fuse. Although the 1959 Field Manual stated that the theoretical casualty radius was 10yd (9m), some fragments were often thrown a good deal further. The replacement for the M2 was the standard issue M26A1; this was a lemon-shaped smooth-bodied bomb whose fragmentation effect was achieved by the presence of a serrated wire coil which lined the casing. It was

lighter than the old grenade, and could be thrown up to 40yd (37m), although some of the fragments would still fly further and it was recommended that the thrower and friendly troops take cover when it was used. There were usually about 1,000 fragments from this bomb, with a hit probability of 50% on troops in the open up to 10yd (9m) away. There was also an improved version of the M26, called the M61.

The 5.56mm Stoner 63 rifle. Although the Stoner rifle never saw widespread use it was an interesting milestone in technological terms. Made by the Cadillac Gage Corporation of Detroit and Michigan, it was intended that the '63' should be the basis of a modular weapons system. During the mid 1960s it was much tested, and production rights were sold in Europe, but the 'system' did not get much further. The Stoner 63 rifle was a little heavy at 9.7lb (4.4kg), was sighted to 500yd (457m), and had a practical rate of about 90 rounds per minute.

Grenades had a couple of uses in Vietnam, which, if not unique, were certainly a part of the character of that war. First was the use of grenades in tunnel clearance operations, like those around Cu Chi. Any explosive blast has its effect magnified in a confined space, but the effect on the Viet Cong was often unpredictable; they dug their tunnels deep with many turns and twists and trap doors. Thus it was that grenades, gas or pyrotechnics thrown into the tunnels often did

A 'tunnel rat' cautiously examines a hole, Colt M1911 in hand. The Vietcong's use of underground tunnels and shelters posed special problems in terms of the weaponry needed to flush them out. Gas, flame, smoke, and grenades were all used, but in the face of twisting passages, water traps and doors, men and dogs had to go underground to be sure. The issue Colt .45in was carried, but its report in such confined spaces could leave its user half deafened and subsequently unable to detect the enemy. In 1966 an experimental 'Tunnel Exploration Kit', with miner's lamp, microphone, and hefty silenced revolver appeared, but even this limited equipment was found to be too cumbersome. Tunnel men therefore adopted a selection of deadly short range arms. These included the Smith and Wesson .38in revolver, various short shotguns and riot weapons, M2 .30in carbine with folding stock, knives, and even foreign pistols like the Beretta and Luger.

not work, and dogs or human 'tunnel rats' armed with revolvers or Colt semi-automatics had to go below. Even less pleasant was the practice of 'fragging'; or using grenades to frighten or kill unpopular officers or career soldiers. Grenades had a reputation for being prone to accident, and it is likely that a number of such incidents were put down to mishap before the technique became known to the authorities.

American use of body armour was especially widespread in Vietnam. Apart from the M1 steel helmet with a variety of camouflage covers, the most ubiquitous piece of armour was the flak jacket. Marine Corps standing orders stated that jackets were to be worn on all combat operations, and one study showed that in fact 73% of the Corps were wearing armour at the time they were wounded, against 19% of the army. There were several models of vest, including the M52, M55

Vietnam saw the use of both the latest technology and the positively medieval. Here a flak-jacket clad member of a river patrol uses a fire arrow against huts.

and M69. The M55 as its numbering suggests, was brought into use in 1955, and continued in production until the end of the 1960s. Its main usefulness was against fragmentation weapons like the grenade and the mortar bomb, and, as the label inside the garment helpfully pointed out, 70% of all combat injuries were caused by such fragments. The protective elements of the sleeveless vest were a weave of 13-ply ballistic nylon and overlapping fibreglass plates, all contained in a cotton shell. In hot conditions it was often worn open, but this was frowned

Montagnard irregulars in Vietnam. The sub-machine guns are old M3 .45in 'Grease Guns'.

upon as it reduced protection. The M69 featured better neck protection, and was encased in waterproof vinyl as well as covered with Oxford cloth. It was closed with either a zipper, or later with Velcro. On occasion it could aid some remarkable survivals: one such was the case of Captain A. Sambucchi of the 35th Artillery. This officer was in a weapons pit when a mortar round exploded about ten feet away, he suffered multiple wounds to his arms, legs, face and head but none through his armour. Another explosion drove a fragment into his chest, but the jacket this time blocked the wound. A fire in the bunker now caused burns to his arms and legs but again his vital organs were protected and he lived.

Communist weapons of Vietnam were much more diverse than those of the US or her allies, partly due to difficulties of supply, and partly because the Vietnamese forces were two armies, the NVA or North Vietnamese Army, and the VC or Viet Cong guerrilla force. When conventional sources of Communist Bloc arms dried up, or were interrupted, the VC in particular resorted to all manner of expedients. Captured weapons, American and French were pressed into use, unexploded bombs were dangerously tapped for explosives, and ingenious devices were improvised from home made materials or rubbish like tin cans and nails.

The most popular rifle was undoubtedly the Soviet designed AK 47, when it was available, and since this has become one of the most widespread and influential arms of the century it deserves detailed attention. The inventor of the AK 47

One of many 7.62mm 'Avtomat Kalashnikova' AK 47 assault rifles captured from the Vietcong. Details visible include the selector lever mounted on the side above the trigger, the sights mounted above and forward of the ejection port, an under barrel cleaning rod and a very tatty sling.

was Mikhail Kalashnikov, a Red Army tank sergeant who took up weapons design after being badly wounded in the battle for Byransk in 1941. His first two essays in the subject were a sub-machine gun and a carbine, but neither were accepted for service. He produced his famous assault rifle in 1947, and it came into service four years later. It was one of the first true assault rifles, a reasonably light, handy weapon firing the reduced-power 7.62mm cartridge developed for the SKS Simonov. Kalashnikov was made a Hero of Socialist Labour in recognition of his efforts. Various improvements and production outside the Soviet Union have produced the the AKM, Chinese Type 56, North Korean Type 58, Polish PMK, East German MPiKM, minor Romanian variations, the Yugoslav M70 and the Finnish M60, all of which have a basic similarity, and the total production of which world wide has been estimated in excess of 70 million units.

Depending on exact model the furniture can be of solid wood, laminated wood, metal, or plastic; the stock is usually fixed but folding models have also been produced in large numbers. The exterior layout of the AK 47 is rather like that of the German Sturmgewehr of 1944, and, like the MP 44, it is gas operated, without a regulator, and with the gas cylinder over the barrel. The AK 47 is capable of selective fire and has a 30-round, curved, detachable box magazine containing 7.62mm cartridges with steel cored bullets. It weighs 9.48lb (4.3kg)

A US Ranger on patrol with a captured AK 47 near the Dong Nai River, 1970. Tough, reliable, and packing a reasonably hefty punch, the AK was often the choice of US Special Forces; it had the added advantage that use could be made of captured ammunition.

unloaded. The AK 47 is reasonably accurate, with good penetration, and well-qualified experts have judged it not significantly inferior to the American M16; it was not unknown for captured AKs in Vietnam to be used very happily by US Rangers. Its main virtues are simplicity and toughness, essential qualities for a true soldier's weapon. Most AKs are equipped with some form of bayonet, the basic Soviet form being a practical looking knife type, whilst the Chinese Type 56 has a folding stiletto which remains permanently attached. The AKM bayonet is interesting in that by clipping it together with its scabbard it doubles as a pair of wire cutters.

Unfortunately for the North Vietnamese there were never enough AK 47s, or Chinese Type 56 assault rifles to go round. Many had to make do with SKS Simonov self-loading carbines, or French model MAS49 rifles. Many of the latter had been captured during the first Indo-China War and subsequently saw use against the Americans. The MAS49 used 7.5mm ammunition and was physically quite a big weapon, firing semi-automatic only. It was therefore relegated to second echelon troops, at least as far as increasing supplies of other arms allowed. The least lucky of the communist fighters did not manage to get semi-automatics at all, and until late in the war there were some guerrillas still armed with bolt action rifles of French, Russian, and Chinese ancestry.

(Opposite page) Triumphant Vietcong atop a shattered armoured personnel carrier. Amongst their weapons are a bolt action rifle fitted with a grenade launcher and, on the right, a Chinese 7.62mm Type 56 semi-automatic carbine. The Type 56 was a close copy of the Soviet SKS, it weighed a handy 8.6lb (3.9kg), had a 10-round magazine, a folding bayonet permanently attached, and was effective up to about 440yd (400m).

A Thai soldier, c.1980, poses with a 7.62mm, Chinese Type 68 rifle. Although similar in general appearance to a Kalashnikov it is easily distinguished by a number of features including a cylindrical gas regulator knob mounted above the barrel, a folding bayonet of SKS type, and the shape of the top dust cover. The Type 68 had selective fire, a 15-round detachable box magazine, and an effective battle range of about 440yd (400m).

The Vietnamese also had a wide variety of SMGs. The best of these was probably the MAT49, a standard in the French Army. This was a 9mm blowback model with a 32-round box magazine. It was compact, weighed 8lb (3.6kg), and was capable of giving a useful volume of fire at close ranges. Unusually for an SMG it was fitted with a grip safety mechanism. Another French SMG, also left over from their period of occupation was the MAS38; this was an earlier model dating back to before World War Two. It was slightly less satisfactory, mainly because its 7.65mm cartridge lacked penetration. The other communist SMGs were a ragbag indeed. They included the old Russian PPsh41, the M3A1, the M1A1 Thompson, and even a few Swedish FFV model 45s.

Pistols were also used, the main examples being Soviet and Chinese. The Tokarev TT33 had been used extensively by Russia in World War Two, and then produced by the Chinese as the Type 54. Both found their way to Vietnam. Similarly the more modern Soviet Makarov, which had itself been largely copied from the Walther came both directly from Russia, and in a Chinese variant known as the Type 59. The Makarov was unremarkable, but was probably preferable to the Tokarev, being lighter, having a safety catch, and was less prone to accident. The Makarov fired a 9mm cartridge less powerful than the European Parabellum, and had an eight-round magazine: Russian examples were identifiable by a star on the grip, while the Chinese Type 59 had its number on the receiver.

In the field of machine guns the picture was again similar in that the Communists relied mainly on a mixture of Chinese and Soviet guns, but they also produced a model of their own, the TUL 1. Remarkably the old Model 1910 Maxim was still seen occasionally, and it could still perform usefully especially if used in ambush or local air defence. From the Soviet arsenal of World War Two came the Degtyarev Pekhotiny DP and DPM, the DshK 38 heavy machine gun, and the SG 43 Goryunov, or their Chinese equivalents. Amongst the more modern weapons was the RPD, a belt-fed light machine gun, air cooled, with a cyclic rate of about 700 rounds per minute. The RPD was often seen with a round drum magazine under the breech, and a 100-round disintegrating belt fed from this. Soviet designers had begun work on the RPD as early as 1943, specifically to make use of their new short 7.62mm cartridge. The gun became a Red Army standard after the war, and the original RPD, as well as its Chinese derivative, the Type 56, found their way to Vietnam.

Probably the newest Eastern Bloc machine gun to be used in Indo-China was the RPK or 'Ruchoi Pulemet Kalashnikov', a light machine gun version of the AK 47. It was first seen in any numbers at the Moscow May Day parade of 1966 and to all intents and purposes was an AK 47 with a longer, sturdier barrel, and a small bipod at the muzzle. Although the RPK has no barrel change facility and a pretty limited capacity in sustained fire it is very light, straightforward, and has a high degree of interchangeability with other Kalashnikov weapons. It can use either AK box magazines or a drum. The North Vietnamese TUL 1 was basically a copy of this gun.

The Vietnamese Communists used a wide variety of hand grenades which either came from the Eastern Bloc, or were improvised. Probably the oldest was the RGD 33, a short stick grenade with a metal handle which could be used offensively, or with a fragmentation sleeve for defence. First used by the Soviets prior to World War Two, it was obsolete, yet still lethal enough by the time of Vietnam. Another bomb of similar vintage was the Russian F1 anti-personnel grenade, known to the Chinese as the Type 1/M33. This had a heavy cast iron body, similar to the American Mk 2, and was best used in a defensive role from cover since some of the fragments produced could still prove dangerous at over 110yd (100m). The RG 42 was also from World War Two, and its Chinese analogue was the Type 42: this was shaped like a small tin can, and though smooth outside, contained an internal fragmentation sleeve, divided up into a diamond pattern. The effective range of these fragments was about 27yd (25m). A more modern Soviet bomb in use in Vietnam was the RGD 5. This was a smaller and lighter grenade than the old models, with the result that it could be thrown a little further and greater supplies could be carried. It was egg shaped and had an effective fragmentation radius of about 16 to 22yd (15 to 20m).

Although a few Japanese and French grenades did turn up in the hands of the VC the next most important source of supply, after China and Russia, was the US forces themselves. Captured grenades were obviously used, but extensive service was made from unexploded US artillery shells, empty ration tins and bamboo tubes. When the realisation dawned that rubbish dumps were a veritable arsenal campaigns were started to 'burn, bash and bury' anything that the VC might find useful. This may have had some effect, but the Americans remained victims of their own huge demand for munitions and home comforts. It said much about the divergent attitudes of the combatants, and emphasised that technology or superior weaponry were not alone enough to ensure success.

Another conflict which had been bubbling away even before Korea was that of Israel with her Arab neighbours. Israel achieved independence from Britain in 1948, and almost immediately the new state was attacked by Egypt, Iraq, Jordan, Syria and Lebanon. Israel won this war as she did conflicts in 1956, 1967 and 1973. Israel had traditionally been dependent on its western ally America, and on imports of weaponry from Belgium and France, whilst her warring Arab neighbours have had a variety of suppliers including the Soviet Union. The Israelis did however realise the importance of a native small arms industry, which would not be affected if outside supplies were cut off.

Perhaps the most interesting of all Israeli small arms is the Uzi sub-machine gun. Work first started on this as early as 1949, under direction of Lt. Colonel Uziel Gal of the Israeli army. The most noticeable feature of the Uzi is its extreme compactness, achieved at least in part by having the bolt recessed to take the face of the breech. This saves a length of about 4in (10cm), and space is further economised by combining the pistol grip and magazine housing. An even smaller version of the basic weapon is the Mini Uzi, like its bigger brother this is 9mm calibre, but weighs only 5.9lb (2.7kg). It can easily be carried under clothing, in an ordinary carrier bag, or tucked away

The 9mm Uzi sub-machine gun, seen here in Dutch service. The Uzi was arguably one of the most influential weapons of the third quarter of the twentieth century, and inspired several other ultra compact 'machine pistols' as well as help launch the Israeli small arms industry. According to one count it has been adopted by 28 countries. The fixed stock, military model shown would usually be fitted with a 25- or 32-round magazine, and weighs 8.15lb (3.7kg). Its cyclic rate of fire is 600 rounds per minute.

Indian army troops, wearing British-type steel helmets and manning a Soviet-made Goryunov 7.62mm SG 43 machine gun. Readily apparent are the folding trail of the carriage, shield, belt feed, and barrel-change handle. Its cyclic rate of fire was 650 rounds per minute with an effective range of 1,100yd (1,000m). Mass produced in World War Two the SG 43 would later see widespread use in Vietnam, Africa, and the Middle East. It was also copied by the Chinese.

Israeli troops firing Galil 7.62mm assault rifles. The Galil is
a gas-operated weapon, loosely based on the Kalashnikov
action. Made in both 7.62mm and 5.56mm it is also found
in at least three differing configurations; the ARM or
'Assault Rifle and Machine Gun' with folding bipod; the AR
or basic 'Assault Rifle', and the SAR or 'Short Assault Rifle',
which has a short barrel and folding stock. It has served
the Israeli armies well since the early 1970s, and can be
fitted with various rifle grenades.

UN troops in the Congo; the sub-machine gun is the 9mm
Model 45 Carl Gustav. Designed in neutral Sweden during
World War Two, and produced at Eskilstuna, the Model 45
was a standard weapon of the Swedish army for half a
century. Minor improvements over time included selective
fire, lock detail changes, a new 36-round magazine and a
bayonet lug. The Carl Gustav saw US Special Forces use as
a silenced weapon in South East Asia, and provided the
model for the Danish Model 49 Hovea and the Egyptian
Port Said SMGs.

in the smallest of spaces inside a vehicle. Uzi weapons have been used not only by Israel but Belgium, Germany, Iran, Ireland, the Netherlands, Thailand, Venezuela and others.

In 1972 the Israeli Army adopted a home-produced weapon as their new standard rifle. The Galil had been developed by Yaacov Liov and Israel Galili, designers who realised the handiness of the AK 47, and were attempting to improve on the Belgian FN FAL already available. The Galil is made in both 5.56mm and 7.62mm calibres, with a fixed or folding stock and with a variety of magazines, including 12-, 35- and 50-round capacities. In the light machine gun version there is a folding bipod under the barrel which can double as a wire cutter. In design the Galil is probably most akin to the AK 47, and the Finnish M62 assault rifle. Accessories for the Galil include muzzle-launched grenades and optional composite magazines.

Until comparatively recently the Israelis did not have their own home-grown pistol unless we count the 'Workers Industry for Arms' copy of the Smith and Wesson .38in, which has mainly been used by Police units. In the period under discussion the military relied on ex-British, and German pistols, and the Italian Model 1951 Beretta.

By the 1970s Israel was also a major exporter of mortars, which were manufactured by the Soltam company at Haifa. The inspiration for several of these products were the mortars made by the Finnish Tampella company, but the Israeli derivatives included various improvements. The 52mm light mortar was a simple design, weighing 17.4lb (7.9kg), which was not equipped with any sights, save a white line on the barrel. The Soltam 60mm mortar was available in several variants, including the 'Standard', 'Long Range', and 'Commando', depending largely on the length of barrel and type of baseplate supplied. The 81mm mortar was similarly made in several slightly varying configurations, including a model with a barrel which dismantles into two sections for ease of movement. Interestingly there was also a 'light' 120mm mortar with pretensions of man portability. Though it weighed 94.8lb (43kg) it could be broken down into three man-sized loads, or carried by mule.

CHAPTER 4

FROM THE FALKLANDS TO THE GULF 1976-2000

ALTHOUGH THE GREAT EAST-WEST CLASH which could have been a Third World War never happened, the 1980s and the early 1990s have certainly not been a time of peace. In the 'first' Gulf War fundamentalist Iran, under the Ayatollah, was pitted for the best part of a decade against Saddam Hussein of Iraq. In Afghanistan the Soviet Union discovered what Britain had already known: that warfare in that country was virtually endemic. In the South Atlantic a military dictatorship revived an ancient claim to territory and was defeated, partly by a Drake-like feat of round-the-world amphibious warfare, and partly by unreliable conscripts only half willing to fight for a regime which waged a 'dirty war' on its own people.

Sporadic outbursts of violence occurred elsewhere; in Africa, in Grenada, but perhaps most persistently in the Middle East, where US involvement in Libya and the Lebanon, the oil problem, and the festering sore of Israel's relationships with her Arab neighbours would finally all become linked with the Iraq question, when the second Gulf War erupted over Kuwait in 1990. Despite huge numerical strength Baghdad's forces proved virtually worthless against a US-led coalition. Even at the time of writing 'low intensity' conflicts simmer on in the ruins of the Eastern Bloc, the former Yugoslavia, the newly independent countries formed from the former Soviet Union, and in South America.

The story of British weapons from the Falklands to the Gulf encompasses some fundamental changes. In 1982 the British Army was equipped on the basis that there were two standard small arms rounds, the 7.62mm for rifles and machine guns, which had been adopted as NATO standard in 1953, and the 9mm Parabellum round for all other purposes. The standard machine gun was the L7 General Purpose Machine Gun (GPMG), a Belgian Fabrique Nationale design (the

A team of US soldiers stand silhouetted in Saudi Arabia before the 1991 Gulf War begins. This war was trumpeted as a triumph for modern military technology, although these men are carrying M16 rifles, little changed from the original 1960s design.

A Canadian soldier with the C8 carbine. The C8 is essentially the US M16A2 carbine in Canadian service, but has full automatic capability, and uses a 30-round plastic magazine. It is built under license at Diemaco, Kitchener, Ontario. Also visible amongst the items on the ground is a LAW 66mm missile still in its travel container.

A British parachutist in the Falklands, with the L7 GPMG, fondly known as the 'Gimpy'. This gas-operated belt-fed weapon was improved from the Belgian MAG, or Mitrailleuse d'Appui Général, and accepted for British Army use in 1961. As seen here in the light machine gun role, it weighs 24lb (10.9kg). Accessories available include a 50-round belt box and a blank firing attachment. Using a powerful cartridge and sighted to 1,970yd (1,800m) it offered considerable bonuses in a support role, even after the introduction of more modern 5.56mm weapons. Note the belt covers seen here, which protected the rounds against icing and damage.

FN MAG) with minor changes for British service. This feeds from a continuous disintegrating-link belt, weighs 24.3lb (11kg) and has a cyclic rate of fire of between 600 and 1,000 rounds per minute.

At the time of the Falklands conflict it had been in service for twenty years, and there were a number of variants. The L7A1 is the basic model, and the L7A2 is different only in that it has provision to mount a 50-round belt box and has double feed pawls in the mechanism. The L8A1, L37A2, and L43A1 are all for armoured vehicles, and the L20A1 is intended for helicopters and aircraft. The L19A1 is unusual in that it features a heavy barrel for sustained fire, but is not general issue.

If the GPMG had been in use for some time, it was as nothing to the age of the service light machine gun or LMG. The L4A3 was nothing more than the World War Two Bren gun slightly modified by rechambering to 7.62mm. It served in many second-line roles, and even in the 1990s can still be found, tucked away in the corners of unit armouries. This longevity is a tribute to the basic soundness of the original Czech design.

Another elderly machine gun used by British forces was the .50in Browning. This veteran of the inter-war period was used by the infantry to give extra fire support, especially at long ranges. It also served in the light anti-aircraft role, both on land and on ship. The age of the Brownings did pose a problem, not through mechanical unreliability, but because there were not enough accessories, particularly tripods, to go round. As a result more had to be urgently ordered, some even from the United States.

The standard rifle of the British Army was the L1A1 SLR. Like the GPMG it was a Belgian design (the FN FAL) and fired the 7.62mm NATO round: it had been in service for about 20 years. Early models of the SLR were identifiable by their extensive woodwork but by the time of the Falklands, most, if not all, had moulded nylon grips and butts. An extra available for use with the SLR was the Sight Unit Infantry Trilux (or SUIT). This enables targets to be engaged in low-light conditions or at longer ranges than is possible with ordinary iron sights. The bayonet provided with the SLR was the L1A3, and, remarkably, this did see hand to hand use by the Royal Marines on Mount Harriet on 11 and 12 June 1982. The L1A3 is a short knife bayonet, and like most modern bayonets is formed from a block of steel by electronic presses and then finished to shape. It has proved useful and durable, being suitable for general purpose applications, unlike the spike and sword bayonets which were fitted to the wartime Lee-Enfields.

Though the SLR was the main infantry arm, special troops did have others. The Special Boat Squadron of the Royal Marines, for example, used not only the American M16, but the M203 grenade launcher and the Colt Commando Carbine.

The standard SMG was the L2A3 Sterling 9mm. The originator of this weapon had been George William Patchett, a native of Nottingham and one-time motorcycle speed record holder. His first

A British Marine in the Falklands with the 7.62mm L1A1 Self Loading Rifle. The British 'SLR' was essentially a home-produced version of the Belgian FN rifle, samples of which had been taken for troop trials in 1955. The L1A1 had a 20-round box magazine, fired single shots only and weighed 9.5lb (4.3kg). This angle of view shows both an attached Sight Unit Infantry Trilux and the permanent carrying handle.

The British 7.62mm L4 light machine gun. Despite the fancy name the L4 was simply the old .303in Bren converted to fire new NATO standard ammunition. For the purist the L4 in fact had several variants, depending on which mark of Bren it had been converted from, the precise model of bipod, and the barrel type. The longest lived of these variants was the L4A4, converted from the Mark III and having a chromium plated barrel. Some were still in the hands of reserve forces in the early 1990s.

The British 9mm, Sterling L2A3 sub-machine gun. The blowback-operated selective fire Sterling entered service with the British Army in the early 1950s, and for some years coexisted alongside the last of the Sten guns. It was to last about 40 years, and perform reliably on many foreign services including the Falklands War and Gulf, before being eclipsed by more modern designs. It is seen here with the butt in the extended position alongside a spare magazine and a few rounds of 9mm parabellum ammunition.

The FN Browning semi automatic 9 mm No2 Mk 1, the British issue version of the world renowned 'High-Power' GP 35 (Model 1935) pistol. Equipped with a 13-round box magazine the Browning weighed 1.79lb (.81kg) and had an effective range of about 50yd (46m). The accessories shown are the British issue holster with cleaning tool, a lanyard, and a spare magazine complete with 9mm rounds. The Model 1935, in its various guises eventually saw service with more than 50 countries. It was also manufactured under license at Rosario, Argentina.

prototypes had been produced as early as 1943, and by the end of the war he had produced an SMG generally known as the Patchett. This was never adopted as standard for the British Army, but in 1949 came a second chance when a contest was organised to find a successor to the Sten. Patchett made various improvements to his original concept, and final tests at Pendine in Wales ended with the declaration that his gun was superior to the rival Birmingham Small Arms design. Although not unlike the later marks of Sten in general appearance and operation, the Sterling is altogether more sophisticated and can be distinguished at a glance from the earlier weapon by its 34-round curved magazine and perforated barrel jacket. The SMG was issued mainly to vehicle crews, as a back up to heavy weapons teams, and to some NCOs. However the open nature of the Falklands terrain meant that there was little action in buildings or at very close ranges, so the SLR was generally more popular.

The weapon of last resort was the 9mm 'High Power' Browning pistol. This had originally been designed before World War Two, and the first model had been in production in the 1930s. The Belgian FN factory which made it was commandeered by the Germans in 1940, and during the war continued to make Browning pistols for them under the title Pistole 640 (b). Belgian resistance workers managed to smuggle the design details out of occupied Europe, and the pistol was put into production in Canada. On the allied side Canadian-made Brownings served not only with the Canadian Army, but the Chinese, and with British commandos and paratroops. The Chinese apparently were particularly keen on the early model, which had a detachable shoulder stock and was sighted optimistically to 550yd (500m).

Belgian production restarted for the world military and commercial markets in 1947. In the mid 1950s Britain decided that the Browning should become standard issue, and gradually began to replace the revolvers then in use. The official designation was 'Pistol, Automatic 9mm FN Browning No. 2 Mk 1'. It was also widely used in Belgium, Canada, Denmark, Germany and the Netherlands; production continued both at Herstal, near Liege, Belgium, and with Inglis of Canada. Probably the biggest advantage of the semi-automatic Browning is its large magazine capacity. Inside the chunky butt is a box magazine holding 13 rounds; unlike many pistols these are not arranged in a single column, one above another, but in two parallel columns. Despite being one of the better military pistols, effective range was still only about 50yd (46m) in the hands of a skilled user, and it could not be considered more than an emergency close range weapon.

Body armour was not on general issue to the British army in the Falklands, although it had been in use for some years for internal security duties in Northern Ireland. Not to use flak jackets as standard for infantry in the war with Argentina was a controversial decision, but in the event this may have been correct. Many of the Falklands casualties were direct hits with high velocity bullets, which armour would not have stopped; and the extra encumbrance would have made marching over the rocky, wet terrain even more difficult than it already was. In general, body armour is at its best in battles of position, in street fighting, or where grenades and mortars are expected to be the major killers. British strategy in the Falklands called for rapid advances, often on foot, over mainly open terrain.

Argentine small arms were remarkably similar to those of the British. Many were Belgian FN products, others were American designs. At first glance it is often difficult to tell a Falklands War trophy from a British issue item; sometimes one

needs to see the maker's marks to be sure. Argentinian infantry, for example, used both the Fabrique National FAL and the MAG; they also used Browning machine guns. In the event this helped the British as they advanced, as soldiers were able to replenish their ammunition supplies from captured Argentine stocks.

Two weapons which were distinctively different to their British counterparts were the SMG and pistol. The most common SMG was the PAM, made by Fabrica Militar de Armas Portatiles Domingo Matheu. This is closely based on the old American M3 'Grease gun' except that it is built for 9mm ammunition. It uses blowback operation, and feeds from a 30-round box magazine. Two versions exist, the basic PAM1, and the PAM2 which features a grip safety.

Another SMG seen in the Falklands was the Halcon, which was developed in the 1940s and issued to the Argentine Gendarmaria Nacional. Production of this gun ended in 1957, but by this time small numbers had been produced both in 9mm and .45in calibres, while there was also a special lightweight model. Some

Some of the spoils of victory, heaps of Argentine munitions, including mortar rounds and ammunition, guarded by a British soldier. Amazingly, the 'fence' around the booty is constructed out of Rosario-made 7.62mm, FN FAL rifles. Variants on the basic Argentine rifle included a heavy-barrelled support weapon and a folding stock version.

Halcons were issued to the air force, and it may have been them who brought them to the 'Malvinas'. Perhaps the most exotic and unexpected SMG used by the Argentinians was the silent, or sound moderated, version of the Sterling. This had been purchased from the Dagenham factory long before the war for naval commando use. Even to the Sterling's own makers this had been a surprising choice, and one which was put down both to inter-service rivalry, and fear of terrorist activity and sabotage within Argentina itself. Nonetheless the Sterling Patchett Mark 5 or L34A1, as it appeared in British military use, was an effective

The Sterling Mark 5, sound-moderated 9mm sub-machine gun. Intended for Special Forces use and known in British service as the L34A1, this version of the Sterling has a large 'diffuser tube' around the barrel. Gas is allowed to escape into the tube and is slowed in an expanded metal wrap. Whilst this makes the weapon very quiet the muzzle velocity of the L34A1 is about 75% of that of the normal weapon, a drawback of many silenced arms. On the other side of the coin the L34A1 is most durable; in one test 60,000 rounds were fired without causing significant barrel wear. In the Falklands it was used against British troops by Argentinan naval Commandos.

weapon, and the Argentine Marines appeared triumphantly with them in the London Sunday Times, just after the invasion.

The standard Argentine pistol was home produced, and went under the title of .45in Ballester Molina. It is also occasionally known as the Hafdasa, from the initials of the manufacturer. Despite the names this is little more than the Colt Model 1911, differing only in details of the trigger, grip, and hammer. It had been introduced in the 1930s and interestingly a few had even found their way into British hands during World War Two. Although not quite up to Colt standards in terms of finish the pistol is reliable and packs a good punch.

If the weapons used by both sides in the Falklands were remarkably similar, there were crucial differences in training and morale, while the British could also rely on devastating support from artillery and naval gunfire. Part of the British advantage could be put down to their special forces, whose work in scouting,

The Russian 7.62mm, AKM assault rifle. The AKM is essentially an updated version of the old AK 47, produced in 1959. It was simplified to aid construction, greater use being made of stampings and pressings than before. A few features aid identification, including a grooved hand guard; bayonet fitting type; three ribs on the receiver top cover, revised sights, and, on this model at least, a muzzle compensator intended to keep the barrel from rising up during shooting. The AKM was widely produced, but generally superseded in the 1970s and 1980s by the AK 74.

spotting, and raiding was extremely useful, but a good deal was also attributable to the sheer endurance of the private soldier in marching across difficult terrain carrying a heavy load. It is worth quoting a couple of instances of the combat experiences of both sides by way of illustration. The first comes from Major General John Frost's account of 2nd Battalion the Parachute Regiment in action at Goose Green:

'Lieutenant Chapman . . . led the section in a swift attack through the line of trenches, using grenades and white phosphorous, machine guns and M-79 grenade launchers as they went . . . About nine of the enemy were killed. It was not possible to tell the exact number, owing to the effect of the burning white phosphorus in the dug out. The unwillingness or inability of the enemy to defend themselves was pathetic: possibly these were administrative troops sent forward from Goose Green on a rotation basis. Most of the Argentine soldiers hid under their blankets, with their rifles propped against the side of the trench.'

The second account of the fighting comes from an Argentinian conscript, in

Daniel Kon's 'Los Chicos de la Guerra'. 'Fabian E.' was with B Company of the 7th Infantry regiment on Mount Longdon on the night of 11 June. Together with two others he had been detailed to defend a 105mm field gun:

> 'We waited for orders, we didn't know what to do. We were alone, and we had a hail of bullets raining down on us. We dragged ourselves a bit further and from behind some rocks we began to shoot towards where we could see the flashes of gun fire . . . I began to shoot first, with the PAM. I fired two rounds, aiming as best I could. They carried on shouting below, louder all the time. According to what we'd been taught, that was wrong, because it gave away your position. After a few rounds my machine gun suddenly jammed, I suppose it was in bad shape because it had been impossible to keep it as clean it should have been. A bit further forward Carlos was still firing his faulty rifle. After my machine gun jammed I took cover again . . . there was nothing we could do.'

Afghanistan has been for centuries an international 'hot spot', both in terms of conflict between Afghans and invading foreigners, and in power struggles between local tribes. In 1978 the Kabul government was at war with local resistance leaders; and at Christmas 1979 the Soviet Army invaded, spearheaded by Spetsnaz units who secured headquarters and airfields ahead of the main force. A ten-year involvement had begun, with the Soviets attempting to prop up a client government against a diverse body of Chinese- and Western-backed 'Mujahideen', or fighters for the faith.

As the conflict became the Soviet Union's own 'Vietnam', Red Army units at the ill-defined front would have first call on the most up -to-date weaponry. Some of it would be captured by Mujahideen, and thus revealed to Western intelligence for the first time. The Afghan government troops were equipped with the earlier range of Soviet small arms based on the intermediate 7.62mm calibre round. Soviet infantry themselves were largely equipped with a second generation

Soviet troops armed with the 5.45mm AK 74. The AK 74 is an updated small-calibre version of the AKM, and is perhaps most easily distinguished at a glance by the presence of a large muzzle brake. This very effectively cuts down recoil, and is a significant aid to accurate shooting: the only drawback is the deflection of gas sideways so that it is inadvisable to stand too close when one is being fired. The AKM weighs 7.9lb (3.6kg) and has a 30-round plastic box magazine.

of Kalashnikovs, all designed to fire a new small calibre bullet in 5.45mm. This family of arms had been introduced in the 1970s, and was first shown publicly in the November 1977 Red Square parade. The basic rifle is known as the AK 74, and is externally little different to the old 7.62mm AK 47. The new weapon has a distinctive long muzzle brake and recoil compensator, while its curved magazine is made from various types of coloured (usually orange) plastic. The AK 74 is no lighter than its predecessor, but is easier to control in automatic fire, largely due to the muzzle brake. The move to a smaller cartridge had mirrored American developments of a decade earlier, and was in line with the trend in NATO. The Russian round has a hollow tip under the nickel jacket, causing it to expand when it hits, which makes it lethally effective. The Afghan tribesmen learned to treat this cartridge with great respect, nicknaming it the 'poison bullet', as few who were hit by it survived.

The Russian 7.62mm PKM light machine gun. During the 1960s a new family of machine weapons was devised in the Soviet Union to replace the old Goryunov and other guns of World War Two vintage. The first of these, seen by Western observers in 1964, was the PK. This was a general purpose weapon which married together the rotating bolt of the Kalashnikov with the cartridge stripper and barrel change method of the Goryunov. Further refinement, and a lighter unfluted barrel, produced the PKM. It is seen here on a tripod for support work though it retains a folded bipod under the barrel. The PKM weighs only 18.5lb (8.4kg), has an effective range of about 1,100yd (1,000m) and feeds from varying lengths of belt up to 250-rounds. (MOD Pattern Room)

A folding-stocked variant is known as the AK 74S, while there is also a short carbine known as the AKSU. This uses the same ammunition and mechanism in an extremely short, compact package. Firing rifle ammunition through such a short weapon creates an immense amount of flash and noise at the muzzle, so the AKSU has an expansion chamber and flash hider fitted.

For extra fire support, the Soviet Army used a similar conversion to the earlier RPK light machine gun. The RPK 74 fires the same 5.45mm round as the AK 74 rifle, although it has a heavier barrel, a bipod and usually a larger 40-round magazine. The 7.62mm cartridge remained in service, however, fired by the belt-fed PKM and SGM machine guns. Heavier firepower was supplied by the 12.7mm DShK and its replacement the NSV, although these were usually vehicle mounted.

Soviet motorised rifle troops, mid-1970s. The tripod-mounted weapons are the 30mm, AGS 17 grenade launcher. Known to the troops as the 'Plamya' or 'flame' this was introduced into Soviet service in 1975, and eventually two per company were issued. It is a belt fed blowback operated gun, and can be tripod or vehicle mounted. With an effective range in excess of 1,100yd (1000m) it can fire about 65 rounds a minute using 29-round belts. Its only real drawback is weight, since the gun itself weighs 37lb (18kg), and the tripod a further 77lb (35kg). The 'Plamya' has seen widespread deployment in Eastern Europe, Chad, Angola, Cuba and Iran. The riflemen flanking the grenade launchers carry 5.45mm AK 74 rifles.

Infantry units were also equipped with the SVD sniper rifle and a number of grenade launchers. The 40mm single-shot BG-15 launcher clips underneath the barrel of an assault rifle, and is a Russian equivalent to the US M203. A more effective weapon is the AGS-17 'Plamya'. This looks rather like a short, stubby machine gun, and is mounted on a light tripod in the infantry role. It fires 30mm grenades out to a maximum of 1,313yd (1,200m) and is fed from a distinctive 29-shot drum magazine on the side of the weapon. Able to fire bursts, it provides a useful source of high-explosive firepower to an infantry company.

The Mujahideen had a rather more colourful selection of arms, varying from the latest American technology to the antiquated and suicidal. Until comparatively recently percussion-type 'jezails', British Martini-Henrys and Russian bolt action Nagants were still to be seen in the hands of the Afghan hill tribes, although Lee-Enfields of both local and British manufacture had predominated. By 1980 the

Mujahideen Afghan freedom fighters in a captured Soviet jeep near Allabad. Amongst them are a typically motley collection of weapons including the Heckler and Koch G3, the AK, GPMG, and Lee Enfield.

Mujahideen had themselves got hold of considerable supplies of Kalashnikovs, many of them from prisoners, but also from Chinese sources. From then on it became usual that older men and snipers would be equipped with .303in Lee-Enfields and the younger troops, who would expect to close with the enemy, would receive whatever AK 47s were available. Eventually Kalashnikov weapons from all over the globe would be used, whether Chinese, Rumanian, Egyptian or captured Russian.

Perhaps the most prestigious of the Mujahideen small arms were East German 5.45mm Kalashnikovs, and Iranian-made G3 rifles. The 'Gewehr 3' weapons were particularly interesting for their truly international pedigree. Derived from a Spanish design they were first produced by the German firm Heckler and Koch in 1959: later they would be made under licence in 13 countries, including places as diverse as Sweden and Saudi Arabia, and see widespread use around the world. The G3 is a counterpart to the FN FAL, and fires 7.62mm NATO calibre ammunition from a 20-round box magazine. Use of sheet steel stampings and plastic furniture keep down costs, but the rifle is still remarkably robust and effective.

An Afghan fighter with a .303in, Short Magazine Lee Enfield. Although some of the Afghan 'Enfields' were made in Britain, many others have since been locally copied, with considerable skill, in the small workshops of the border towns of the North West Frontier. Some of the copies are so good that it takes close examination to determine their origin, which is sometimes given away by incorrect markings or misspellings. Ammunition is still made in Mexico, India, Pakistan and possibly elsewhere.

The Heckler and Koch G3 rifle. Closely related in design terms to the Spanish CETME, the 7.62mm G3 was for 30 years the standard rifle of the German Bundeswehr. It has also been widely produced elsewhere, and saw service in both Afghanistan and the Gulf. Variations and accessories include a bipod, silencer, a G3 SG/1 sniper rifle, and G3K 'short' or carbine version. A G41 rifle has also been developed in 5.56mm. The selective-fire G3 is a delayed blowback operated weapon, is sighted to 440yd (400m), weighs 9.7lb (4.4kg) and has a 20-round magazine. (MOD Pattern Room)

Afghan anti-government forces also had a considerable variety of machine guns, including old Czech ZB 26s, as well as more modern Soviet and Chinese designs. The Soviet heavy machine guns DShKM 12.7mm and 14.5mm KPV were known respectively to the Afghans as 'Dashika' and 'Zigroiat'. Some of the Afghans' most potent weapons were their hand-held missile launchers, which were both Soviet and western. These included captured RPG-22 and RPG-7 anti-tank rockets, and American Stingers and British Blowpipe anti-aircraft weapons. The resistance used mortars whenever available, and had quite large numbers of Soviet and Chinese 82mm models, and smaller numbers of larger calibre models from several countries. Mines were especially popular and used with almost reckless abandon by all parties, creating large numbers of civilian casualties. Some of the nastiest mines in use were the plastic-bodied varieties, which are extremely difficult to detect. Some, like the PFM-1 'butterfly' were dropped from helicopters, and lay armed, until touched, for many months. Against organised Soviet forces the Mujahideen adopted a guerrilla style of fighting, relying extensively on ambush and surprise attacks on outlying garrisons. Eventually the pro-Soviet Kabul government would outlive the Soviet Union itself, and after the Russians withdrew, the Afghans returned to fighting each other.

Whilst conflict continued in Afghanistan, another major war was underway in the Gulf. The Shah of Iran was overthrown in 1979, and replaced by the fundamentalist regime of Ayatollah Ruhollah Khomeni. In September 1980, Iraq under Saddam Hussein took advantage of the turmoil and invaded, with the immediate objective of control of the Shatt-al-Arab waterway. Iran suffered heavy losses, and turned away more and more from regular troops, to lightly armed irregular infantry, the 'Pasadaran' and the paramilitary 'Basij'. The 'human wave' attacks of these units, countered by Iraqi entrenchments, gas and artillery are believed to have led to 80,000 deaths in the Basra battles alone.

Interestingly the Iranian arsenal of small arms included a good number of weapons left over from the time of friendship with the west. Amongst the guns used in the war with Iraq were included the Colt M1911 pistol, the Israeli Uzi SMG the Heckler and Koch G3, and the old Browning M2 .50in heavy machine gun. These were backed up with American 60mm M19, 81mm M29, and 107mm M30 mortars, as well as heavy Israeli Soltam mortars. Anti-tank and anti-aircraft weapons were drawn from both sides of the iron curtain, in the form of recoilless rifles, RPG-7 and SA-7 missile launchers, and TOW heavy anti-tank missiles. Small arms ammunition was manufactured locally at the state-owned factory in Teheran, but demand was such that more was imported from elsewhere. The war finally ended in July 1988 with no winner, but Iraq had certainly failed in its strategic objectives. Iraq was left with a huge legacy of debt, much of it owed to the tiny oil rich state of Kuwait.

On 2 August 1990, Iraq invaded Kuwait, and the scene was set for a second Gulf War. With United Nations approval, the US and 22 other countries deployed troops to the Gulf in operations 'Desert Shield' and 'Desert Storm'. Half a million men faced each other on either side of the border. Aerial assault, tanks, and 'high tech' weaponry paved the way for Iraqi defeat, but the men who took and held the ground were, as always, infantry soldiers equipped with small arms. Most of the Iraqis' hand-held weapons were from the Eastern Bloc arsenals, with the ubiqui-

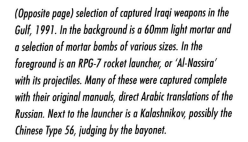

(Opposite page) selection of captured Iraqi weapons in the Gulf, 1991. In the background is a 60mm light mortar and a selection of mortar bombs of various sizes. In the foreground is an RPG-7 rocket launcher, or 'Al-Nassira' with its projectiles. Many of these were captured complete with their original manuals, direct Arabic translations of the Russian. Next to the launcher is a Kalashnikov, possibly the Chinese Type 56, judging by the bayonet.

The US M249 light machine gun or 'SAW' Squad Automatic Weapon in the Gulf. The M249 SAW was developed from, and is almost identical to, the 5.56mm Belgian Minimi, which was first exhibited in 1974. Along with weapons like the Colt CMG-2, the Stoner, Rodman, Maremont XM 233, and the Philco-Ford XM 234 it was soon under consideration for US Army service. A decision as to which gun to adopt was however long delayed, at least in part because the US procurement agencies wished to know which calibre NATO would decide on before choosing. After a decade the Minimi was finally selected, and slight modification produced the M249. Amongst the weapon's desirable features are its lightness at 15.2lb (6.9kg), an easy change barrel, and its ability to use belts, belts in boxes, or 30-round box magazines. There is also a short 'Para' version. The weapon has a cyclic rate of up to 1,000 rounds per minute, and a muzzle velocity of 3,000ft/s (915m/s). Notice the gunner's goggles to protect him from the fine Saudi sand .

tous AK 47, and its later AK 74 and Romanian AKM variants heading the list. A local variant of the Soviet weapon, known as the 'Tabuk' was also produced. Other items of Soviet ancestry included large numbers of RPG-7 rocket launchers, called by the Iraqis the 'Al-Nassira', some of which were even used from the decks of fast moving patrol boats; while there were also Tokarev pistols and most models of Soviet machine gun. Amongst the heaviest of the machine guns was the elderly model 38/46, an improved version of the Soviet World War Two Degtyarev 12.7mm.

The standard Iraqi sniper rifle was the Soviet 7.62mm Dragunov, or SVD, which had already seen extensive service in Afghanistan and elsewhere. While most other nations stayed with the traditional bolt action rifle as their sniper's weapon, the Soviets had plumped for a semi-automatic design based on Kalashnikov mechanics. It fires a 7.62mm bullet, although it uses the older full-powered cartridge rather the Kalashnikov intermediate round. This rifle feeds from a 10-round box magazine, and though long and not terribly easy to handle, is good at its task and quite capable of achieving hits at 875yd (800m) in the hands of a skilled user. In the Iraqi army it was issued one per section to the Republican Guard and one per vehicle to mechanised units, and to other infantry units as available. The Iraqis also produced their own model of the Dragunov, known locally as the 'Al-Kadisa'. There is also a Chinese copy known as the Type 79.

The Iraqis were faced by a huge coalition of nations, each with their own troops who were equipped in their own way. The US Army used much of which had already been seen in Vietnam fifteen years earlier, but there were a good number of additions to the arsenal. One of these was the M249 squad automatic weapon or 'SAW', which was replacing the M60 machine gun. The M249 is fundamentally the Belgian Minimi 5.56mm light machine gun, which had been unveiled as early as 1974, and is also used by Australia, Canada, Italy and others. It is gas-operated, and capable of either belt or magazine feed, although most users carry it with a plastic ammunition box which holds a 100-shot disintegrating belt. This is a

The US 40mm MK 19 Mod 3, grenade launcher. Developed by the US Navy, this grenade launcher first appeared as a prototype in 1967. It saw use in Vietnam and number were made for Israel in 1974. A major US contract for the improved 'Model 3', shown here, was awarded in 1983. The MK 19 is an air-cooled blowback automatic, capable of firing armour piercing as well as high explosive grenades, and by using a belt feed can project up to 350 shells a minute. This is awesome firepower when one considers that the gun weighs 78.3lb (35.3kg), and can, at least for short distances, be carried by its crew. Notice the gunner's covered plastic helmet, nicknamed the 'Fritz' due to its similarity in outline to the German M1935 headgear.

light, portable and effective machine gun for the squad fire support role, although the 5.56mm ammunition loses its effectiveness at long range faster than the older 7.62mm cartridge of the M60. Another weapon which had first seen service in Vietnam, and which saw widespread use in the Gulf, was the Mark 19 grenade launcher. This is the US equivalent to the Russian AGS-17, but is a much heavier and more powerful weapon. It fires 40mm grenades which are fed from a belt, and can put down withering area fire out to about 2,000yd (1,850m). It is heavy and bulky though, and is usually seen mounted on vehicles or helicopters.

One of the more controversial new weapons was the M9 Beretta pistol. In the mid-1980s the US authorities had held tests to find a successor for the now elderly Colt M1911. One of the most interesting contenders was the SIG-Sauer 226, which had been especially designed for the purpose, but the winner of the competition, selected in 1985, was the Beretta 92SB. There were minor alterations demanded to the grip which resulted in a new designation, 92F, and 315,390 of these pistols were ordered for American forces. The US Army now christened the pistol the 'semi-automatic, 9mm M9', and it was agreed that further production would be in the US. Various sections of government and industry were aghast that a foreign weapon had been selected, and for more than two years debate would rumble on. Smith and Wesson, for example, were particularly aggrieved to have been passed over on the apparent technicality of a firing pin energy test which was

A US Marine Corps 'Boarding Team' c.1990. Their weapons include the Beretta 9mm, M9 pistol, also known as the model 92FS, which is standard issue to the Marine Corps and Coast Guard as well as the Army, Navy and Airforce. The lead man has a Remington M870 Mark 1 shotgun. Selected as a result of competitive trials in 1966 the Marine Corps Model 870 is essentially similar to the civilian gun, but has a modified choke to the barrel and is often seen with different stock configurations. It is a 12-gauge weapon with a seven-shot tube magazine under the barrel, and is fitted to take the M7 bayonet.

The US M60 machine gun and M16 rifle in the Gulf. The M60, seen here on a tripod mounting, remained useful in a support role due to its longer range and heavier bullet. It was not therefore entirely replaced by the M249 SAW. Textbook 'sustained fire' with the M60 was a controlled 100 rounds a minute in short bursts, 'rapid' was 200 a minute, but this required frequent barrel changes. In 'cyclic' fire 550 bullets would be used per minute, with the recommendation that the barrel be changed after just one minute. 'Rapid' fire against ground targets was the norm, with reversion to 'sustained' once a local 'fire superiority' had been attained. 'Cyclic' was to be reserved for dire emergency, or for enemy aircraft.

wrongly calculated, and there was much questioning over the wording of the original specification.

One particularly contentious point was whether the army expected to get 5,000 rounds out of its pistol before failure, or whether this was merely an average to be expected over several guns. Also debated was the Non Developmental Items (NDI) concept, where procurement agencies were especially interested in obtaining equipment which was already fully developed. At the root of the question however was the shock of adopting a non-American handgun, a matter which struck at the heart of US pride, but a dilemma which had already had to be faced by most nations the world over.

It is interesting to note that, even before the latest political changes, South Africa had also adopted a pistol with startling similarity to the Beretta. In theory at least she could not buy the Italian gun, because at the time sanctions were being imposed by the international community. Instead South Africa began to make her own version, the Lyttleton Z-88, 9mm. Developed in 1986 and going into production three years later the 'Z' in its title was taken from the name of the late T.D. Zeederberg, formerly general manager of the Lyttleton company. Since then they have gone on to design their own Vektor SP1 pistol

A US Navy SEAL with M4 Colt Carbine and M203 grenade launcher. Mechanically similar to the 5.56mm M16A2 the carbine's main differences lie in a shorter barrel length and a sliding butt which make the weapon handier, especially for Special Forces use.

Although the US Army retained the M16 as its standard longarm the 'black rifle' had undergone one significant change since the 1960s. The M16A2, introduced in 1983, no longer had a full automatic fire capability; instead it was able to fire single shots, or three-round bursts. This was an interesting development, and perhaps reflected a realisation that economy of fire was not the American infantryman's strongest suit. In any case the Canadians, who also used M16s, retained the full auto provision. Other changes in the M16A2 were more subtle, such as a slightly heavier barrel with a modified twist in the rifling; a new flash suppressor and muzzle compensator; a new sight; and a moulding behind the ejection port designed to prevent spent cartridge cases flying into the face of a left handed user. The revised rifling and sight were due to the introduction of a new NATO standard round, the SS109. While a 5.56mm cartridge, and of similar dimensions to the earlier American M193, the new Belgian-designed round has different ballistic characteristics to its predecessor.

Even before the Falklands conflict, the British Army had been looking for a replacement for the SLR. Bullpup designs, with the magazine mounted behind the grip and trigger, had come under consideration as early as the late1940s, with an experimental design, the EM 2, also known as the '7mm Rifle, Automatic, No. 9, Mark 1'. For the time this was a remarkable departure, in that it took the German and Russian concept of the intermediate-powered cartridge a stage further, giving the weapon an optical tube sight fitted built in to the carrying handle. By using a bullpup configuration, the chamber and mechanism were behind the grip, and the rifle could be made exceptionally compact. The EM 2 was approved for service, but never became a general issue, as NATO instead standardised on a full-powered 7.62mm round and the British Army chose the SLR.

The bullpup idea made a comeback in the 1970s, this time in a new weapon called, without startling originality, the Enfield Individual Weapon. This used an even smaller 4.85mm cartridge, and was submitted for NATO trials in 1977 to 1979. It did not then succeed, but pointed the way to the new British standard weapon, the SA 80.

It was actually October 1985 before Small Arm 1980 was formally issued to the army, and so the official title of the new rifle would become the L85A1. The main difference to the 1970s prototype was calibre, for the L85A1 was in 5.56mm NATO standard. It uses a 30-round box magazine, and is normally fitted with a SUSAT (Sight Unit, Small Arm, Trilux) optical sight. Loaded and ready it weighs a fraction under 11lb (5kg). There is also a slightly heavier squad light machine gun version, the L86A1. This has a thicker barrel, a bipod, and a butt hand grip to steady it, although the barrel is fixed and it feeds from the same 30-shot magazine as the rifle. Accuracy on the range is exceptional, especially with the optical sight fitted.

The reality of the first few years of service has been disappointing, and teething problems with the system have included both the serious and the ludicrous. Dangerous looking cracks were the cause of one investigation, and a magazine catch which snagged on webbing and dropped the soldier's ammunition had to be altered. The bayonet, which is a cast socket mounted design, was found to have weaknesses, and most strangely of all, insect repellent from the soldiers' faces was found to melt the material of the butt. All these questions can be, and no doubt have been, addressed; but there is one drawback which will always affect bullpup automatic weapons with magazines, and this is that in the prone position it is sometimes difficult to achieve

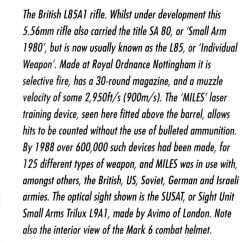

The British L85A1 rifle. Whilst under development this 5.56mm rifle also carried the title SA 80, or 'Small Arm 1980', but is now usually known as the L85, or 'Individual Weapon'. Made at Royal Ordnance Nottingham it is selective fire, has a 30-round magazine, and a muzzle velocity of some 2,950ft/s (900m/s). The 'MILES' laser training device, seen here fitted above the barrel, allows hits to be counted without the use of bulleted ammunition. By 1988 over 600,000 such devices had been made, for 125 different types of weapon, and MILES was in use with, amongst others, the British, US, Soviet, German and Israeli armies. The optical sight shown is the SUSAT, or Sight Unit Small Arms Trilux L9A1, made by Avimo of London. Note also the interior view of the Mark 6 combat helmet.

The British L86A1 Light Support Weapon, caught as a cartridge is ejected from the breech. The 5.56mm L86A1 is essentially a heavy-barrelled version of the Individual Weapon, fitted with a bipod, seen here in the swung down position. It replaced the various L4 Bren conversions, and saw service in the Gulf.

sufficient elevation against a higher target. The more one pushes ones face to the ground the more the magazine gets in the way. The consistent bad press for the L85A1 is such that it makes one wonder whether the public is being prepared for the purchase of a new (perhaps non-British) weapon.

In the Gulf the L85A1 was the standard infantry weapon, but the Sterling SMG and the L1A1 SLR were still sometimes to be seen in the hands of support troops. British special forces spurned the new rifle and instead went their own way with their small arms. One eight-man SAS patrol was recorded as carrying four Minimi 5.56mm light machine guns, four M16 assault rifles with M203 grenade launchers, eight 66mm LAW anti-tank missiles, and a selection of grenades, explosives and pyrotechnics. Amazingly one member of this patrol was later to complain that they could have done with more hardware, namely at least one silenced pistol.

The French FA MAS rifle. The St Étienne-made FA MAS is in several ways a remarkable weapon; its strange shape is obvious, but it can also be made to eject its spent cartridges in either direction, making left or right handed use a practical possibility. The issue model carried in the Gulf was fitted with a small bipod and had a smaller trigger guard than the example shown here.

Long before the Gulf war the French Army had given up their old MAS Model 49/56 rifles, and had themselves adopted a bullpup weapon. Developed in the 1970s and issued in the 1980s, the 5.56mm Fusil Automatique MAS or FA MAS is a compact and handy design. The FA MAS has a 25-round magazine and small holes in the side indicate at a glance how many shots are left. Three types of fire are possible: single shot, three round bursts, or fully automatic. The sights are contained in a trough which also acts as the carrying handle. At first sight the shape of the weapon is strange, and has led French troops to christen it 'Le Clairon', or the bugle. It has proven to be effective and reliable, and other states who have adopted it include Djibouti, Gabon, Lebanon, Senegal, and the United Arab Emirates.

Arab states within the UN coalition included countries which had been supplied from both East and West. In the former category were both Syria and Egypt, which had at various times been regarded as client states of the Soviet Union. Egypt had once been mainly equipped by Britain, but from 1954 began to receive arms from both the Soviets and Czechoslovakia. During the Gulf war, the Egyptian Army had mainly AK 47 and AKM rifles. Interestingly the Egyptians also have two types of pistol not normally encountered elsewhere. One is the Helwan, which is a copy of the Beretta 951, made under licence, and the other, the Tokagypt, is a version of the Soviet Tokarev made in Hungary. The seven-shot semi-automatic Tokagypt features minor improvements over the Russian model, such as a better shaped grip and a safety catch, but has not been a great success and seems mainly to have gone to the police rather than the army.

Amongst the Arab states supplied from the West were the countries of the 'Gulf Co-operation Council': Saudi Arabia, Oman, Qatar, United Arab Emirates,

Bahrain, and Kuwait itself. Predominantly these used weapons from Western Europe. Oman and Saudi Arabia made the interesting choice of the Austrian 5.56 mm Steyr AUG (Armee Universal Gewehr), as their standard arm. This futuristic looking bullpup is in fact a modular system, enabling quick conversion from assault weapon to light machine gun. Various options include single, automatic, or controlled burst fire. The AUG was first adopted by the Austrians as early as 1977, and other customers have included Eire, Morocco, Indonesia, Australia and

Nigerian troops in the Gulf, wearing helmets of an obsolete US style and carrying 9mm Heckler and Koch MP5 sub-machine guns. The very popular selective fire MP5 was developed in the 1960s and has mechanical similarities to the same manufacturer's G3 rifle. Weighing only 5.5lb (2.5kg) the MP5 feeds from either a 15- or 30-round magazine, and has a muzzle velocity of 1,312ft/s (400m/s). There also exists an MP5SD silenced version, and an even shorter MP5K.

The remarkable Austrian 5.56mm AUG or 'Armee Universal Gewehr'. The AUG has been one of the most successful designs of the last quarter of the twentieth century, and is novel in several respects. It is part of a modular system, has a 1.5 times magnification optical sight built into the carrying handle, and by the use of lesser or greater trigger pressures will fire single shots or automatic bursts. The AUG weighs 7.9lb (3.6kg), and can be fitted with 30- or 42-round magazines. The example pictured is in Australian service, and is fitted with MILES, or 'Multiple Integrated Laser Engagement System', a training device which transmits to the harness of other troops taking part in exercises, showing hits scored.

This Croatian fighter's dress sense may be Hollywood in inspiration but the firearm is conventional enough, being the 7.62mm M70AB2 assault rifle. This was a derivative of the Kalashnikov, and an issue arm of the old Yugoslav Army. Apart from the folding stock the M70AB2 has the distinction having of a permanently-attached flip up sight for rifle grenades, which, when raised, cuts off the gas supply to the piston. The body armour worn appears to be the side laced US M69 type, rather than the standard Yugoslav 'Bullet Resistant Jacket'.

New Zealand. The AUG has a one-piece plastic moulding which incorporates the butt, grip and most of the body. The steel receiver and barrel are attached to this, while the receiver also incorporates an integral carrying handle and optical sight. The AUG can stand a good deal of rough treatment, and has established a reputation as an excellent system. Other Arab states of the 'Co-operation Council' had weapons supplied from France, Italy, Germany and Britain.

While the Falklands, Afghanistan and the Gulf wars have been conflicts of note in the 1980s and 1990s, they have by no means been the only places in which conflict has taken place. And while the United States, Britain, the Soviet Union, France, Belgium and Germany have produced many important weapon designs, they are by no means the only countries with arms manufacturing capability. Most states with any industrial capacity are capable of building small arms, while many are able to modify existing designs, or even create completely new ones.

An example of this is given by the armaments industry of the former Yugoslavia, which has produced a range of copies of Soviet weapons combined with indigenous designs. Notable amongst the former must be counted those pistols manufactured by Zavodi Crvena Zastava. The most ordinary of these are the Model 57, Model 70, and Model 70A, which are essentially copies of the Soviet Tokarev. Slightly more unusual is the Model 70(k) a short 9mm semi-automatic, with an eight-round magazine, initially intended for police use. The Revolver Model 83, introduced in 1987, and intended for military and police use, is available in .357in Magnum, .38in Special and 9mm and was sold commercially in different barrel lengths.

Since the collapse of the old Yugoslav state, 'snipers' in Bosnia and Croatia have frequently made headlines in the media; especially when the victims are patently non-combatants, or United Nations peacekeeping troops. More often than not such incidents are the result of random fire from ill disciplined irregulars and militiamen using ordinary weapons like the Yugoslavian versions of the Soviet SKS and AK 74. The Yugoslavs did however have their own specially dedicated sniper weapon, the Zavodi Crvena Zastava M76. This uses the basic Kalashnikov mechanism, albeit somewhat strengthened, and has something of that weapon's external appearance, but is chambered for the elderly 7.92mm Mauser cartridge. Also slightly out of the ordinary are the M80 and M80A assault rifles; again these have the basics of the tried and trusted Kalashnikov, but were produced in US and NATO calibres, being intended for export. Serbian troops have also been seen with the M56 SMG in 7.62mm, a weapon which has similar operating principles to the old German MP 40.

Switzerland and Sweden are two nations famed for their neutral stances, and have not been involved in any significant combat since the nineteenth century. Even so, both countries have maintained their own high-quality small arms industries, and despite small populations, show every sign of continuing to do so. Switzerland in particular is famed for the fact of its near universal militia, with most adult males keeping a service rifle at home, ready for the time that they should be called for duty.

The Swiss national arms production facility is the Schwizerische Industrie Gesellschaft (SIG), and since World War Two this has produced various home-grown models, although often based on foreign concepts. The Sturmgewehr 57, a rather heavy but reliable semi-automatic rifle in 7.5mm, was influenced by both German Heckler and Koch, and Spanish CETME ideas. A later 5.56mm SG 530 was also developed. In the 1970s it was decided that a new system was required, but various delays meant that manufacture of the new gun would not start until 1986, and the service issue would not be until 1990. Thus it was that

A Swiss soldier with the 7.5mm Sturmgewehr 57. Standard issue in the Swiss army from the 1950s to the 1990s, the Sturmgewehr 57 was a reliable if somewhat hefty assault rifle. It was closely related to the 7.62mm, SIG 510-4, had a cyclic rate of about 500 rounds per minute, and fed from a 24-round box magazine. It is seen here with an infra red lamp for use at night.

A member of a Spanish boarding party on patrol during the first Gulf War. The weapon is a CETME Model 58 rifle. The 7.62mm CETME firers a slightly weaker round than the standard NATO but otherwise identical in dimensions. The CETME feeds from a 20-round box magazine and has an effective range of 656yd (600m) A 5.56mm version has since been developed, known as the CETME L. Notice also the high collared, wrap-around style, body armour in camouflage material.

although the latest Swiss assault rifle has borne other designations it was finally titled the SG 90. It is a superbly made 5.56mm weapon with the magazine in front of the trigger in a traditional layout. It has an innovative plastic skeleton butt, which can be folded away to one side if desired. The 20- or 30-round magazines are transparent plastic.

The standard Swedish arm, chosen in 1980 and introduced in 1984, is the AK5, 5.56mm assault rifle. Though made in Sweden the gun is an FN design, slightly modified. The starting point was the FNC, and to this the Swedes have added various refinements for operations in cold climates. A better grip and an enlarged trigger guard, for example, enable the user to wear winter gloves.

Spain also continues to make its own small arms at the Empresa Nacional 'Santa Barbara', though in fact the latest Spanish Army 5.56mm assault rifle, the CETME model L, is fairly traditional. CETME stands for 'Centro de Estudios Tecnicos de Materiales Especiales', or Technical Centre for the Study of Special Materials, and after World War Two this body had set out to design a new weapon for the Spanish Army. The starting point had been the German experimental Mauser Sturmgewehr 45, unfinished at the end of the war, from which the

Spanish produced the CETME 58, and subsequently the CETME Model C. Much of this design work was later incorporated in the Heckler and Koch G3 when German small arms manufacture restarted. The CETME Model L, which first entered service in 1988, follows the same line of development but makes extensive use of plastics and is chambered for 5.56mm. It weighs 7.5lb (3.4kg), has a folding bipod, a 30-round magazine and can fire single shots or fully automatic.

India, which has managed to avoid a major war since its 1970s battles with Pakistan, now shows signs of developing its own small arms industry beyond

South African troops c.1990 armed with the 5.56mm R4 rifle. During the imposition of sanctions South African small arms procurement was always problematic. The R4 was in fact based on the Israeli Galil, and is produced at the Lyttleton Engineering works, Pretoria. It is gas operated, selective fire, and uses a rotating bolt system: the magazines are a substantial 35 rounds. Notice also the smoke grenade carried by the soldier seen in profile.

old British designs. Most notable in this respect is the 5.56mm INSAS assault rifle, made by the Indian Small Arms Factory of Kanpur. This incorporates a catholic collection of features culled from some of the leading arms of the last half century. It is just under 3ft (1m) in length, with a 20- or 30-round magazine: the pistol grip and receiver show Kalashnikov influences, whilst the magazine housing has the same dimensions as that on the M16. The cocking handle is similar to that found on Heckler and Koch rifles, and the gun can fire single shots or three round bursts. Despite its 'pick and mix' approach to design it is a well-balanced and promising weapon.

In terms of small arms design, the last decades of the twentieth century have confirmed the direction taken from 1939 onward: towards more and more light automatic, or semi-automatic weapons in the hands of the front line soldier, and greater anti-vehicle capability. Also obvious is the trend towards assault weapons of relatively small calibre, intended primarily for engagements at under 330yd (300m). Most developed nations have already taken up, or intend to take up, an assault rifle in 5.56 or 5.45mm calibre. Many of these rifles have a controlled burst fire capability, as well as, or instead of, fully automatic fire.

Semi-automatic pistols have now ousted revolvers, to finally become the norm amongst military handguns, a process which has taken much of the century. Recent contenders in the field of military semi-automatic pistols have included the Spanish Llama models 82 and 87, which serve with Spanish forces; the Greek Hellenic Arms EP 7; the British Sterling Spitfire; the Brazilian Imbel ,which is yet another reworking of the Colt M911; various models of Beretta from Italy, and the plastic-framed Glock from Austria. Most fearsome, if somewhat unmanageable, are the Israeli Desert Eagles, huge automatic pistols available in calibres up to and including .50in 'Action Express'. At the really exotic end of the military pistol market, and presumably only purchased in small numbers for special forces, are a Czech 4.5mm underwater pistol which fires a dart, and the Chinese 'knife pistol' in .22in calibre.

A new category of weapon which seems to be emerging is the Personal Defence Weapon (PDW) intended for soldiers who do not require a rifle as their primary weapon. Modern armies have a myriad of personnel, such as drivers, signallers, artillerymen, technicians, engineers etc, who really only require a weapon for self-defence. To fulfil this role, manufacturers have been experimenting with new materials and concepts, and have concentrated on a range of pistol/SMG hybrids. Interesting weapons in this super-pistol, or mini-SMG category include the Czech Skorpion, which was actually introduced as early as 1963; the short-lived Sterling Para Pistol; the Ingram Model 10, which was developed

The Czechoslovak Model 61 Skorpion sub-machine gun. Even under Communism Czech arms designers showed innovation and a measure of independent thought. The 7.65mm Skorpion, designed at Omnipol at the end of the 1950s is an excellent case in point, and, like the Uzi was one of the first successful really small sub-machine guns. Since the round was rather light the Skorpion was best employed as a vehicle crew personal defence weapon, or as a weapon of surprise, but larger calibre guns were produced subsequently. The 7.65mm Skorpion weighs just 3.5lb (1.59kg) and uses a 10- or 20-round magazine.

about 1970 and subsequently repackaged as the Cobray; the Heckler and Koch MP 5K, the Israeli Micro-Uzi and the Steyr TMP. Perhaps the most exotic of all in this area is the grandly named Bushman Individual Defence Weapon, a British gun which may be best described as an ultra-compact SMG. Its natural rate of fire is a magazine-emptying 1,400 rounds per minute, but an electronic regulator keeps this down to something more manageable. US Special Operations Command has actually issued a requirement for a weapon of this general sort, and Heckler and Koch has made a gun to match the specification. This is the 'Offensive Handgun Weapon System', which has a polymer frame, mechanical recoil reduction, sound suppressor and laser sight.

Another remarkable weapon mid-way between pistol and SMG is the 9mm Calico M950, made by Calico Incorporated of Bakersfield, USA, and which first appeared in 1989. The Calico is a modular system which allows a longer or shorter weapon to be assembled from interchangeable components, but its most notable feature is its huge magazine capacity. A 'small' magazine holds 50 rounds,

The Calico M-955AS light sub-machine gun. The Calico, seen here with a full butt and forward hand grip is one of a few 'personal defence' or very close combat weapons developed in the early 1990s. Note the extraordinary top-mounted large capacity drum magazine.

while a larger model holds 100 shots. Both magazines are tube-like arrangements which fit on top of the gun, and store the cartridges in two helical layers. The ammunition feed is therefore from the top, whilst spent cartridges eject underneath. The Calico weighs just over 2lb (1kg) when empty, which is light for the firepower it bestows.

Fabrique Nationale of Belgium have probably taken the most radical step in developing a PDW, in that they have designed a completely new round in 5.7mm calibre. It is fired by an unusual-looking weapon, which in the main is formed from a one-piece plastic moulding. The P90 has a rectangular, oblong appearance, with the pistol grip and foregrip blending into the body. There is an optical collimating sight above the barrel. It is a short, bullpup weapon which feeds from a translucent plastic 50-shot box magazine which lies horizontally along the top of the receiver. It can fire single shots or on fully automatic, and is claimed to be as accurate as an assault rifle out to about 220yd (200m).

Experiment continues with ideas like the caseless round, and various forms of electronic assistance, but since the collapse of the Warsaw Pact, the 'peace dividend' is beginning to apply, both in terms of smaller forces and in reduced procurement budgets. One early casualty amongst advanced weapons projects was the Heckler and Koch G11. This remarkable rifle has an overall plastic casing which also forms the stock, pistol grip and carrying handle/optical sight. It fires a unique 4.7mm telescoped round, with the bullet embedded in the propellant. The cartridge is also completely caseless, and once fired there is nothing left to eject from the rifle. It feeds from a 50-shot box which lies along the top of the weapon. Inside there

The Belgian FN P 90 Personal Defence Weapon. Announced in 1988 the P 90 was designed, in the same way as the old US M1 carbine, to be a weapon for second line troops. Since it is only 15.6in (400mm) long and has a 50-round magazine it might also be a useful weapon for assault in confined spaces. Unusually the P 90 uses a new 5.7mm cartridge; also the translucent magazine is top mounted, with the ejection of spent cartridges downwards. The gun weighs 6.17lb (2.8kg), and has a cyclic rate of about 900 rounds per minute.

is a rotary chamber, which gives the rifle a fearsome rate of fire in a controlled three-round burst. The barrel, breech and mechanism are independently mounted inside the casing, and recoil backwards as a unit. They don't hit the rear stop until the third round is fired, so the weapon does not begin to rise until all the bullets are on their way. While the G11 was a startling new technical development, the end of the cold war has seen the project shelved, with only a few weapons made.

The unique Heckler & Koch G11 automatic rifle. The barrel, breech and mechanism are independently mounted inside the casing, and the recoil is thus not transmitted to the firer until the last round of a 3-shot burst has been fired. It also makes use of specially-developed caseless ammunition which feeds from horizontal top-mounted magazines. This is the K2 variant, as entered for the US Army Advanced Combat Rifle competition. It has a bayonet fitted, and sports a Litton M845 night sight in place of the normal integral carrying handle/optical sight.

The US Army also looked at advanced technology for its projected M16A2 replacement, the Advanced Combat Rifle (ACR). Four designs were trialled, including a modified G11. One was a Steyr rifle, while the other two were from American companies, namely Colt and AAI. Technologies examined included flechette 'dart' rounds, duplex cartridges with two bullets, and advanced plastic materials. In the end the project was shelved, as the cost of a new development was felt to be too high for any likely advantage in performance. Perhaps the current range of assault rifles is so effective that there is little further development left in the concept of a weapon firing a lump of lead down a long tube at the enemy.

At the other end of the scale in terms of modernity it is noticeable that many weapons, long thought to be obsolete, are still in service or, in the mid-1990s are only just reaching the scrap yard. Some, like the Bren and the AK 47 remain because they have proved their worth many times over; others have simply been passed on cheaply to Third World states. Hungary and Turkey for a long time produced pistols which were essentially copies of the German Walther PP; the Hungarian weapon being known as the WALAM, and the Turkish as the Kirrikale. Bolt action Mausers are even now seen in Africa, Haiti, and elsewhere; SLRs appear in the Indian sub-continent and in British ex-colonies. Some remainders are simply bizarre, like the odd Sten gun seen in the hands of the Mexican Zapatistas, or the consignment of 1930s .38in Enfield revolvers which by 1994 had resurfaced in Britain after service in the Middle East.

One area which has remained old fashioned and steadfastly refused to move with the times is that of the sniper rifle. Despite experiment with other sorts of sniper weapon, new bolt action rifles seem to appear all the time, doubtless

because they have yet to be bettered in terms of accuracy. From the Austrian SSG 69, which first came out in 1969 with a modern plastic stock but an ancient bolt, have followed many others. These include the Norwegian NM 149S, the Swiss SIG-Sauer SSG 2000, the Finnish Sako TRG-21, and the Parker Hale Models 83 and 85. The main dissenter has been the Russian Army, who have moved to a semi-automatic weapon with the SVD Dragunov.

Britain adopted a new bolt action sniper rifle in 1986 in the form of the L96A1, whose main concessions to modernity were a green plastic stock and a light aluminium frame. The barrel is assembled onto the frame rather than the stock, and so if the stock is damaged it remains likely that the weapon will still

An Italian mountain trooper armed with the BM 59 Ital Beretta 7.62mm rifle. Amazingly, Italy continued to make and use this family of small arms based on the US Garand for many years after World War Two. Various modifications included folding stocks, bipods, large magazines, pistol grips, and grenade launchers, but the mechanical essentials were unchanged, and guns were also made under license in Indonesia and Morocco. The basic BM 59 had a 20-round box magazine, weighed 10.1lb (4.6kg), and was effective to about 656yd (600m).

The Accuracy International AWP, 7.62mm sniper rifle. From this commercial model was developed the very similar British army L96A1 sniper rifle which was adopted in 1986. Both weapons have a ten shot detachable box magazine and are clad in high impact plastic. The standard infantry sight is the 6x Schmidt and Bender, but there are also special anti-terrorist sights. Army requirements stated 'first shot' accuracy at 656yd (600m), and reasonable 'harassing fire' accuracy at 1,100yd (1,000m).

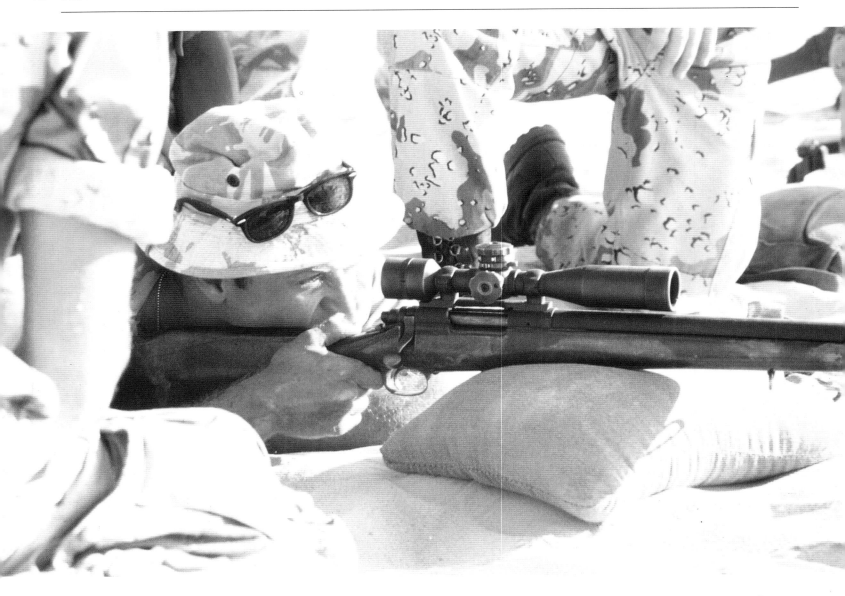

function accurately. The usual sight is the Schmidt and Bender telescopic zoom. The United States Army uses another bolt action weapon of traditional appearance. The M24 has a synthetic stock, while the barrel is attached to an aluminium block. In US service it has a Leopard Ultra scope. France has used two models of sniper rifle since 1980, the FR-F1 and the FR-F2; the latter, introduced in 1984, is distinguished by a thermal sleeve covering the barrel. This is believed not only to protect it but to keep it at an even temperature, thus reducing the infra-red signature of the weapon.

One new development in this field has been the advent of the long-range anti-materiel rifle. The best known of these is the Barrett Light Fifty M82A1. This large semi-automatic weapon fires the .50in Browning heavy machine gun cartridge, and is deadly at about 2,200yd (2,000m). It can be used against high-value equipment such as electronics and signalling systems, light vehicles, fire control systems or parked aircraft or helicopters. It is also deadly to personnel. The M82 is in service with a number of forces, and provided a unique long-range capability to US special forces in the Gulf war, where at least one kill was recorded at over 1,750yd (1,600m).

The Barrett M82A1 .50in calibre, semi automatic sniper rifle. The mechanism is based on short recoil principles, and by using the same cartridge as the Browning heavy machine gun, the Barrett is well suited to long range sniping. Its penetrative ability is also remarkable, shooting through flak jackets and light vehicles which might defeat a smaller round. Recoil is considerable but mitigated somewhat by a Solothurn-type muzzle brake; the gun is also heavy at 33lb (14.97kg). (MOD Pattern Room)

(Left top) A US Marine Corps sniper in the Gulf armed with the 7.62mm, M40A1 sniper rifle. The Remington made M40A1 is a conventional bolt action heavy-barrelled rifle, intended for single shot accuracy at medium to long ranges. It has a five round integral magazine and weighs 14.48lb (6.57kg); the telescopic sight seen here is the Marine Corps standard, 10x magnification.
(Left) The French FR-F1, or Fusil à Répétition Modèle F1, 7.5mm sniper rifle. Based on the obsolete MAS 36 bolt action the FR-F1 is virtually identical to two other guns intended for sporting and 'big game' purposes. Effective to about 875yd (800m) it has a 10-round magazine and weighs 11.5lb (5.2kg).

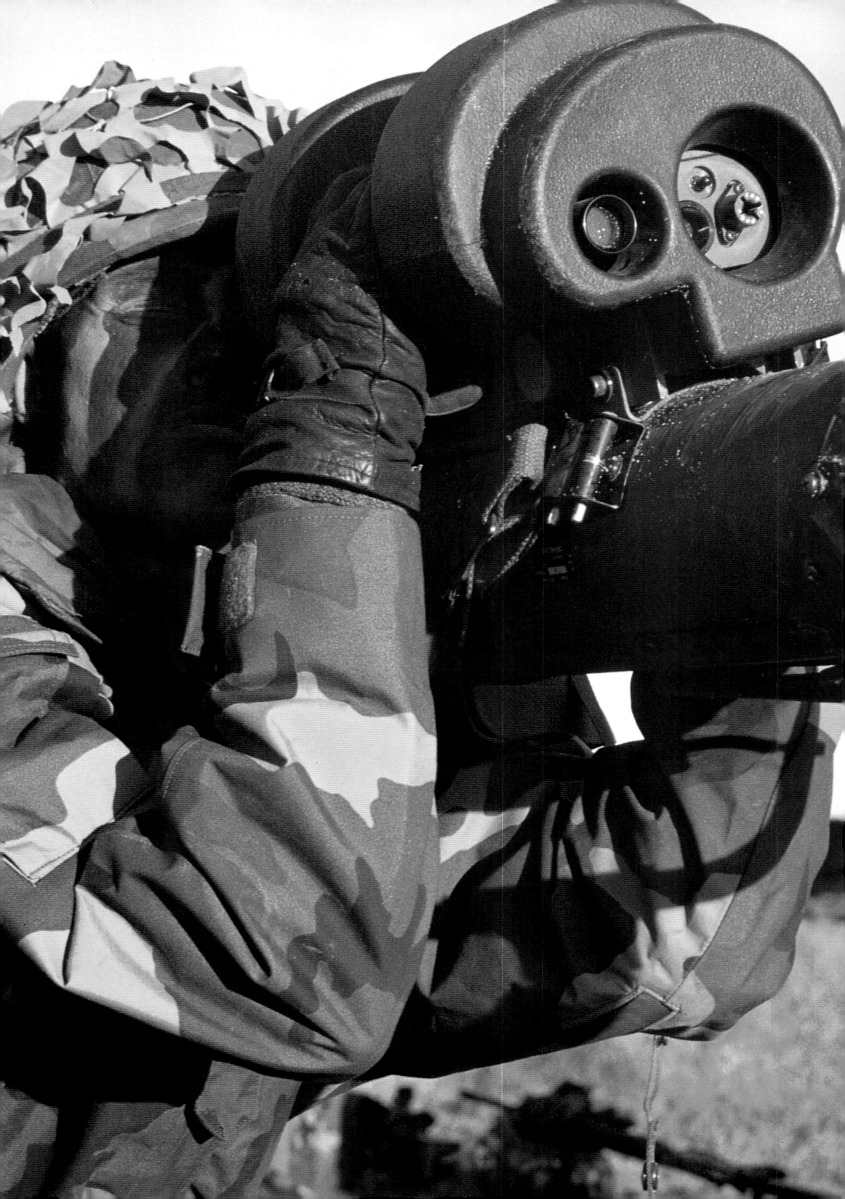

CHAPTER 5

MEN AGAINST MACHINES

T HOUGH THERE HAVE BEEN SIEGE ENGINES and horse-powered vehicles for centuries, the story of men using special weapons against vehicles and aircraft is almost exclusively one of the twentieth century. Armoured trains were used in the Boer War, but field guns, explosives on the track or a bent line were enough to deal with them. Only with World War One, when tanks and aircraft were used extensively for military purposes for the first time, did it become imperative that the infantryman have some means of defence.

The tank actually made its debut in the hands of the British on the Somme on 15 September 1916. Though the numbers were small its impact on the German infantry was spectacular enough. In the words of Frank Mitchell's 'Tank Warfare':

> 'As soon as they saw these fearful iron monsters lumbering out of the mist towards them, the majority turned and fled in terror. A few stout-hearted machine gunners stuck to their guns and blazed away defiantly at the creatures sides, but when they found that bullets were powerless they, too, dived like rabbits for cover, just in time to escape the ponderous tracks that crushed their puny machine guns into the mud.'

One German officer referred to them as 'fire vomiting iron dragons', and a German newspaper called them 'the Devil'. Even in the first attack, however, one tank at least was hit and knocked out by a field gun, whilst many others suffered mechanical failure. Tanks were not invulnerable.

The problem for the infantry was to find something more portable than a field gun, but still powerful enough to stop a tank. The Germans came up with a couple of possible answers very quickly. The first was the simple hand grenade. Early British tanks often had vision ports rather than periscopes, and built up so much heat inside that they usually travelled with open hatches. Also the top decking of the vehicle was very thin. A brave man who could get a bomb through a hatch, or on top of the tank, might hope to knock it out. The British soon responded by putting frames of chicken wire, otherwise known as 'anti-grenade netting' on top of the tanks. The next German ploy was to wire seven grenade heads to a single stick, and create a 'concentrated charge', which could also make an impact on bunkers.

At about the same time, armour piercing 'K' bullets were put into use against tanks. The 'K' round had in fact been in existence for some time, intended to

A US infantryman aims a Dragon anti-tank missile. The wire-guided missile comes as 'round of ammunition', sealed in its launch tube, which is clipped to the sight unit. Once the missile is fired, the empty tube is discarded.

The German 13mm Mauser 'Tank-Gewehr' of 1918. This was the first true anti-tank rifle, and was essentially a huge, single shot, bolt action weapon. It weighed a hefty 39lb (17.69kg), but had a muzzle velocity of around 2,950ft/s (900m/s) and an ability to penetrate 1in (25mm) of armour at 220yd (200m). (MOD Pattern Room)

give snipers and machine gunners better long range penetration against protected targets, but it was discovered that the tungsten-carbide core could pierce parts of the Mark I and Mark II tanks. In 1917 it was ordered that all German infantry soldiers receive 5 rounds, and machine guns a complete belt of the special ammunition expressly for use against tanks. With the advent of the thicker-skinned British Mark IV tank the 'K' bullet became almost useless, but the Germans were already preparing a heavy duty answer; the first anti-tank rifle. This was the Mauser Tank-Gewehr of 1918. Essentially it was nothing more than a giant bolt action rifle with a small bipod. A single-shot weapon, it used 13mm bullets with steel cores: armour penetration was only about 1in (25mm) at 220yd (200m), but this was greater than the thickness of any tank armour of the time.

Allied troops scarcely had to worry about tanks because the Germans never built more than about 20 of their own and captured perhaps another 15. Many of these were quickly knocked out by artillery, mishap, and in at least one case, by tank to tank action. Even so Britain did evolve a novel and handy anti-tank weapon. This was the Rifle Grenade No. 44, which looked like a tin can with a canvas skirt, mounted on a metal rod. It was pushed rod-first into the muzzle of a rifle, which was then loaded with a blank cartridge. Firing the rifle shot out the grenade, which would explode on impact: the canvas skirt helped to ensure that the bomb landed nose first. It is not known whether any were successfully deployed against the few enemy tanks, but the No. 44 would have been quite a useful anti-building and pill box weapon.

In the interwar period most of the development of man-portable anti-armour

The Browning M2 machine gun uses a .50in cartridge inspired by that of the Mauser Tank-Gewehr, and even in the 1990s retains a useful capability against the myriad of light vehicles and helicopters that populate the modern battlefield.

weapons concentrated on anti-tank rifles. Much work was done on mines, obstacles and anti-tank guns proper, but it was only the AT rifle which was widely issued to the infantry, and which could be carried and deployed by one man. To take the main AT rifles of the period in chronological order, the first was probably the Polish Karabin Przeciwpancerny WZ 'UR' of 1935. This had much in common with the original T-Gewehr, but was pared down to a minimum to reduce weight. It was also equipped with a five-round magazine, and, although the bullets were only 7.92mm, the case was oversized, giving a very high muzzle velocity of 4,198ft/sec (1,280m/sec).

The British Boys AT rifle was also designed during the middle 1930s and was named after its designer, Captain Boys. The Boys had a five-round detachable box magazine, and some of the recoil was absorbed by a barrel which slid back on firing, but the anti-armour performance was no better than that of the Polish gun. The first large order of Boys rifles was made from Birmingham Small Arms in late 1936, and the army was substantially equipped with them by the end of the first year of war. Although the factory was badly hit by enemy bombing, orders continued to be placed until January 1942, by which time both tank and weapon advances had made the Boys hopelessly out of date. Even so there were

The British Boys .55in anti-tank rifle. The Boys was named after one of its designers, Captain Boys, the Assistant Superintendent of Design at Enfield, who also had a hand in the development of the .38in Enfield revolver. The Boys weighed 36lb (16.32kg), had a five-round magazine, and could penetrate .83in (21mm) of armour at 328yd (300m). BSA produced about 69,000 of these anti-tank rifles, with further orders placed in the US and Canada. (MOD Pattern Room)

further experiments, including a version with a cartridge necked down from the standard .55in to .303in. Apart from seeking higher velocities it was also hoped that the Boys would prove suitable for long range sniping, and it is interesting to note that this line of enquiry has been subsequently developed with modern weapons like the American Barrett M82 .50in sniper rifle.

Just about the most unusual AT rifle, and one which was barely man-portable at 152lb (69kg), was the Japanese Kyuana Shiki, or Model 97, of 1937. This was a gas operated fully automatic 20mm, with a seven-round box magazine. A burst from this weapon was awesome, if often ineffective, because controlling it was virtually impossible for a single man. Japanese troops preferred to dig this gun into a prepared weapons pit, and use it on predetermined aiming points because of its extreme unmanoeuvrability. It was capable of penetrating .6in (15mm) of

The defence of the Romney, Hythe and Dymchurch light railway, Kent, 1940. The train contains at least two Boys anti-tank rifles and four Lewis guns, two of which are mounted on anti-aircraft pintles, and two behind shields. More usual transport applications were in tracked 'Bren Carriers' and trucks.

The monumentally unwieldy Japanese Kyunana Shiki 20mm, or Model 97 anti-tank rifle. Weighing 152lb (68.93kg), and being 80.75in (2.04m) in length, the seven-round, gas operated, fully automatic Model 97 was surely the ultimate expression of the anti-tank rifle. It scored some success against US light tanks in the Pacific, but armour penetration was still limited. (MOD Pattern Room)

armour, and provided useful weight of fire in certain circumstances, but was completely incapable of dealing with more modern tanks like the M4 Sherman.

In the late 1930s, the Germans began to think of replacing their old anti-tank weapons. There were three main models produced before the futility of using AT rifles against modern tanks was admitted. These were the Panzerbuchse Models 38, 39, and 41. The 1938 model used a large cartridge reduced to 7.92mm, but was still only single shot. The 1939 model AT rifle was also single shot, but much lightened and simplified. Many of these were subsequently cut down and used as grenade launchers, in which role they were known as Granatbuchse Model 39. The Panzerbuchse Model 41 was a more unusual weapon, based originally on an idea for an aircraft-mounted strafing cannon. Two Solothurn designers got working on this and from it developed a semi-automatic anti-tank rifle. Armour penetration was good, but still not good enough considering how well protected tanks of 1941 had become. On the Eastern front they proved useless against the T-34, although a number were later handed over to the Italians.

The Finns produced a new AT rifle in 1939; and this was made in both single shot, and semi-automatic versions. One point of interest was that it could be fitted with a small pair of skis for snowy conditions. The Russians introduced two new AT rifles in 1941, both of them in 14.5mm calibre. The PTRD was a single

The Russian PTRD 14.5mm anti-tank rifle. Arguably one of the best anti-tank rifles, the PTRD was capable of defeating 1in (25mm) of armour at 550yd (500m). It was long, at 79in (2m), but at 38.14lb (17.3kg) not exceptionally heavy for this type of weapon. (MOD Pattern Room)

shot weapon with a monstrous cartridge, capable of a muzzle velocity of over 3,000ft/sec (914m/sec). Although there was no magazine, the spent cartridge was recoil ejected. The other model was the PTRS, which had a five-round magazine and improved recoil absorption. Although more user friendly when actually firing, it was heavier and less robust. Both the PTRD and PTRS were able to penetrate about 1in (25mm) of armour at 550yd (500m); a not very impressive performance against the latest Panzers.

Although it was rocket weapons which ultimately replaced anti-tank rifles, in the middle war years there appeared a bewildering variety of man-portable anti-tank equipment. The last AT rifles coexisted with anti-tank grenades, rifle projected anti-tank grenades, satchel charges, spring projectors and flame weapons. Anti-tank grenades relied on two possible effects. First, an explosion in contact with an armoured plate may not necessarily pierce it, but may cause scabs of metal to detach on the inside, or it may blow out rivets, or damage vulnerable parts like tracks or externally stowed fuel. Secondly, 'shaped charge' grenades could actually punch holes through armour. Shaped or hollow charges have a cone-shaped gap in their nose, and when the explosive detonates the force is concentrated on the middle of the spot at the base of the cone. The result is a narrow jet of gas which burns forward through the armour. The effect is greatly enhanced if the interior of the cone is lined with a thin layer of metal (usually copper), which is forced through the armour in a molten stream.

The first British grenade to make use of the hollow charge effect was the No. 68 rifle grenade. Looking like the rear end of a mortar bomb, it was fired by a

Indian army troops in the 1970s. Except for the presence of the FN self loading rifle the scene could be straight from World War Two. In the foreground is an SMLE rifle fitted with a cup discharger: although usually used to project Mills bombs this could also throw the No. 68 anti-tank grenade.

cup discharger fitted to a standard SMLE rifle. It was used in small numbers in France in 1940 and in the western desert, finding its way to the Home Guard in 1941-1942. It had a range of about 100yd (91m) and was claimed to be able to penetrate up to 2in (51mm) of armour. The other British anti-tank bombs were the numbers 74, 75, and 82. No. 74 was the sticky bomb, invented in 1940. This was an extremely nasty device, more dangerous to the user than the target and heartily disliked by the infantry. It comprised a spherical glass flask of nitro-glycerine coated in stockinette and glue. Once a safety cover and pin had been removed the bomb was thrown or simply smashed against the tank. It was supposed to stick there until, five seconds later, the nitro-glycerine exploded. The bombs travelled in a box like a small metal suitcase, and special practice bombs were provided, made of white painted wood with a metal ring around them.

The No. 75, or Hawkins bomb, was a dual purpose mine or grenade. Looking like a small water bottle or oil tin it was ignited by crushing. The idea was therefore either to place it in the path of enemy vehicles or throw it in front of a tank. Another possible method was to tie a number of them to a string, and working from cover, pull them out suddenly across a roadway, before an enemy convoy. The No. 82 or Gammon bomb was an interesting concept in that the explosive and the igniter travelled separately, and were married up in the quantities required by the soldier. The Gammon was effectively a small bag with a fuse on top. The required amount of plastic explosive was pushed into the bag depending on the type of target. Half a stick of explosive was enough for blowing in a door or attacking a dugout, but two sticks were recommended for taking on a tank.

The Red Army was particularly keen on anti-tank grenades, which fitted in well with their aggressive ethos on close combat. The three main Soviet models were the RPGs -6, -40 and -43, all of which were stick types. The RPG-6 and RPG-40 had metal handles whilst the RPG-43 had a wooden handle. All three were stabilised in flight by cloth streamers and were percussion bombs, designed to explode on impact. RPGs -6 and -43 were both hollow charge bombs, and the RPG-6 was arguably the best of the bunch having an armour penetration of 4in (100mm), and it could also be used as an anti-personnel bomb. The Germans had a particularly fearsome group of anti-tank hollow charges, varying between 4.5 and 22lb (2 and 10kg) in weight. Obviously only the lightest of these could be thrown, whilst the heaviest were placed. Looking like large upturned funnels, the 'Heft Hohladung' grenades could be attached by magnet to a tank and, with penetration through armour upward of 4.5in (110mm), there was little that could withstand them. They were widely used against bunkers and fortifications as well as tanks. The Germans were so impressed with these weapons, that to prevent the Allies making use of their own versions, they covered the upper surfaces of many of their tanks with a rough coat of 'Zimmerit' anti-magnetic paste.

Before passing on to true rocket weapons it is worth considering that strange British hybrid the PIAT or Projector Infantry Anti-Tank, which was developed from the earlier Blacker Bombard. The major parts of the PIAT system were the launcher, with its trigger mechanism and giant spring, and the bomb. After much wrestling, the powerful spring was cocked and the bomb placed in the firing trough. Pulling the trigger allowed a spigot to shoot forward into the tail of the bomb. The bomb was pushed violently out of the trough and at the same time the

The PIAT or 'Projector Infantry Anti-tank' which entered British service in 1942 bridged the gap between anti-tank rifles and the advent of effective rocket weapons. It was heavy and clumsy at 32lb (14.5kg), and devilish to cock, but capable of penetrating 2.9in (75mm) of armour. This example has been sectioned to show the huge launching spring, the strength of which made the PIAT so difficult to cock. The picture also shows the shaped charge bomb with its impact fuse on the extended nose spike. (MOD Pattern Room)

cartridge in its tail was detonated. The bomb then shot off to a range of up to 200yd (183m) and was capable, by dint of its hollow charge warhead, of penetrating 3in (76mm) of armour. Discharge self-cocked the projector for a second round. It was also useful against buildings and fortifications, and the lack of rocket backblast meant that it could be safely fired from inside a building. The PIAT was hard work to cock and highly unpleasant to fire, but in 1942 was one of the better anti-tank devices available to the infantryman. Something in excess of 100,000 of these were made by ICI.

It was the Germans and Americans who really pioneered anti-tank rocket weapons. Rockets had been perceived as militarily useful in both Europe and China since the medieval era. In the Napoleonic Wars the British horse artillery had maintained a rocket troop which had occasional successes against both enemy positions and cavalry. Perhaps the first serious proposal for a rocket as an anti-tank weapon came from the American Dr Robert Goddard in the summer of 1918; his tubular launcher supported by a crude tripod was not unlike the old British 'Congreve' rockets, but pointed the way to an intriguing possibility.

It was another American, Colonel Skinner of the US Army, who put the vital ingredients of hollow charge and rocket together in a highly practical form. He had been working on the idea for some time when finally in 1942 his prototype came for testing at Aberdeen proving ground. Immediate success led to an order for 5,000 rocket weapons from the General Electric Company on 19 May. The name Bazooka came from the GIs, who thought that it resembled the home-made trombone played by the radio comedian Bob Burns. These Bazookas were delivered in a month, and since the war on the Eastern Front had reached a critical stage, a few were sent to Russia, and a later batch to North Africa. The weapon

A British PIAT team cover a road junction. The PIAT's practical anti-tank range was about 110yd (100m), but it could also be used as a bunker busting device at up to 770yd (700m). Perhaps the greatest exponent of the PIAT was Fusilier F.A. Jefferson of 2nd Battalion Lancashire Fusiliers, who won the VC for the destruction of two enemy tanks in quick succession, at Monte Cassino in May 1944.

A US 2.36in Bazooka team lurking in the snow. The 2.36 in Bazooka was, for its time, one of the best anti-tank weapons in use. It weighed only 13.23lb (6kg), and was capable of penetrating 3.17in (80mm) of armour out to 380yd (350m). This picture shows the loader inserting the projectile: the weapon itself has crude snow camouflage in the form of strips of white cloth wound around the barrel.

performed very well, being able to pierce 3in (76mm) of armour, but some were captured, aiding the Germans' own rocket anti-tank programme which was also gearing up in 1942. In the event the Germans would produce two very different hand-held projectors, the Panzerfaust and the Panzerschreck.

The Panzerfaust was a remarkable departure, a single-shot disposable tube with a large-headed hollow charge rocket projectile, thrown by a black powder charge. The story of its development was pieced together by British Intelligence in September 1945, mainly by means of interview with Dr Heinrich Langweiler, the inventor, at Weilburg near Wetzlar. According to him the first experiments were made in the summer of 1942 as a result of the appearance of the T-34 tank on the Eastern Front.

The first prototype was a tube, only 13.7in (350mm) long, into which a hollow charge bomb on a short stick was inserted. The whole thing weighed only 5lb (2.3kg), and was held out at right angles to the arm; there were no sights, and hits were thus secured as much by luck as judgement. This weird device did how-

ever prove that it was possible to combine the principles of hollow charge and recoilless rocket propulsion. It also provided the weapon's first name, the Faustpatrone or fist cartridge. It was quickly realised that the weapon needed better sighting, and in December 1942 there appeared the Faustpatrone 1, or Gretchen, later to be officially designated the Panzerfaust (Klein) 30m. This had a longer tube, sights, and fired a bomb 4.2in (105mm) in diameter, at a muzzle velocity of 98ft/sec (30m/sec). The armour penetration was 5.5in (140mm), sufficient to defeat the frontal armour of the T-34, KV, and Sherman tanks.

The German Panzerfaust pictured c.1943. The Panzerfaust could be fired from a variety of positions, prone, kneeling or standing, and could also be used under the arm, or over the shoulder, providing the back blast was not trapped. The Panzerfaust 30 'Gross' shown here weighed 11lb (5kg) and was capable of penetrating in 7.9in (200mm) of armour at close range. German propaganda stressed how easy the Panzerfaust 'wonder weapon' was to use, illustrating the point for the newsreels with patriotic, but non technically-minded, housewives. Allied propaganda decried it as a 'weapon of embarrassment', although tank crews soon learned to respect it.

Further improvements soon produced the Panzerfaust (Gross) 30m which was demonstrated at Kummersdorf in March 1943. This weighed 11.25lb (5kg), and had an armour penetrating capability of 7.8in (200mm); enough to destroy any allied tank then in existence. At this point 3,000 of each model were ordered for troop trials on the Eastern Front. Results were good, so mass production was initiated in October 1943. Production targets were set of 100,000 'Klein' and 200,000 'Gross' per month, and these figures were actually achieved in April 1944. The destructive capability of the Panzerfaust (Gross) 30m proved excellent, and at least one instance where a Panzerfaust hit a Sherman in the side, the jet passed through and blew a hole in the far side.

Development now concentrated on increasing range, and to this end was created the Panzerfaust 60m; with a thicker firing tube and larger propellant charge. Range and muzzle velocity were thereby improved. The army also expressed interest in a Panzerfaust with an anti-personnel capability, and the Sprengfaust was duly developed. This used a remarkable bomb, which, instead of having a hollow charge, bounced into the air on first contact with the ground and exploded into a cloud of fragments. Complexity ensured that this never reached full production status. In September 1944 a further range increase was achieved with the Panzerfaust 100m. That winter, with the Ardennes offensive in full swing, Panzerfaust production reached amazing levels. According to armaments minister Albert Speer, 997,000 were made in November; 1,253,000 in

December; and 1,200,000 in January 1945. At the same time a new and even more deadly version, the Panzerfaust 150, was coming on stream. This not only increased the range yet further but finally introduced the desired anti-personnel capacity, in the form of a fragmentation sleeve to be fitted to the standard bomb. It was perhaps fortunate for allied tank crews that the war ended when it did. At this point there was under development the Panzerfaust 250, capable of a range of 220yd (200m), and of reloading. Low level aircraft might not have been safe either because special sights and an anti-aircraft version of the bomb were then under investigation.

The development of the other German anti-tank rocket projector, the Panzerschreck, began with a demonstration at Kummersdorf in March 1943. Here the officers of the Heereswaffenampt, or Army Weapons Office, were shown an American Bazooka captured in Tunisia; they were so impressed that work began

The German Panzerschreck together with its 88mm rocket projectile. First used in 1943 the Panzerschreck was an effective anti-tank weapon, capable of dealing with virtually any Allied tank. The example seen here has a shield to protect the firer against the vicious back blast of the projectile; users of the first model had to be content with steel helmet and gas mask. (MOD Pattern Room)

on a German version. The weapon they produced was actually larger than the American precursor, having a 3.4in (88mm) bomb, electrical firing, and very often a small shield to protect the face of the firer. The troops would sometimes call the new weapon the Ofenrohr, or stove pipe, due to the shape and belching backblast of flame and smoke on firing. That it was such a success was due not only to a lucky capture, but to previous German experiments such as the tripod mounted LG40 gun.

After World War Two pace of development slowed and when interest was rekindled it was mainly in two areas, wheeled and vehicle mounted recoilless or missile weapons, which do not concern us here, and hand-held rocket weapons. Korea was a shock to the system for both sides of the Iron Curtain, for it pitted the weapons of the former allies against each other for the first time. The West discovered that the old 2.36in (60mm) Bazooka was not really capable of a definite one-shot kill against a T-34, while the Eastern Bloc discovered that it had no effective infantry anti-tank weapon which was not also suicidal. The American answer was simple: they had been working on a 3.5in (89mm) version of the Bazooka before the end of World War Two, but the project had been shelved at the end of hostilities. The 3.5in 'Super Bazooka' was now brought into production. It proved very effective, though in the event it would see more use against machine gun nests and infantry in Korea, because the Communist forces used relatively few tanks. The weapon would subsequently become a NATO mainstay, and saw service with many countries.

In Britain this weapon was dubbed the '3.5 inch Rocket Launcher', and was issued during the 1950s on a scale of three per infantry company. Each team was intended to have six rockets, with a further six rockets per tube available at short notice. The launcher could be fired by one man, but really needed a second to act as ammunition carrier and loader. The official manual stated that it was capable of defeating all but the frontal armour of the heaviest tanks. The rockets would fly for over 900yd (820m), but engaging a tank at anything much over 150yd (137m) was found to be impractical. The danger area to friendly troops from the backblast on launching was a 25yd (23m) triangle to the rear of the firer. Regarding tactical use of the launcher the following helpful advice was given to trainees:

> 'When in the open, the kneeling position is best, but whenever possible the launcher should be fired standing, from a fire trench or suitable position which will give protection from ground and air, and should be of such a shape and size that Nos. 1 and 2, (the crew) and their equipment. . . are immune from being crushed by a tank.'

Early pattern American 3.5in launchers were fitted with a bipod, but later models, and apparently all the British ones, did not have this feature. Although bigger and bulkier than its predecessor, the 3.5in was light at 15lb (6.8kg), and

The post-war Soviet 73mm SPG 9 recoilless gun, pictured in the mid 1970s. Recoilless guns were in considerable vogue as infantry support weapons in the period between 1950 and 1980, but only the lightest of them could really claim to be man portable. Even this example, which is at the smaller end of the scale weighs in at 101lb (45.7kg) with an added 26lb (12kg) for the stand. Nevertheless the SPG 9 had a respectable performance, being able to deal with 15.5in (390mm) of armour, and it had a maximum range of 1,420yd (1,300m).

carriage was made easier by the fact that releasing a barrel lock allowed it to be folded. Ultimately it proved useful enough to remain in service with some countries until the 1980s, and close copies would be manufactured in Spain and China.

The Russians began a new series of RPG weapons in the 1950s, but the basic elements, i.e. a tube with large projecting rocket head and spring-loaded hammer and cap for firing, came straight from the German Panzerfaust. The first general issue model was the RPG-2; this was reloadable, and it was possible to fire up to six rounds a minute in emergencies. It had an effective range of about 160yd (150m). Maximum armour penetration was about 7in (180mm). The Chinese also manufactured the RPG-2, but under the designation Type 56, and with a modified rocket round.

In the Red Square parade of November 1962 Western observers first became aware of a new Soviet anti-tank weapon, which they christened M62 for obvious

An Egyptian RPG 7 anti-tank rocket launcher seen with the ordinary flip up sights, and no projectile loaded. The calibre of the RPG rocket is 3.37in (85mm), and the warhead overhangs the end of the 1.6in (40mm) launch tube. It can penetrate 13.1in (330mm) of armour, and engage moving targets at up to 330yd (300m). Large stationary targets may be hit at 550yd (500m). The RPG 7 has achieved very widespread use in eastern Europe, Africa, Asia and the Middle East, and has been locally produced in several countries. (MOD Pattern Room)

Polish soldiers on exercise, c.1990, with an RPG 7 rocket launcher, mounted with a PGO 7 optical sight. This launcher has a dummy projectile loaded. The soldier in the background has a 40 mm BG-15 grenade launcher fitted to his Kalashnikov. First seen in Afghanistan in 1984, this has a range of about 460yd (420m).

The Soviet AT-3 'SAGGER' was one of the first man-portable anti-tank missiles to be deployed. Two missiles and the sight unit were carried in an aluminium case, which doubled as a launch platform. Once he fired the missile, the operator had to track it in his sight, using a small 'joystick' to guide it towards the target. Movement of this sent electronic commands down the thin wire which was paid out behind the missile. To hit a moving target under combat conditions took a high level of skill from the operator, whose aim had to remain steady during the flight of the missile. But even so, Egyptian SAGGER teams gave Israeli tank units a nasty shock during the 1973 Arab-Israeli war.

reasons, but later more accurately called the RPG-7. This improved model had better sights, greater range, anti-personnel capability, and the ability to penetrate 12.5in (320mm) of armour. The RPG-7 benefits from having a nozzle arrangement rather than a simple tube, and the main rocket motor is not activated until the projectile is at least 33ft (10m) clear of the tube. Predictably the Chinese have also produced a version, which is known as the Type 69. In 1968 a handier folding Russian launcher appeared, called the RPG-7V. RPGs of various models saw extensive use in Afghanistan; often as not in the anti-personnel role. Further development produced another new model, the RPG-16, in the 1980s. Apart from European Warsaw pact countries the RPG series has also seen widespread use in Africa, Asia and the Middle East.

Another small Soviet anti-tank weapon is the RPG-18; but this is distinctively different to the models mentioned above, and much more similar in configuration

to the American M72 LAW (see below). In carrying mode it is a 27in (700mm) tube, which telescopes out in readiness for firing. It weighs only 8.8lb (4kg), and is labelled with a series of drawings and simple firing instructions. It is effective to about 220yd (200m) with an armour piercing capability of 11.7in (300mm). At the other end of the scale came the Sagger missile, one version of which was intended to be man-portable with motor rifle and airborne units. Nonetheless it had to be set up on the ground, and the rocket, almost a metre in length, was capable of penetrating over 15.6in (400mm) of armour.

Sagger was extremely difficult to steer, and has since been replaced in Russian service by two other man-portable systems. The AT-4 Spigot, a wire guided missile equivalent to the MILAN (see below) with a range of about 2,200yd (2,000m), and the smaller AT-7 Saxhorn, which is closer to Dragon in concept (see also below) and has a range of about 1,100yd (1,000m).

In the West there have been many more diverse weapons brought into use against tanks since 1950. The Belgians, for example, continued to experiment with anti-tank rifle grenades, and produced in that year the Mecar-made Energa. It was adopted by several countries, including Britain. For firing, the Energa was fitted over the muzzle of the rifle on a special adapter, and was launched using a blank cartridge. A flip-up sight on the adapter aided aim, but little accuracy was expected beyond 110yd (100m). According to the 1953 manual the virtues of the Energa were lightness, versatility and power; it was easy to carry, could be used against concrete and light vehicles as well as tanks, and was capable of defeating all but the frontal armour of the heaviest tanks. Two adapters were issued per infantry section, with ten spares in battalion store. Each section had six grenades on hand, with a further three in reserve. A more recent version, the HEAT-RFL-75 Super Energa, claims to be accurate to 164yd (150m) against moving targets by means of a rocket boost.

In terms of home grown British developments the work of Sir Denis Burney for some time led the field. It appears that his objective was to produce a practical shoulder-fired recoilless gun, but impracticality of scale and cut-backs left only a wheeled version to pass into production. Britain therefore depended

The Russian AT-4, anti-tank weapon. Originally known by the unglamorous acronym 'FAGOT', the AT-4 was actually developed in the 1960s, and entered service in the 1970s. It is a SACLOS or 'Semi Automatic Command to Line of Sight' weapon, and bears many similarities to MILAN. The complete firing unit weighs a total of 88lb (40kg), and the missile is able to penetrate 1.6ft (.5m) of armour out to a maximum range of about 2,200yd (2,000m).

The Belgian FN 'Bullet-Thru' grenade, pictured c.1990. The rifleman does not need to use special propellant cartridges with this weapon, instead he merely clips the grenade on to the muzzle of his rifle and fires a normal round. The bullet passes through hollow central axis of the bomb, but the high pressure gas is trapped, providing the propelling force to launch the bomb. This was essentially similar to the method used in the French 'VB' grenade, and the German Model 1917 Wurfgranate. The 'Bullet-Thru' weighs 11oz (.32kg) and has an effective radius of about 11yd (10m). Shown here fitted to the FNC 5.56mm rifle, the grenade has a range of about 330yd (300m).

The Swedish Carl Gustav 84mm medium anti-tank weapon. Being a rifled, breechloading, open ended tube, the Carl Gustav enjoyed many of the benefits of the Bazooka, rifle, and hollow charge weapon all in one package. By the 1970s the 'Charlie Gee' was in use with the Swedish, British, Canadian, Norwegian and Danish forces. It weighed 31lb (14.2kg) and could penetrate 1.3ft (.4m) of armour at up to 490yd (450metres), using a shaped charge High Explosive Anti-tank (HEAT) round. This projectile with its distinctive long nose is shown in the centre of the group of ammunition. The other shells are high explosive, smoke, and illumination. Also shown are the protective caps used to cover the muzzle and breech of the launcher in transit. (MOD PATTERN ROOM)

mainly on foreign designs for hand-held anti-tank capability, not only the Belgian Energa, but the American LAW, and the Swedish Carl Gustav. This last proved to be a very effective medium anti-tank weapon which has only recently been superseded. It is an 84mm shoulder-fired recoilless gun, capable of engaging armour at 550yd (500m), and infantry (using a high explosive round) at 1,100yd (1,000m). It was normally served by a crew of two, one loading the breech, the other aiming and firing. Accuracy was aided by a rifled barrel, and an armour penetration of 15.6in (400mm) was claimed; enough to deal with main battle tanks.

The weapon which has replaced the Carl Gustav in the British Army has an even more fearsome performance, for the LAW 80, made by Hunting Engineering and Royal Ordnance, can pierce over 23.4in (600mm) of armour. This is a one shot, disposable, 94mm rocket weapon with a built-in spotting rifle to increase the probability of a hit. The LAW 80 is highly effective, especially in conjunction with the 'Adder' system, with which a number of unmanned LAW 80s can be set up and fired remotely in a preplanned manner. The one serious disadvantage is weight, for 22lb (10kg) is quite a lot for a single shot light weapon, and it does not

The British LAW 80, 'Light Anti-tank Weapon'. From 1987 the single-shot LAW 80 began to replace the Carl Gustav as the British infantry's prime anti-tank weapon. The projectile initiation of the LAW 80 is entirely non-electric, making it more reliable, even after a long period of storage. The tube itself is of a wound filament construction, and aim is aided by the inclusion of an integral spotting rifle which has five pre-packed rounds of ammunition. The LAW 80 saw use in the Gulf, and, although most Iraqi armour was cleared quickly by allied tanks, the new anti-tank weapon proved its worth in the bunker-smashing role.

seem likely that an infantry section would be able to carry many rounds.

In America there have been various successors to the old 3.5in Super Bazooka. Perhaps the longest lived and most widely used has been the M72 2.6in (66mm) LAW, which was also copied by the Soviets (see above). The M72 weighs only 5lb (2.36kg) and consists of a single round in an aluminium tube. Like the Soviet model the tube opens telescopically, causing the simple sights to pop up. A small trigger bar above the centre of the weapon is depressed to fire it. For such a small and handy device the performance is very good; it being possible to

US troops advancing c.1974; carried with them are single shot M72 Light Anti-tank Weapons. The biggest advantage of the M72 LAW was its lightness, an infantry squad was not significantly inconvenienced by carrying several and they had the capacity to destroy all but the heaviest of main battle tanks.

(Opposite page) The US Dragon medium anti-tank weapon on firing. Development of the Dragon began in 1966 with the awarding to McDonnell Douglas of a $35 million contract: US Army tests began in 1971, and four years later the system was operational. By the 1980s Dragon was the US Army infantry's main anti-tank system. The basic wire-guided Dragon M47 weighs 32.2lb (14.6kg), has a range of about 1,100yd (1,000m), and apart from an ability to penetrate armour can punch through 3ft (.9m) of reinforced concrete. There have been two improvements, the Dragon II and the Dragon II+, which have led to increases in performance. The Dragon is widely used by many countries including Israel, Iran, the Netherlands, Spain, Switzerland and parts of the former Yugoslavia.

engage moving targets up to 164yd (150m) away, and to achieve armour penetration of 11.7in (300mm).

The Americans have also made use of a number of recoilless rifles, of which the 3.5in (90mm) M67 could be man-ported. In the 1980s recoilless weapons gave way to Dragon, a tube launched, optically tracked, wire guided system, capable of operation by one man. After firing the operator keeps the sight cross hairs on the target, and any directional changes are relayed to the missile by wires which pay out behind it. The main tube of the launcher is disposable, but the sight tracker unit is kept and re-used for the next shot. Dragon is now being replaced in US service by the AT-4, a Swedish-built single shot rocket launcher rather like the British LAW 80.

Although several other countries, including Italy and Israel produce their own hand-held rocket anti-tank weapons, it is the French and German systems which have gained greater currency in recent years. The French make both LRAC 89 and MILAN, which stand respectively for Lance-Roquette Anti Char de 89mm and Missile d'Infanteries Leger Anti Char. The LRAC is a lightweight bazooka-type arm also capable of firing anti-personnel rounds, as well as penetrating up to 15.6in (400mm) of armour. The MILAN, which is also made in Germany and the UK, is in service with many countries. It is intended primarily for infantry use from a defensive position and is wire guided. Like the American Dragon the system is in two parts, a factory-sealed missile pod, and the guidance and tracking unit which can be attached to fresh rounds. MILAN has proven to be

British MILAN or 'Missile d'Infanterie Léger Anti-Char' crew, c.1990. The crewmen wear ballistic nylon Mark 6 General Service helmets, and have a second missile at the ready. The MILAN was originally a French design but was produced with German co-operation, and its international status has been confirmed by the fact that it is also made in Britain and has been sold both inside and outside NATO countries. The missile is wire-guided, weighs 26lb (11.8kg) in its launch pack, has a range of about 2,200yd (2,000m) and contains a shaped charge warhead. The reusable launcher weighs 36.2lb (16.4kg) and when set up on the ground has a 360 degree traverse.

A fighter in the former Yugoslavia armed with the locally made 44mm, RB M57, anti-tank launcher. Derived from the German Panzerfaust the M57 is 39in (1m) long, weighs 17.9lb (8.1kg), and fires a missile weighing 5.38lb (2.44kg). Its range is about 220yd (200m) and it can penetrate 1.25ft (.38m) of armour.

exceptionally effective and can engage tanks and fortifications at ranges of up to 2,190yd (2,000m).

Post-war German developments in the anti-tank field include Lanze and Panzerfaust 3, both of which owe a good deal to the original World War Two Panzerfaust design. As in both the original Panzerfaust and the Soviet RPG-7, the warhead overhangs the end of the launch tube and is therefore not limited to the diameter of the tube. Both weapons also have low velocity launchers, keeping down overall weight and the distance from which the firer can easily be detected.

Austria, already noteworthy for the success of the AUG assault rifle, has created a further stir since the late 1980s with its 15mm Steyr Anti-Materiel Rifle. In many ways this has the appearance of an ultra-modern anti-tank rifle, though of course something as light as this would not have any hope of tackling a main battle tank. The AMR is therefore intended to take on lighter vehicles, aircraft on the ground, and communications targets; and it can be imagined that in the hands of special forces such a rifle could well do damage out of proportion to its size and cost. The only real question mark therefore is why, despite experiment, anti-tank rifles were not kept in active use for the same reasons after 1942. It is also apparent, that, although less powerful, the American Barrett .50in M82A1 sniper rifle in use with US Navy SEALS and the SAS, is much lighter and could perform many of the same functions whilst being more suitable in the anti-personnel role. The same may also be true of the Hungarian Gepard and Destroyer long-range sniper rifles, in 12.7mm and 14.5mm respectively. Nonetheless the Steyr AMR is an impressive weapon with little recoil for its size. It has a bullpup configuration, an eight-shot magazine, and the ability to penetrate 1.65in (40mm) of armour at 875yd (800m) using a fin-stabilised projectile. Its 44lb (20kg) weight is somewhat offset by the fact that it can be split into two pieces for carrying.

In general terms truly man-portable anti-aircraft weapons have proved less fruitful than their anti-tank brethren. The reasons for this are essentially straightforward: even when flying low an aircraft is likely to be several hundred yards from the man trying to shoot it down, and though larger than a tank, moves many times faster and in less predictable ways. To engage successfully, an anti-aircraft weapon will usually require a fixed mounting with all-round pivot; factors hardly conducive to remaining man-portable. Tanks by contrast have to traverse the terrain to attack, and may well be vulnerable to the enemy soldier especially if unsupported by friendly infantry. Moreover, an armoured vehicle is comparatively slow moving, and intelligent use of the field can improve the tank hunter's chances considerably; he will know for example that tanks are likely to have to cross certain bridges, will prefer tracks and roads to ditches, bogs, and minefields, and will be especially vulnerable in built-up areas where they can be struck from a few feet away

Though fanciful claims have been made for man-portable weapons, and even for soldiers with rifles, the kill rate against aircraft with anything less than a ground-mounted missile, or multiple anti-aircraft gun mountings, is almost negligible. Demonstrations of this have been provided since 1980 in both the Falklands and the Gulf. Indeed it is fair to say that the most important use of a hand-held anti-aircraft weapon remains the ability of its user to discourage air attack, and to interfere with the pilot's mission. Streams of tracer bullets coming

Mines are also useful anti-armour and anti-personnel weapons for infantry units in defensive positions. Modern designs have sophisticated electronic fuses, while their plastic casing makes them difficult to detect with mine-clearing equipment. This Afghan Mujahideen fighter is demonstrating the use of a mine to his colleagues.

British troops man a .303in Hotchkiss light machine gun on an early AA mount. Introduced to British service in 1916 the Hotchkiss Mark I was essentially the French machine rifle model 1909, known to the Americans as the Benét-Mercié. Like the other Hotchkiss models it was strip fed, until the introduction of a slightly modified Mark I model. In British service it was first issued to the cavalry: the gun was fairly handy, but was seen as inferior to the Lewis. Like the Lewis, it was also used as tank armament.*

upwards from a number of machine guns can easily disrupt a pilot's concentration and throw his aim off.

Until after 1945 there were few ways indeed that the infantry could strike against aircraft without the aid of heavier 'flak'. One method which was, and remains, almost universal is the use of AA mounts for machine guns. One of the first was a cart wheel struck on a post on which the gun could be balanced or lashed to provide all-round fire. By 1915 designers were working on more durable stands, tripods, and monopods, which from 1916 to 1918 would become semi-permanent fixtures in airfields and camps. The only other significant modifications to the standard machine gun, apart from multiple mounts and ring sights, were a plethora of new magazine types and belt holders, intended to make rapid traverse and elevation more practical and to make more rounds available. Examples which spring readily to mind are the drum magazines used with the Bren gun and MG 34 in World War Two.

One other weapon, which at first glance seems improbable for the anti-aircraft role, was the light mortar. Nevertheless mortar bombs rise to a considerable vertical height, and before the end of World War One methods of employing them against aircraft were being investigated. One mortar actually so deployed was the British Stokes, which could be moved around by men with reasonable rapidity, and which was fitted

A pipe-smoking British officer watches practice with a .303in Vickers machine gun on an anti-aircraft mount. The main difference to the standard tripod is obviously in terms of elevation, but special sights help the firer judge the correct amount of deflection, while a belt box makes tracking and traversing easier.

Field Marshal Walter Model in conversation with Grenadiers on the Eastern Front, c.1944, one of whom carries an MG 42. Interestingly the weapon is on a bipod, but is fitted with an anti-aircraft 'ring' sight and a 50-round drum magazine. The MG 42 had a very high rate of fire for a single barrelled air-cooled weapon, making it especially useful in the anti-air role.

with an AA sight. The big problem with the use of mortar bombs against aircraft was getting them to explode at the vital moment, and thus it was that various expedients including cables and parachutes were experimented with in an attempt to improve lethality.

Though of minimum utility, rifles were also pointed skyward in the hope of bringing down enemy fliers. Most people realised that this was essentially a deterrent or morale-raising exercise, so beyond training the infantry to 'aim off' in front of fast moving aircraft, and to work as a unit in order to maximise the amount of lead in the air little else was done in this direction. An exception were the Japanese who actually produced a version of their Arisaka rifle with a monopod

British light air defence, 1980s-style. A simple monopod holds a standard 7.62mm L7 GPMG, which has no belt box or anti-aircraft sights. The usefulness of this setup against fast-flying jets or armoured helicopters must be questionable.

Light air defence, 1940s-style. These New Zealand troops have a .303in Bren light machine gun on a special 'AA' mounting during World War Two. The Bren was used with a variety of anti-aircraft mounts of which this 'Tripod, anti-aircraft' was perhaps the most common. Where a two man team was available one would aim and fire the Bren with his left hand gripping the carrying handle as he traversed the weapon. The 'No 2' would act as loader. If a third man was on hand, one man would act as section commander, spotting and directing fire. Brens were also seen with large drum magazines for anti-aircraft use.

and anti-aircraft sight. One well known expert has described this arrangement as more of a 'psychological crutch' for the user, than a serious threat to allied aircraft. In any event the Type 99 rifle had its AA sight deleted in 1943, a tacit admission perhaps that its presence had been a luxury rather than an integral and useful part of the gun.

With World War Two came the use of missiles against aircraft as a viable proposition. Most were launched from static launchers, like the Home Guard 'Rocket Batteries', or fired from other aircraft, but hand-held rocket weapons like the Bazooka and Panzerfaust suggested that a man-portable device might be possible. Also developed during the war were guidance systems for larger scale missile projects, which, if they could be made small enough and light enough, could be applied to a hand-held device. In the 1950s these elements were brought together to create the shoulder-launched AA missile. One of the first to be successful was the American Redeye, which was developed at the end of the decade. Redeye's added advantage, which gave it hopes of success against low level aircraft, was its infra-red sensor which enabled the missile to home on the heat of an aircraft engine. The gunner tracked the enemy aircraft through an optical sight, and was informed by means of a buzzer when the rocket was ready for launch. A large scale contract for Redeye missiles was placed with General Dynamics of Pomona California in 1964.

A Russian SA-7 anti-aircraft missile in Yugoslavia c.1992. First seen in action with the Egyptians after the Six Day War, the SA-7 was also used in Vietnam, though with better success against piston-engined aircraft and helicopters than jets. A mainstay of eastern European armies it weighs 23.4lb (10.6kg) with a 20.3lb (9.2kg) missile. A later improved model is known as SA-14.

Interestingly the first Soviet shoulder-launched AA missile was very similar to the Redeye, and it is believed that it was developed due to an example of the American arm reaching Russia via Scandinavia. The SA-7 Grail, as it became known, first saw action with the Egyptian Army in the late 1960s. Although somewhat cruder than its American precursor it had similar performance, and claimed a maximum slant range of 1.24 miles (2km). Later models, including the SA-7A, and SA-7B, incorporated refinements such as proximity-fused missiles, and an automatic self destruct after 15 seconds. The series has seen use throughout the old Warsaw Pact and in Egypt, Syria, former Yugoslavia and East Africa.

Britain began to issue the Shorts Blowpipe in the 1970s, but this was rather different to either the American or Soviet weapons. Blowpipe's guidance system depended not on infra-red, but on a transmitter in the aiming unit. If the operator keeps aiming his sight on the aircraft the missile heads for the centre of the view field; adjustments can be made by means of a thumb control. The missile responds by means of nose-mounted control surfaces which serve to steer it in flight. It explodes either on contact with the target or close by, due to a proxim-

British troops with the Short Brothers Javelin anti-aircraft missile launcher. Javelin is the 1980s update of the Blowpipe, and features a TV camera in its guidance system as well as a new warhead and two stage rocket motor. The earlier Blowpipe demanded a high level of skill from the firer, and Javelin is an attempt to make operation easier under combat conditions. The missile canisters are disposable but the launch unit is saved for reuse. On the ground is a bipod mounted 7.62mm L7 GPMG.

ity fuse. The aiming unit is a reusable element, and once a missile has been used can be detached from the old missile pod, and relocated to a new one. The missile and aiming unit together weigh 46lb (21kg). This weight, combined with the need to manually track the target makes Blowpipe difficult to use and demands a high standard of skill and training from the firer.

Since initial deployment a new and improved version, similar in general appearance but known as Javelin, has been issued. Javelin benefits from greatly improved miniaturisation of the electronics, and employs a solid state television camera. The missile is automatically tracked and steered by the sight unit, and is said to be much more accurate and easier to control. The missile has a separate nose and tail section which are both free to rotate independently which gives a very quick response to guidance corrections. Javelin has a range of about 2.5 miles (4km).

The French are another nation which have developed their own anti-aircraft missile capable of being shoulder-launched. Their weapon is the Mistral, or SATCP as it is otherwise known. Once fired the gunner need take no further action because the Mistral homes on the infra-red emissions of aircraft engines, and explodes by means of a laser proximity fuse. Against low level targets ranges of 2.5 to 3.7 miles (4 to 6km) are claimed, depending on the size, type and number of aircraft engaged.

By 1976 the Americans had realised that both Redeye and the SA-7 were fundamentally out of date, not least because they were vulnerable to infra-red countermeasures. The search was therefore begun for a successor. In 1983 this new weapon was revealed as Stinger, a weapon similar in general appearance to the old Redeye but with numerous improvements. Not least of these was the incorporation of an electronic 'Identification Friend or Foe' system, intended to prevent the shooting down of friendly aircraft. Delivery of the system to US forces began in 1986. In American use Stinger teams are usually two men with two launch units, who can assist each other, or fire independently. Stinger has seen active service with Afghan Mujahideen, who used it against Soviet helicopter gunships. It proved to be remarkably effective.

The Bofors RBS-70 is a Swedish light air-defence system, although it barely qualifies as manportable. The target is tracked through the sighting system, and the missile is steered using a laser beam. This makes it immune to most radar or infra-red countermeasures, while the tripod mount and seat allow the operator to remain alert during long watches.

Launching the US Stinger anti-aircraft missile. Produced by General Dynamics, the Stinger was first introduced in 1986. It incorporates optical aiming with infra red homing, and the missiles have dual thrust rocket motors, and a separate boost motor. Stinger is much more effective than the earlier Redeye or SA-7, and is able to differentiate between its target and most types of decoy flare. Unlike Blowpipe or Javelin, the missile guides automatically once fired, allowing the operator to take cover if necessary. The complete equipment weighs 29.6lb (13.4kg), but whilst the missile tubes are disposable the launch pack is reused for subsequent shots. An M134 Tracking Head Trainer set and an M60 Field Handling Trainer help to keep down the expense of instructing new recruits.

CHAPTER 6

LAW, CRIME AND TERROR

THE POLICE OF MOST NATIONS have really only been recognised as a body worthy of specialist arms and armour in the past hundred years. In the eighteenth and nineteenth centuries law enforcement bodies were often highly localised, and rapidly supplanted by the militia or other quasi-military forces when armed or violent adversaries were encountered. It is no accident that some modern police agencies still carry military sounding titles, be it the Spanish Guardia Civil, the Russian Militia, or the Irish Garda. Often even policemen in purely civil organisations such as those run by English or American counties were ex-soldiers, and their senior members would attend parades wearing campaign medals and swords. The semi-protective traditional helmet of the British 'Bobby' was itself modelled on a nineteenth century military pattern.

As a result, police arms in 1900 were motley indeed. To take the British example, all officers would be equipped with a hardwood truncheon for everyday use, but firepower would be a mixture of the officially issued and the privately owned, including shotguns, military revolvers and rifles. Only the Irish Police had a special revolver, the Webley RIC (Royal Irish Constabulary), which also equipped the colonial forces of Australia and South Africa. The poor weaponry of the London police was shown up dramatically over Christmas 1910 and New Year 1911 when a criminal gang, under the leadership of 'Peter the Painter' was cornered in Exchange Buildings, Sidney Street. A police sergeant and an inspector were killed, and Home Secretary Winston Churchill had no option but to call out the military in the form of the Scots Guards. Despite an exchange of fire and the building being burnt, Peter the Painter escaped. It was believed that his gang had been equipped with Mauser automatics. Soon after this incident the Metropolitan Police adopted the Webley .32in automatic pistol, as did the forces of Cairo, Adelaide and several other cities.

The other side of the coin was that, in Britain at least, there was relatively little armed crime. Gun control was therefore virtually non-existent, and it was perfectly legal to own revolvers for self-defence or shotguns for sport. As late as the end of World War One, trophy military rifles, and even machine guns were given out to members of the public who had done particularly deserving work towards the war effort. There were also many privately held military arms belonging to Volunteers, officers, and target shooters. Doubtless both the responsible

Officers of the Salem, Massachusetts Police Department in a training exercise. The two men covering have 9mm automatics, while the uniformed man is wearing lightweight body-armour under his shirt. The officer nearest to the suspect has a side-handled baton clipped to his belt.

The British Metropolitan Police Webley .32in semi-automatic pistol. Adopted in 1911 the .32in Webley was an eight-round gun which weighed 1.26lb (.57kg) and had a muzzle velocity of 300ft/s (274m/s). It was handy to carry, but lacked real stopping power and was subsequently replaced by larger calibre revolvers.

attitude to firearms prevailing, and the existence of the death penalty had an influence on the lack of crime using guns. It was only after World War One, and with the fear that Bolshevik revolution would spread from Russia and Germany to Britain, that there was any attempt to control weapons in private ownership. Even then it was only military weapons which interested the authorities. At the same time, with millions of surplus weapons flooding on to the market, police forces had the opportunity to purchase anew, and make moves towards standardisation. Thus it was that all over Britain police forces adopted Webley revolvers, usually ex-service Mark VI, .455in models.

Here the European and American policies on law, crime and gun ownership sharply divided. America was not yet cheek by jowl with the perceived Communist menace, there were fewer surplus war arms, and in any case the right to gun ownership was enshrined in the Constitution. The 'Wild West' was nowhere near as wild as Hollywood might have us believe, but nevertheless on the frontier gun ownership was still commonplace. The vast rural states of the west and mid-west needed huge numbers of shotguns and rifles for pest control and hunting, and the National Rifle Association would become a powerful lobby on behalf of the shooter.

As the 1920s progressed crime in the US became more organised, and criminals gained access not only to pistols and shotguns but to the 'Chicago Piano', the Thompson sub-machine gun, which was to be almost a status symbol for the gangster. The first recorded use in gang warfare came on 25 September 1925 when the Frank McErland and 'Polack' Joe Saltis gang attacked O'Donnell's in Chicago. In the hyperbole of one crime reporter the new weapon was described as a 'diabolical machine of death' which was the 'greatest aid to bigger and better business the criminal has discovered this generation'. It seems that Al Capone got hold of three Thompsons in February 1926. Later that year his own headquarters at the Hawthorne Inn was shot up by members of a rival gang armed with SMGs. A thousand rounds were fired but no one was killed. Probably the bloodiest and most notorious Thompson killings came on St.

Valentine's Day 1929, when 'Machine Gun McGurn' and Fred Burke disguised as police shot seven people.

Against this background it is hardly surprising that the armed policeman was the norm in America. Several forces formed their own SMG-armed squads, and revolvers were standard, carried at all times, and backed up with a shotgun or two in cars. Despite police efforts armed crime continued to rise. In June 1933 came one of the most bizarre incidents, when 'Pretty Boy Floyd' and two other men attempted to spring Frank Nash from police custody, using SMGs.

Clyde Barrow was one of the most notorious and best armed outlaws of the 1930s, and is shown here armed with both a shotgun and bolt action rifle. He was ambushed and killed on 23 May 1934 with Bonnie Parker near Gibsland, Louisiana by local law enforcement officers and Texas Rangers. In the car with them on the fateful day were three M1918 Browning Automatic Rifles and over 100 loaded magazines stolen from a Beaumont National Guard armory.

In thirty seconds they killed four agents and Frank Nash. Indeed few famous criminals of the period seem to have been without a Thompson; 'Ma Baker' went down with one in her hands, as did 'Baby Face Nelson'.

In some parts of the United States police training techniques were well advanced by the 1930s. At Camp Perry the police training school included a moving automobile target, and the famous Hogan's Alley, in which 'criminal' and 'innocent bystander' targets could be made to appear at doors and windows. The Hogan's Alley idea, which has since become common the world over, had its genesis in military training, and had been brought to the US by Captain Deeming, who had prepared a similar 'French Village' for the national shooting match at Calwell, New Jersey in 1919.

(Below) Massed FBI firepower on the range, c.1935. The weapons are of many types and calibres and include the Browning Automatic Rifle, the Thompson sub-machine gun, bolt action rifles and shotguns.

(Right) An FBI man, c.1935, with the 'Monitor', a law enforcement version of the Browning Automatic Rifle (BAR). Main differences between the military BAR and the Monitor were the shorter barrel of the latter, complete with a large compensator at the muzzle to help reduce the effects of recoil. The Monitor never sold in large quantities, as plenty of ex-military BAR's were available more cheaply.

Bank clerks and storekeepers also took up arms in the fight against crime. One unusual weapon in use in the 1930s was the Harrington and Richardson Handy Gun, a pistol firing a shotgun shell and intended, so its makers stated, 'as a weapon of defence for the home, office and bank, and as a small game gun for the hunter. Also for the automobilist against hold ups.' Rival models were also manufactured, such as the Stevens Autoshot and the Ithaca Autoburglar. At the same time Colt offered a conventional revolver to the potential crime victim in the shape of the Banker's Special, a short .38in which was also adopted by the US Railway Mail service.

The US Colt 'Official Police' .38in revolver. Appearing in 1926 as a development of the 'New Navy' model of 1889, the 'Official Police' saw a good deal of service, both in law enforcement, and to a lesser extent in the military. The Colt company claimed that by 1936 the 'Official Police' was living up to its title by being the standard hand gun of the departments of New York City, Chicago, Los Angeles, St. Louis, Portland, and the State police of Pennsylvania, Maryland, Connecticut, Michigan, and Missouri. Produced in a number of calibres the 'Official Police' was a simple and sturdy six shot weapon, weighing 2.1lb (.96kg). (MOD Pattern Room)

During the second quarter of the century many of the world's police forces were changing from large calibre revolvers to either revolving arms based on a .38in cartridge, or automatics. It was not surprising that the US should lead the way, having already pioneered .38in police revolvers with the Smith and Wesson Military and Police model of 1899;

nor that the Belgians and Germans, early exponents of the automatic, should have soon begun using them as police arms. What was remarkable was that the Chinese should adopt automatics as early as the 1920s, and that one of their prime choices was the old C96 'Broomhandle' Mauser. This was imported into China, not only by Mauser, but in copied form by the Spanish company, Astra. Some copies were actually made by the Chinese themselves.

Meanwhile Britain and America continued almost exclusively with revolvers, and whilst the .38in Special cartridge, first introduced in 1902, remained popular for police work for many years, there were other important developments. In 1935 came the very powerful .357in Magnum cartridge; twenty years later appeared its big brother, the .44in Magnum. This really is the biggest and most

The 1970s-vintage monstrous long-barrelled .357in Magnum Colt Python revolver. Available in black or stainless steel the Colt Python has been described as the 'Ultimate' revolver. In police terms however demand for large .357in Magnum revolvers, which had proved extremely popular over the preceding two decades, was already in decline by the time the expensive Python reached the market. (MOD Pattern Room)

powerful round that is likely to be practical in a policing context, despite the advent of even more monstrous ammunition since. Immortalised by the 'Dirty Harry' films, the Smith and Wesson .44in Magnum revolver can not only routinely kill and blow an adversary off his feet with a single round, but is also exceptionally heavy, difficult to conceal and has a vicious recoil. Understandably, perhaps, variants of the .38in Special and the .357in Magnum revolver have remained more popular. Amongst these were stainless steel and different barrel weight versions of the updated Military and Police Smith and Wesson, the Air Weight with an alloy frame, and the Highway Patrolman.

As the Webley began to show its age British police also began to adopt American arms. It is perhaps surprising that they were unable to opt for an Enfield or Sterling product, but the revolvers chosen were mainly Smith and Wesson Models 10 and 19. It is also ironic that Smith and Wesson would eventually land up as part of a British multinational, the Tomkins group. Not until the 1970s did British and American police forces really begin to consider changing their revolvers for automatics, and the British were perhaps even slower than usual in addressing the question because of a bungled attempt on the life of Princess Anne. On this occasion a bodyguard with an automatic failed to return fire due to a jam.

The Brazilian Taurus .357in Magnum. Produced at the 'Forjas Taurus' or 'Bull Forge' at Porto Alegre, the .357in Magnum was just one of many models produced to satisfy the South American market, which by the last quar- ter of the twentieth century was large indeed. The six shot Taurus bears similarities to Smith and Wesson arms. (MOD Pattern Room)

In America police forces still use a mixture of revolvers and automatics but the latter are now the clear leaders. Amongst the models favoured are various updated versions of the old Colt .45in, the Smith and Wesson 645, the Browning 'Hi-Power', and a number of other European designs. The European guns include the German 9mm SIG-Sauer Model 226, several models of Glock, and the Italian Beretta automatic, which also equips the US military and the French Gendarmerie Nationale. The Smith and Wesson 645 shows particular promise, having already been adopted by a number of agencies including the Police Department of Montabello California. Pleasing results have been reported including a significant improvement in range scores, ease of handling in rapid fire situations and controllable recoil despite the .45in round. Finally it seems likely that the Beretta is to be widely adopted in Britain. The Japanese police are possibly the only significant exception to the trend to automatics in the last quarter of the century, having taken up a new revolver.

The 9mm Heckler and Koch P7 semi-automatic, together with two magazines. Developed with police use in mind the P7 had, by the late 1980s, become a popular pistol in many countries. Its users include the German police and army, and several US police forces. The gun's most interesting feature is the long safety lever at the front of the grip, which has to be held firmly before the gun can fire. The standard P7 weighs 1.72lb (.78kg), and has an eight-round magazine: a P7 K3 variant uses a special short cartridge.

As far as firearms procurement for police agencies is concerned it is worth noting that this is not normally so centralised as that of the military. British and US police forces have a fair degree of latitude, not only in the choice of weapon, but in matters of training and organisation. To take the British example the Firearms Officer in many county forces is a senior policeman who organises training and operational matters. In others the Firearms Officer is a civilian employee who spends much of their time dealing with licence applications. This semi-autonomy may not matter normally but shows up badly when different forces have to deal with licensing matters and adopt totally different standards, and it could be catastrophic in the case of a serious firearms incident which happened to cross a county boundary.

In the US there is even a tendency for several different arms to be used by officers of the same force. A good example is the Los Angeles police department which, in the mid-1980s, decided that the .38in revolver should remain as its standard arm, but that men undergoing training could opt for the 9mm automatic. Additionally several other smaller models could be carried in plain clothes. Another major police agency in California allows its uniformed officers to carry a Colt, Smith and Wesson or Ruger double action revolver in either .38in Special or .357in Magnum. In plain clothes any gun is allowed with a barrel as short as 2in (51mm). The result is a total lack of standardisation in either guns or ammunition. This is justified on the grounds that it is an important concession to the officers concerned who feel safer, and that it makes concealment of weapons easier, particularly for female or smaller male officers.

In Britain between 1910 and 1966 only 24 policemen were murdered whilst on duty, and even now, despite a several-fold increase, armed robberies are still uncommon enough to be newsworthy. Murders with guns each year are counted in tens, and indeed so few people are killed in this way that a single bad incident, like the 'Hungerford Massacre' of 1987, can distort a whole year's statistics. Even so a few criminals have succeeded in building up formidable arsenals. One such was the Sten gun, five revolvers, tear gas pistol, two rifles, four shotguns and 992 rounds of ammunition held by John Henry Childs and Henry Mackenny who killed six people in the 1970s. They were caught as a result of the 'Security Express' robbery, in which they took part in 1979. In 1994 a Liverpool arms cache, believed to have been related to a drug dealing gang, was found to contain a dozen military weapons, including assault rifles and Czechoslovak SMGs.

In the US, by contrast, gun crime is a commonplace. In New York in 1990 alone there were 1,500 killings with guns, and in the same period police seized 17,000 illegal firearms: nationally firearms killings regularly exceed 30,000. Perhaps the most heartrending aspect of American gun crime is the growing involvement of children. In the second half of the 1980s, 71 pupils and teachers were shot dead in school and over 200 more were wounded. Altogether the yearly average of children under 14 killed by firearms had reached 230 by the early 1990s. Very often this last category involved accidents where children shot themselves, or each other; in California for example it was usual for at least one child to die each year playing 'Russian roulette'. Connecticut introduced a 'trigger lock' law directed at least partly at this problem, which stated that guns kept in the home must be fitted with a device to prevent them being fired accidentally. In New York many problem schools have instituted 'frisks' with a metal detector in order to try to keep weapons out of the classroom. Gun control is a highly charged issue in the US, and one made more difficult by the fact that there are both State and Federal edicts on the subject. One Federal effort in the early 1990s aimed at cutting gun deaths was the Brady bill, which introduced a time delay in the purchase of firearms. One would suspect however that this would have a pretty marginal effect, since few criminals decide to a commit crime, then take a trip

One of the most familiar sights on the highway. In this case officers of the Salem Police Department with holstered automatics.

A British Metropolitan Police officer demonstrates the 'plain clothes' use of the Austrian 9mm Glock 17 semi-automatic. With the gun holstered and the cap concealed the officer may pass for any other bystander: with the gun drawn and a swift call of 'halt! armed police' he is ready to engage armed criminals. The open jacket reveals cloth-covered body armour. The Glock 17 is a popular arm and has been used by the Austrian police and army, as well as police and Special Forces elsewhere. It is a simple construction of 33 parts, based on the Browning system. The receiver is made of high resistance polymer, and there is no manual safety. Once the pistol is cocked, it can be carried safely, while all the user needs to do is pull the trigger to fire. The Glock weighs 1.4lb (.62kg) empty and has a capacious 17-round magazine.

down to their local gunstore in order to buy a gun to execute it. In an experimental scheme in Brooklyn money has been given out to those handing in firearms, with no questions asked, and it is interesting to note that virtually the same technique was applied after the American invasion of Haiti.

In Britain too there are periodic amnesties, but no money has changed hands except when semi-automatic long arms were banned and legal shooters were left seriously out of pocket. These British amnesties started in the 1960s, and the latest and most successful was that of 1988 which coincided with changes in the law updating the 1968 Firearms Act. The 1988 amnesty, in which the present writer was actively involved, netted 50,000 weapons, and although some of these were fearsome in the extreme, few can have been used for any criminal purpose since many of them were trophies of the World Wars and clearly had not been fired since. Amongst the more unusual items to be handed in were a Model 1866 Winchester, a Schwarzlose heavy machine gun and a flintlock New Land Pattern pistol of the Oxfordshire Yeomanry dating back to about 1820. Home Office co-operation allowed museums to save many historic pieces for national and local collections.

It can reasonably be argued that in the British instance, tightening gun control is not the answer to firearms related crime. Most crimes with firearms are committed with illegally held weapons, very often sawn-off shotguns. Increasing controls on the legally held arms therefore has very little impact on the crime statistics. It may be that more rigorously enforcing the existing law, and heavy punishments for illegally held arms, combined with frequent amnesties, would be a better strategy. The current approach of hitting legal shooters harder by introducing new law is politically expedient in that the public get to see that 'something is being done', but the only impact it has is to push some of the legal shooters, willingly or not, into the definition of criminal. Better police training on firearms, and the enforcement of existing laws would be likely to be more productive, but it is not happening because no one can make political capital from this more systematic approach. Whilst gun law remains an emotive subject, significant advances have been made in the field of forensic ballistics. It is now possible to tell a good deal about a crime weapon, and by implication the criminal, from the examination of the cartridge case, the bullet, and the damage done by the round. Cartridge cases alone can offer at least four different types of forensic evidence pointing towards the firearm used. Most obviously, the make of cartridge, the metal type, length, and calibre will whittle down the type of arm and the number of outlets through which such weapons and ammunition can be obtained. Less obvious are three types of mark which may be left on the cartridge by the crime weapon. First is the indentation of the striker on the percussion cap; this may be central or offset, deep or shallow, regular or oddly shaped. Second is the impression of the face of the breech on the base of the cartridge, formed when the cartridge is expanded against it on firing. Third is the mark of the extractor, which may scrape or dent the spent cartridge as it ejects it from the gun.

The bullet itself yields a good deal of information. Again size, weight, metallurgical composition, and calibre are useful; but what may tie a bullet to a particular gun is microscopic examination. The barrel of every rifled gun leaves the marks of the 'grooves' and 'lands' on the bullet, and also evidence of any irregularity in the bore. Suspect weapons are tested by firing a similar round then placing both the test bullet and the crime bullet under a stereoscopic microscope. If the bullets have been fired from the same gun the lines and scratches will match. Deformation of the bullet, or lack of it, may also be useful in determining the path of a bullet's flight, the materials through which it has passed, and maybe even whether it was shot close to, or well away from, the target.

More conclusive evidence of the distance from which a shot is fired is likely to come from a victim's body. Powder burning for example tends to increase with the closeness of a shot, and can be critical in distinguishing a murder from a suicide. It is difficult to shoot oneself from more than a foot away, but murders are quite often committed from a range of several feet or yards. Absence of powder burns therefore tends to point to foul play, or accidental shooting, rather than suicide. Unburnt powder from the crime scene may also prove useful; its

The Ingram Model 10, or 'MAC 10', 9mm sub-machine gun. Gordon B. Ingram originally worked for the Police Ordnance Corporation where he designed his first moderately successful arm, the Model 6 sub-machine gun. This sold to various police forces and armies in Asia and South America in the 1950s. He later moved to the Military Armament Corporation, and in 1970 came up with his much better known Model 10. This compact and simply made weapon, also available in .45in ACP, weighed only 6.3lb (2.84kg), and was soon popular both with law enforcement officers and the criminal fraternity. Its most widespread deployment has been in South America and the US, but it was also bought in Europe and Israel. The Model 10 has the cyclic rate of fire of 1,100 rounds per minute, is threaded at the muzzle to fit a sound suppressor, and can accept 16-, 30-, or 32-round magazines, not shown here. Military Armament collapsed in 1975, but the Model 10 has since been sold by another company under the title 'Cobray'. (MOD Pattern Room)

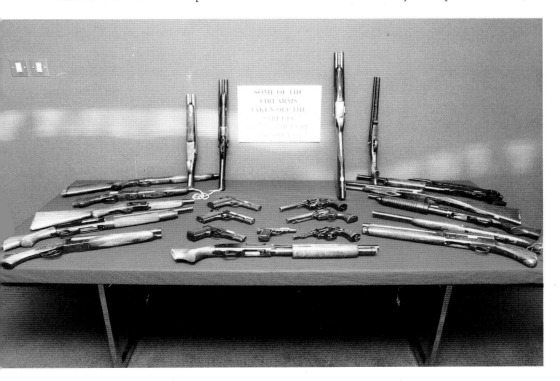

Britain is a country where armed crime is still regarded as unusual, yet this is just a selection of weapons taken off the streets by a Scottish police force in January1994. Shown are 15 sawn-off shotguns, three revolvers and four automatics. Police forensic scientists will examine weapons like these to see if their characteristics match those of any bullets/shot found in currently unsolved crimes.

structure and chemical analysis may say something about the weapon as well as the ammunition. A sawn-off, or very short-barrelled gun spews out more unburnt grains at the muzzle than a long-barrelled one, which gives the extra fraction of a second required for complete combustion within the bore. Pathological evidence is also likely to be important; and can include details such as the path of the shot through the body and the size of the entry and exit wounds. Shotgun wounds are very different from pistol or rifle wounds; the degree of spread of the charge may help to determine not only the firing range, but whether a weapon was sawn-off, and the angle from which it was fired. The pellets themselves may be of lead or steel, hard or soft, and vary in size and weight with the type of cartridge used.

Another form of testing used in explosive cases is the chemical analysis of swabs taken from a suspects' hands. This gained popularity in the 1970s, in connection with the IRA bombings of bars and other targets on mainland Britain, but has since faced a good deal of criticism, and a revision of procedures, as several persons convicted on this type of evidence have subsequently been freed. The main problem with this test was that the same chemicals which are left on a suspect after handling explosives may get there by perfectly legitimate means, and may come from other things, for example fertilisers, or the coatings on playing cards. Against terrorism, forensic science and police work often appear to be engaged in a gruesome race. With the advent of fingerprinting, gloves and then surgical gloves became popular with criminals. As police forces became expert in tracing arms consignments by the serial numbers on firearms, these marks were removed or defaced. When infra-red and X-ray procedures were evolved for reading even defaced marks the terrorists took angle grinders to their arms and gouged out whole panels to defeat the new technology.

One weapon which was feared would be very difficult to combat was the Austrian Glock 17 pistol. With a frame, trigger and magazine all of plastic it was thought that existing X-ray airport security would be rendered obsolete. Media scares were increased by the rumour that Libya had ordered 200 pistols, and that these could soon pass into the wrong hands. In fact the Glock still has a steel barrel, and must use conventional metal-cased ammunition.

Perhaps the worst misinterpretation of forensic evidence came in the most famous ballistic case of all; the assassination of John F. Kennedy in 1963. The mistakes in the autopsy, and the inexact understanding of the weapon, a 6.5mm Italian military Mannlicher-Carcano, opened the way for all sorts of theories about second and third assassins, and 'magic bullets'. Neither of the two doctors who examined Kennedy on 22 November 1963 had ever performed an autopsy involving a gunshot wound, in spite of the fact that one of them, Commander Humes, was Chief Pathologist at Bethesda Naval Hospital, and the other, Colonel Finck, was Head of Wound Ballistics at the armed forces Institute of Pathology. Worse, inadequate photographs were taken since an FBI agent barred the normal photographer, and the original notes were destroyed because they had become soaked in the President's blood. Amazingly the pathologists erroneously concluded that one of the two bullets which hit Kennedy fell back out of the same hole through which it had entered, and that the other hit him low in the back of the head. The errors were compounded by failure to section the brain and its subsequent loss, and the mis-weighing or non-weighing of other bodily organs. In the light of this inadequate report the wounds to John Connally, another occupant of the car, and the fact that one apparently little damaged bullet turned up on his stretcher, appeared either miraculous or sinister. Only by having other gunmen did it appear possible that so many wounds and bullets could appear.

The explanation presented to the House of Representatives Select Committee in 1979 was relatively mundane – though surprising to those who had no conception of the power of a military rifle cartridge with full metal jacket. Lee Harvey Oswald had fired three times, missing once. One bullet entered the President from behind and passed out through the front of his throat without hitting any bone, went into Connally, nicked a rib and passed through his wrist, before finishing against his thigh, slightly embedded. A second bullet clipped the top of the President's skull, shattering it, and then broke against the front windscreen strut.

This was all proved beyond reasonable doubt by analysis of the bullet found, and a tiny fragment of metal retrieved from Connally. They were identical in content. Furthermore the bullet which had struck Connally had done so sideways, as it would have done if it hit the President first. Lastly it became clear that the exit wound in Kennedy's throat had at first been ignored, because those who treated him had enlarged the hole to make a tracheotomy. To disbelievers it is worth pointing out that the sort of rifle and cartridge used in the attack was capable of penetrating 12in (305mm) of brick or 18in (457mm) of sand. A similar amount of human tissue presented no real obstacle, and Oswald's shooting, whilst very good, was by no means miraculous. He was a qualified Marine Sharpshooter, had rested the rifle on a pile of books, and was able to shoot from above and behind his victim as the car was moving slowly away. He shot reasonably swiftly, but three

One of the most celebrated murder cases in history is that of the assassination of President John F. Kennedy. This is the scoped Mannlicher-Carcano rifle used by Lee Harvey Oswald, and which forensic evidence shows fired the shots which killed the President. Many have refused to accept the official story of this event, and a whole industry has sprung up which promotes a wide range of conspiracy theories.

shots in eight seconds was well within the capabilities of the weapon, given that the first round was already in the chamber. The fact that the vehicle was receding slowly into the distance, rather than going across the line of sight made the shooting rather easier. The forensic ballistics cannot prove the existence or non-existence of a 'conspiracy', but they do show that the shots which killed the President came from one gun, and that the gun was in the book depository building.

Subsequent events have shown it to be perfectly possible for unbalanced individuals to plan and execute assassination attempts on celebrities without the necessity of a conspiratorial group, or even any logical reason. The attempted assassinations of President Reagan, the Pope, and the tragically successful killing of John Lennon, are all cases in point. Such events have also helped to make the bodyguard, whether working as an individual, or as an employee of a company or official agency a commonplace. In the 1950s even major public figures often made do with a single man, sometimes not even a trained specialist, and without any means of communication: by the 1990s the bodyguard business had become big business, with training schools and their own repertoire of tactics in driving and deployment as well as skill at arms. The whole concept had became such a fixture of public life that films like 'The Bodyguard', or 'Line of Fire' could be major box office successes.

The most difficult form of armed crime to legislate against, predict, or stop, is the deranged mass murderer who is happy to kill anyone, and to be killed himself. The phenomenon is distinctly different from the 'serial killer' who may kill more but over a period of time. Probably the first classic example of this type was

Italian security men during a sweep of the harbour at Venice in preparation for a VIP visit. The sub-machine gun is a 9mm Beretta model 12. This weapon went into production in 1959, and has since equipped the Italian Army as well as being sold in South America and Africa. It is a selective fire blowback weapon with a forward pistol grip and a mechanism in which a bolt extension wraps around the barrel, leading to greater steadiness in operation than most weapons of this class. It takes various magazines up to 40 rounds, and claims an effective range of 220yd (200m).

Charles Whitman who climbed a tower at Austin University Texas, in 1961, and calmly killed 16 students by sniper fire. Since then there have been many similar incidents. So far as there is any pattern, these assassins are usually white, in their thirties, withdrawn, obsessionally tidy, and prone to occasional bursts of temper. There are of course exceptions to the rule, and one such was 16-year-old school girl Brenda Spencer, who, in 1979, sprayed her San Diego school playground with bullets, killing two adults and wounding eight children. When she was asked why, she was said to have replied that she 'did not like Mondays'. Some other American incidents have included the 21 killed in the San Ysidio 'McDonald's massacre' in California in 1984; and the 16 killed by ex-Marine Gene Simmons in Arkansas in 1988. The worst single incident of mass killing in US history was carried out by Jo Hennard in October 1991. Hennard, an unemployed veteran, shot 22 people in a Texas cafe. Having driven a truck through a window, he fired more than 100 shots from his pistol before shooting himself.

Many other countries have had isolated occurrences, including Australia, Canada, and France. The Canadian incident is one of the most extraordinary. In this case Marc Lepine shot 14 at Montreal University in 1989. Oddly, the carnage was not totally random: Lepine entered room C234 of the Department of Engineering clutching a semi-automatic Mini 14 Sturm Ruger, saying that he wanted 'feminists in men's roles'. He sorted out the male from the female engineering students and shot only the women.

The one British case has been all the more shocking for its singularity. Michael

Ryan, a misfit with a gun obsession and a desire to kill his mother, killed 16 and himself, in Hungerford, in 1987. The episode caused, or gave excuse for, major changes in the law which had been basically unchanged for twenty years. The Government proceeded to introduce sweeping changes in all areas, including new shotgun certificates, new police powers, changes to weapons categories, and to the regulations concerning museums. It is worth noting that Michael Ryan did not use a shotgun or a museum piece in his rampage, but a Chinese version of the AK 47, which was semi-automatic only, and an M14.

At the same time efforts were also made to control knives, and several sorts of martial arts weapons. It is true that knives are in fact used in many more assaults than guns, but legislation in this area is virtually useless, unless it is to increase the penalty for a threat or an actual attack. After all, most attacks are not carried out with 'combat' knives but kitchen knives, craft knives, and razors, none of which can be practically banned or licensed. Again the measures chosen were cosmetic rather than practical.

Part of the British answer to armed crime has been arms for the police, but not for all policemen at all times. Weapons have largely been concentrated in the hands of specialists in 'armed response' and 'diplomatic protection' groups. The public is perceived to have a natural aversion to the armed policeman, although every weapons-related crime is used to prepare society for that concept. In the case of Scotland Yard the main armed response unit is SO19, a total of nearly 200 officers in several locations, with a training centre at Lippets Hill, Essex. Within the force SO19 are sometimes mockingly known as 'Ninjas', due to their black overalls, hoods, and gas masks. Weapons available to the unit include Heckler and Koch MP5 semi-automatic carbines; sniper rifles; Remington 12-bore pump-action shotguns; Glock 9mm pistols; Smith and Wesson .38in revolvers, and various gas and stun devices. Gas grenades are not only hand thrown, but projected by means of the Webley-Schermuly launcher. Forced entry is something of a team speciality, and apart from old fashioned sledge hammers, compressed air rams and solid shotgun projectiles are used.

The Metropolitan Police have had something like SO19 since 1967, when the first full time training centre was set up with a team of only ten officers. What is relatively new is the idea of an Armed Response Vehicle, a car permanently equipped with weapons, and which may already be out on patrol when directed to an incident. The officers, usually a group of three, can immediately use their arms if they think life to be in danger, and can otherwise be given permission to do so over the radio by the control room chief. The scheme first came into use in 1991, and by 1994 there were known to be 12 such teams in use; in that year also the regulations requiring permission to take the guns out onto the street were relaxed. Even though the British response to the armed criminal has been toughened it is still restrained by American standards, where the first response is likely to be an armed patrolman, and the next step may well be the fully fledged Special Weapons And Tactics (SWAT) team. Though these vary from city to city they are likely to include snipers, pyrotechnics, a selection of semi-automatic weapons, all carried by specialists in close assault. Despite such firepower this response may not be an over reaction, since it is not unknown for drug gangs in particular to have access to machine pistols, and other weapons equal or superior to those used

A French Police marksman on a roof top at the Paris air show during the visit by President Mitterand. Marksmen in this role can provide an observation and deterrent function, although a determined assassin could probably get close enough to throw a bomb or get a shot off before they could react.

A US police 'Special Weapons and Tactics' team practice their entry drill. The point man prepares to smash in the door with a compressed-air ram whilst his colleagues line up to enter the building. They are armed with Colt 9mm sub-machine guns, weapons developed for police use from the M16 assault rifle.

Classic British policing equipment, including handcuffs, whistle and the short straight hardwood batons, also known as 'truncheons' or 'staffs', in use from the nineteenth century until the 1990s. The British police baton is rooted in antiquity and tradition, and mimics the shape of the old 'tip stave', in use in the seventeenth century, and surmounted with an ornamental crown, which actually unscrewed to reveal a void in which a warrant was contained. The Metropolitan Police standardised on a 15.5in (.39m) truncheon in the 1890s, with a slightly shorter model for plain clothes and senior officers. These were made of crocus, perpinga or rosewood, and the styles and materials remained constant for a century. Occasionally twentieth century examples are found decorated with coats of arms and dates, usually these are presentation pieces for retiring officers.

by the law enforcement agencies.

Remarkably, there are two police weapons which have changed relatively little during the twentieth century; one is the baton, nitestick, or truncheon, and the other is the shotgun. American batons show perhaps the greatest diversity, with side-handled models, telescopic types, and a variety of styles and materials. Britain has shown greater attachment to tradition, sticking pretty conservatively to a short straight model which would have been familiar to the village constable of the eighteenth century, and even this is often concealed in a long truncheon pocket. Only in the 1990s have there been British experiments with side-handled batons, and these have been carefully orchestrated with public relations in mind. Doubtless there is concern that any radical departure might have human rights implications, especially since some of the more exotic forms of baton have associations with

The British 'bobby', 1990s-style. A British Metropolitan policeman, fully armed for close assault. The Bristol body armour with 'hard' plates protects from neck to groin, and the ballistic helmet is fronted with a visor, in this case worn over the respirator. The machine pistol is the 9mm, Heckler and Koch, MP5. This is backed up not only with a semi-automatic pistol but a 12-gauge pump action shot gun, with pistol grip but no stock.

totalitarian regimes, and even with outright torture. This is especially the case with some Chinese models which are not only electrified but specially shaped for easy insertion into the orifices of the human body.

Law enforcement shotguns have perhaps shown more changes since 1900, but there are relatively few significant innovations if one excepts the invention of the semi-automatic shotgun about the turn of the century. Even now most police shotguns are of the pump-action variety. Perhaps the best known security shotgun is the Italian Franchi SPAS 12 which was introduced in 1983. This can operate either as a pump-action or a semi-automatic, has a pistol grip, an eight-shot mag-

A range of ASP police batons. Above are two S24 side-handled batons. Made of synthetic material, this style has been inspired by martial arts weapons. Left are two models of F16 telescopic baton, seen here both extended and collapsed. While perhaps not as versatile as the side-handled baton, the telescopic variant combines ease of carrying with a reasonable level of protection for the officer.

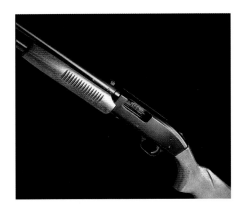

azine, and weights 9.6lb (4.35kg). It retails in the US at about $700. Even more up to date in terms of styling are the 1988 Holmes Model 88 shotgun, which has the looks of an assault rifle, and the Mossberg 500 bullpup, a design of 1986. Nevertheless both these futuristic looking types are pump-action weapons, a mechanism which would have been familiar to many officers in 1900. Even more comprehensible to the constable of yesteryear would be many of the more conservative designs, amongst which should be numbered the Mossberg 500 Security; the Remington Model 870 Police; the Ithaca Model 87; and the Winchester Defender, all of which are traditionally configured pump-actions, differing significantly only in materials from the nineteenth century original.

One way in which the police and potential assassination targets have pro-

Two patterns of police/military shotgun. The American Mossberg Model 500 (top) is a12-gauge pump action weapon available in a number of models, with or without stocks. The Italian Franchi SPAS 12 (above) is a ferocious-looking semi-automatic designed from the outset for paramilitary use. The strange-shaped butt can hook under the arm to allow single-handed firing. Shotguns are deadly at short ranges, although dissipation of the shot at longer range limits the chance of injury to bystanders. They can also be used with special solid shot, non-lethal plastic shot or CS gas rounds. As the US Army's 1984 manual on 'Civil Disturbances' observed, 'The riot shotgun is an extremely versatile weapon, its appearance and capability have a strong psychological effect on rioters'.

tected themselves is with body armour. As long ago as World War Two a few generals and political leaders had begun this trend, as was exemplified by Hitler's armoured peaked cap. Yet it is really only since the 1960s that armoured vehicles and body armour have become common. Innovations have included the heavily armoured 'Pope Mobile', and armoured podiums for speech making: the use of body armour has also become more imaginative with garments like the Kevlar-reinforced trench coat, as modelled by Henry Kissinger in the Middle East, or the similarly strengthened golfing jackets favoured by President Gerald Ford. United States police agencies really woke up to the significance of body armour in the 1970s. In 1974 there were132 federal, state and local officers killed in the line of duty; 128 of them were slain with firearms and most of the murder weapons were hand guns of .38in calibre or less. Body armour was widely introduced soon after, and although the number of incidents rose, the number of police fatalities fell to 94 in 1978.

The modern US policeman is likely to wear garments manufactured by one of six major manufacturers of personal protection; American Body Armor; Armor of America; Burlington; Second Chance; Sierra; or Smith and Wesson. Vests are made both 'soft' and 'hard' in that they can be simple layers of Kevlar and nylon, or reinforced with ceramic and metal plates. The armour is also made for men and women, and different models can be worn either inside or outside the normal clothing. Concealed armour is useful during undercover work, is perceived as less confrontational, and may lull an assailant into attacking the protected body whilst ignoring the more vulnerable head or limbs. Some armour is just too bulky to hide, but gives excellent protection. American Body Armor's High Coverage

An officer of Salem Massachusetts Police Department demonstrating the concealed wearing of body armour. Light 'vests' of this type are made by several manufacturers including Second Chance, Smith and Wesson, and American Body Armour. Second Chance alone claim that 350 lives had been saved by 1985 as a result of wearing their concealed armours. Note also the revolver in a 'quick draw' holster; though if the shirt has to be opened first this is a weapon of last resort.

Tactical Armor is one such type which provides protection against hand guns, shotguns and SMGs, and with add-on ceramic plates can stop rifle bullets. Armor of America's Sacramento Vest is similarly impressive, able to stop a 7.62mm high velocity rifle bullet at 26ft (8m) when fitted with special inserts.

Armours are usually graded as to the type of bullet they will resist, and it is rare for a vest to fail to stop the calibre of ammunition which it has been designed to intercept. Even so, it is notable that exposure to moisture and long term wear and tear can degrade the ballistic performance of body armour. It is also worth noting that a growing number of US criminals are carrying firearms of a heavier calibre, such as the huge Desert Eagle in .44in Magnum, or even .50in Action Express, which requires a very heavy grade armour to stop. The US National Institute of Justice has produced its own standards for the ballistic performance of police armour. These are tougher than the manufacturers' own ratings on several counts, most importantly because they fail any vest which exhibits a back face deformation of 1.7in (44 mm). Perhaps because of these factors only 25% of US police officers were believed to be wearing armour on a regular basis in 1994, a surprising statistic when it is considered that even the lightest vests would stop some rounds, and would have a protective effect against fragments and spent bullets.

The Israeli Military Industries Desert Eagle semi-automatic pistol. Originally offered as a sporting arm the 'Desert Eagle' has since been sold for military purposes, and, apart from the original .357in Magnum calibre, has also been made in .44in Magnum, and .50in Action Express. It is gas operated, and has a locked breech and rotating bolt. The magazine holds nine rounds, and the gun weighs 3.88lb (1.76kg). Hollywood, and the gun's massive size have made the Desert Eagle something of a status symbol with the criminal fraternity.

An officer of the Royal Ulster Constabulary on street patrol, Northern Ireland c.1990, with a Ruger 5.56mm, Mini 14 rifle. The US-made Sturm Ruger Mini 14 was first introduced commercially in 1973, and as the name suggests its basic mechanism is similar to that used in the American M14 service rifle of the late 1950s and early 1960s. There have been various improvements to the Mini 14 over the years, and it has been sold to several law enforcement agencies. It weighs 2.9kg, and can be fitted with various magazines, the largest holding 30-rounds. The effective range is about 330yd (300m).

In Britain police body armour is gaining popularity. By the early 1990s the Metropolitan Police alone was believed to have 3,000 sets of body armour, and its use was spreading to other cities. Less obvious is the fact that police rainwear sometimes has ballistic nylon or Kevlar layers. Marksmen or armed police wear visible flak jackets, and in Northern Ireland this has become the norm, with Bristol body armours being issued to the RUC. One unusual British product is the anti-knife jacket, made by Security Equipment Supplies. This is almost like a lightweight version of a Roman scale armour, having a metal section fronting the Kevlar packs. Other countries making their own body armour include Belgium, Germany, Israel, and Switzerland. The German Police and Border Police for example, as well as some banks, make use of Berka IWKA armoured vests. These are extremely light, but can easily resist a 9mm round at 33ft (10m).

Perhaps the most specialised of body armours are the 'EOD', or Explosive Ordnance Disposal suits. Outside the purely military sphere the EOD suit is most likely to be seen in use dealing with terrorist bombs, alongside such aids as

remote-controlled EOD robots. In Britain the Ministry of Defence has produced at least four patterns of EOD armour and these cover most of the body, although the ends of the hands often have to be left exposed so that the technician can work on the device. The basic requirement of the British EOD suit is believed to be that it can withstand a 5lb (2.3kg) nail bomb going off 3ft (1m) away.

As the weaponry of law and order has improved, so has that of the terrorist. This is at least in part because the terrorist's weapons are often bought or stolen military weapons, and partly because nation states sometimes support terrorism within ideologically opposed states. This has usually been associated with the old Eastern

Bloc, or with certain Middle Eastern states, but it is also true that from other perspectives western sponsored groups could be seen as terrorist, as in the case of the 'Contras' in Nicaragua. In the British instance, the soldier was most likely to find himself faced in the 1930s and 1940s by Indian, Arab, or Israeli terrorists armed with stolen Lee-Enfields or other bolt action rifles, shotguns, and locally made copies of military rifles or grenades. As in Northern Ireland larger bombs were likely to be made from commercially available nitrates, or blasting powders with simple fuses. In

The British EOD (Explosive Ordnance Disposal) protective suit Mark 2, c.1985. During a quarter century of 'troubles' in Northern Ireland, and in other bomb incidents in the UK, the Royal Army Ordnance Corps, known irreverently as the 'Bang Gang', has been a familiar sight. The work of bomb disposal is usually lonely as only one man at a time is risked, explaining his finding and actions to his colleagues at a distance by radio. 'Wheelbarrows' or robots with cameras, probes, 'hands', and shot guns are often used, but sometimes only a man will do. The EOD suit is made by Galt on the Isle of Wight, and, including helmet weighs a total of 48.5lb (22kg).

The nail bomb. In this crude but sometimes effective terrorist device, nails take the place of shrapnel or a metal bomb case.

the modern context the terrorist arsenal is likely to be much more formidable. The Czech plastic explosive Semtex seems to have supplanted gelignite as the terrorist's favourite, and bombers can use quite sophisticated triggers. Apart from timers there are switches sensitive to alterations in pressure, which are especially useful against aircraft and where a device may be placed inside electrical equipment such as a cassette player to confuse searchers. In other instances bombs are triggered by a broadcast signal, or a cable running to an observation point. This last was something of an IRA speciality, bombs being placed inside culverts under lonely country roads and exploded when a Land Rover patrol or other target appeared.

Other explosive devices which have turned up in terrorist and guerrilla hands are legion. Common choices have included Soviet S2-3 and S2-6 demolition charges, blocks of Belgian Trialene, several products of Chilean explosives companies, and the American Charge Demolition M11. All can be used to make anti-vehicle and anti-property weapons, or in conjunction with timers, and/or extra fragmentation materials, anti-personnel bombs. In Africa particularly, military landmines have been in frequent use by guerrilla forces. Many of these were

The aftermath of a car bomb at the Rhein-Main air base in August 1985. As little as 2.2lb (1kg) of explosive placed skillfully can blow a car apart. The exponents of terror tactics have evolved two main modus operandi. The first is to steal a vehicle, plant the bomb, and get someone (either an unwilling hostage or a suicide bomber) to drive it to the target. The other approach is to booby-trap the car of a selected victim, as was the case in the murder of British politician Airey Neave by the Irish National Liberation Army (INLA). Often only a 'finger tip' search of the debris, and thousands of hours of forensic work will provide clues to the origin of such an attack.

of Soviet provenance and perhaps the most frequently encountered was the TM-46, a metal-cased anti-tank mine, along with its similar cousins the TMN-46, TM-57, and TM-62. The flat, circular TM-46 has also been copied and manufactured elsewhere by nations as diverse as Bulgaria, China, Egypt and Israel. Yugoslav, Czech and British anti-tank mines of obsolete pattern also turn up in guerrilla armouries. The Soviet wooden-bodied family of anti-tank mines have also proved popular, the best known of which is the TMB-B. This is armed by tilting a central board of the wooden box, and when the mine is run over by a vehicle the board breaks, igniting the fuse. A useful characteristic of the wooden mine is its difficulty to detect, a feature shared with the more modern plastic varieties such as the Chinese Type 72.

Claymore-type mines, both military and home made, are also found in the hands of the more sophisticated guerrilla and terror groups. The main features of this family of weapons are that they are placed above ground, they include a charge and a fragmentation element, and that they are directional in effect.

Incendiary devices of various degrees of sophistication are also popular terrorist weapons. At the simplest end of the scale 'Molotov Cocktails' or petrol bombs are used in riots all over the world. Often these are no more than a lemonade or a spirit bottle with a wick, but they can be improved by techniques such as weakening the bottles to break easily, or by the addition of additives, like rubber, which cause the burning liquids to stick. The name Molotov Cocktail stems from the Spanish Civil War, when they were employed against Nationalist tanks. Slightly more sophisticated are timed incendiaries, designed to set light to vulnerable targets such as shops after the terrorist has left. Packed into very small boxes they can be slipped into coat pockets, tucked amongst stock and papers, and waste a good deal of security force effort in detecting. The economic impact of such attacks can be out of all proportion to the effort expended, and may have the effect of setting the business community at odds with the government. Such no doubt was the logic of the much bigger City of London truck bombs, and the destruction of the Baltic Exchange, which at the very least caused major disruption to traffic flows over a long period.

Another weapon which few terrorists are likely to be able to manufacture but which can occasionally be obtained commercially or by captures from the military

are thermal charges and thermite bombs; these burn at tremendous temperatures, and can even burn under water. Reaching 2,000 degrees centigrade, thermal weapons are capable not only of starting fires but of welding together metals or destroying heavy equipment. A textbook use is to put one down the barrel of a tank or artillery piece, thus ruining the bore and seizing the breech.

In terms of small arms many terror groups have long since graduated from the World War Two army surplus items like rifles and Thompsons, and the home made 'zip' guns which characterised the Mau Mau in Kenya, and Eoka in Cyprus. Direct or indirect import of the most modern arms available became the best route, and from 1950 to 1990 the Eastern Bloc powers and Libya were identified as the main sources of supply. Amongst the most sought after items in terrorist circles are RPG rocket launchers, explosives, Czech machine pistols, and all models

A masked petrol bomber during a riot in the Bogside, Northern Ireland. The petrol bomb or 'Molotov cocktail' is one of the simplest weapons to make, but also difficult for the security forces to counter. Its constituents can be bought almost anywhere, and it can be deadly; yet an 'appropriate' level of response is difficult given that shooting outright may lead to public sympathy for the rioters, especially where the press, as here, are close at hand. Plastic or 'rubber' bullets, and 'CS', or 'tear gas', are possible answers. Another countermeasure devised by W.R. Blake of the Tulsa ordnance company in 1975, was a .410in shotgun which fired golf balls at the malcontents, with progressively more powerful cartridges to match the level of threat.

The need for riot control equipment is not a new phenomenon. This image shows British police officers c.1910 with one of the first purpose made riot devices, the so called 'Gladstone shield'. Made of steel, the Gladstone was almost circular, convex, and with a small vision slit: it was marginally better than a trash can lid for the intended task. At least one example was 'recovered' by Police officers during a riot 70 years later. (Greater Manchester Police Museum)

Home made 9mm sub-machine gun captured from Protestant paramilitaries in Belfast. With 9mm ammunition relatively common, many terrorist attempts to build their own arms have resulted in weapons which seem to take the Sten or the Sterling as their inspiration.

of the ubiquitous AK 47. Perhaps one of the most extraordinary weapons to turn up in terrorist hands was a Soviet heavy machine gun, mounted on a lorry, which was captured in an army versus IRA shoot-out in 1992. Another weapon, in Ireland, but unlocated at the time of writing was a Barrett sniper rifle, whose .50in ammunition is easily capable of piercing flak jackets. It might have been thought that the fall of the Berlin Wall and the end of Communism in the former Soviet Union might lead to a diminution in weapons from the east. In fact the effect has been to make the supply rather less ideological, and rather more commercial. Various 'investigative reporters' from the west who have visited the Commonwealth of Independent States, or the warring corners of the old empire claim to have found for sale not only small items like Kalashnikovs or grenades, but far more dangerous items like tanks or plutonium.

One facility that terrorists are now unlikely to get in the former Eastern Bloc is training. At one time it is believed that groups like the PLO, the Red Brigades, and IRA were frequently trained in Eastern Europe, and especially East Germany. Now many commentators look to the Middle East, and particularly to the Lebanon, a source of long term discomfort to Israel. It is interesting to note that several terror groups have achieved, or are seeking to achieve, a more legitimate political stance in the 1990s; foremost amongst these are the ANC, latterly the official government of South Africa, the PLO, and the IRA. Whether this is a natural development in that it simply follows the well-trodden path of Israel and many African and South American groups, or whether it has been brought about at least in part by the new patterns of supply must be a matter for speculation.

An arms cache, captured by the security forces in Northern Ireland, containing more than 40 Kalashnikovs, plus pistols, grenades, explosives, and ammunition. The import of arms to the province with which to continue the 'armed struggle' goes back to at least the eighteenth century when much of the weaponry came from France. By the time of World War One, Loyalist volunteers had stocks of antique Swiss Vetterli rifles, and Republicans were looking to Germany, as well as conducting their own internal Civil War south of the border. After World War Two both sides were using war surplus, as well as seeking imports from the Communist bloc. 'Fund raising' to finance campaigns took the form of appeals in the US as well as extortion and crime at home. The biggest ever capture of arms for Northern Ireland was made by French customs, who, in 1987 seized 50 tons of ammunition, 1,000 Kalashnikovs, and miscellaneous other weapons bound for the Provisional IRA, from Libya, on the trawler Eksund.

The SAS at the Iranian Embassy siege, Princess Gate London, May 1980. In a 12-minute storm of stun grenades and small arms fire five terrorists were killed and 20 hostages were freed. This success which rekindled the public's interest in, and appreciation of the SAS, was no accident. For some time the regiment had operated a 'Counter Revolutionary Wing', to which three-year postings were made. Training included not only 'Close Quarter Battle' and 'Body Guard', but 'the Killing House'. This was occupied by dummy targets, and taught the soldiers to rapidly identify and engage hostile targets while preventing injury to hostages. Visible in this picture is the Heckler and Koch MP5, with a torch mounted on the receiver.

The booby trap has been a favourite weapon of the terrorist, special forces, and retreating armies throughout the twentieth century. It is difficult to make generalisations about them since their success depends much on their diversity, and the degree to which they can fool an enemy into believing them innocuous. Sometimes indeed it is the very fear of the booby trap and the bomb, which become the weapon; a hoax call, an empty cardboard box or an upturned plate in the road, looking like a mine, can all have the desired effect. Convoys can be halted, rail transport disrupted, and police and army time wasted.

In World War Two allied sabotage agents used a variety of ways to trigger

booby trap bombs, relying principally on a number of officially made and issued switches. One of these was the pressure release switch, shaped like a tiny box. When there was no pressure on it the lid would snap open, setting off a percussion cap and fuse. This had many applications; it could be placed under a heavy book, under a toilet seat, or a tempting souvenir, and when these were lifted a bomb would be exploded. Other triggers relied on pressure; they could be left on rail lines, or under floorboards, or under a mat. 'Pull' switches were often used with a trip wire, or could be triggered as a door or window were opened. Both terrorist organisations and regular armies have issued their own manuals on booby trapping, the latter differing from the former mainly in that they also offer advice on identification and safe disposal. One such publication was the US Department of the Army Field Manual 'Booby Traps', of 1965. In the military the use of booby traps was seen as supplementary to minefields, and although usually laid by specialists, all troops of the US forces were intended to have a basic knowledge. Amongst the 'nasties' noted by the manual were methods of attaching bombs to dead bodies, fixing anti-lifting devices to mines, using one bomb to attract a crowd and killing them with another, and the conversion of mortar shells, grenades, and other munitions. Some of the most bizarre and unexpected suggestions included wiring radios and televisions to explode when turned on, and the use of a mouse trap as a pressure release switch.

Also noted by US intelligence were a number of devices used by foreign powers since 1939. Soviet methods included exploding balls, frogs, and household objects; Cognac bottles were used to disguise incendiary liquids. Nazi German tricks included a special exploding chocolate bar, the Japanese had a bomb disguised as a tobacco pipe, while the Italians had a particularly nasty exploding headset. A number of these items were more effective than their small size would suggest since the victim was likely to be holding them in close proximity to the head or body when they exploded. Despite such exotics the basic principles of the successful booby trap remain constant: the use of local and innocuous looking materials is the best aid to concealment; dummy booby traps often repeated lead either to carelessness or paranoia, and an appeal to greed or curiosity is often effective.

An FBI hostage rescue team in training, with 9mm Heckler and Koch MP5 sub-machine guns. The German MP5 has become the weapon of choice for many of the world's hostage rescue and anti-terrorist teams. It uses a similar mechanism to that of the G3 rifle, firing from a closed bolt to give high levels of accuracy. This precision is essential where innocent hostages are being held.

CHAPTER 7

SPORT AND LEISURE

T HE MOST REMARKABLE FEATURE of twentieth century weapons for sport and leisure must be their diversity. In the nineteenth century most people in Europe and America would have been familiar with at least some of the weapons of the duel and the hunt, but the twentieth century has seen not only new weapons for traditional pursuits, but whole new areas opened up. Amongst the most important of these must be clay pigeon shooting, air weapons, modern fencing, re-enactment, and the still young and controversial game of paintball. Collecting weapons has also become an end in itself, for the private individual as well as for the great institutions and the very wealthy.

Target archery is arguably one of the oldest weapon sports, practice against inanimate targets being a vital preparation both for war and the hunt. A significant revival took place on both sides of the Atlantic in the second half of the nineteenth century, with the American National Archery Association being formed in 1879; this being perhaps a strange juxtaposition as some Native Americans were still using the bow for practical purposes at that time. In the twentieth century target archery has become a widespread leisure activity, and a high tech Olympic discipline. Apart from crossbows, which are equipped with stocks and triggers, there are four major types of bow. These are the traditional long bow, usually of yew with horn nocks to take the bow string, and a pull often in excess of 100lb (45kg); beginners' bows which are much less powerful and usually of glass fibre or lemon wood; composite bows with a laminated structure; and compound bows, with short powerful limbs, pulley wheels and adjustable weight and draw length.

There was a fad for metal bows in the early part of the twentieth century, amongst the best of which were the Swedish Seefab bows, but fashion has proved fickle, and the shooter has proved wary of the damage that can be done if they break. Many bows now have stabilisers or weights added, to improve balance and cut vibration. Traditionally bowstrings were of linen thread, but since the 1950s many man-made materials have been used, so that fibres like Dacron and Kevlar have become popular. Arrows similarly used to be of wood with feather fletchings, the most traditional feather being that of the goose, but latterly aluminium and glass fibre shafts have become common and the feathers are often replaced with plastic vanes. A modern arrow will usually be classified both by weight, and by spine rating, which indicates the degree to

The huge Holland and Holland 4-gauge 'Saurian gun', with its dinosaur decoration. The weapon 'as art' has a history which goes back to classical antiquity; and as a collectors' piece the 'Saurian gun' follows in this tradition.

which the arrow will bend under a given load. Apart from ordinary target arrows there are also 'fru fru' arrows with blunt ends, field arrows, and arrows for hunting with bladed heads.

The modern Barnett crossbow, by Barnett of Wolverhampton, England, complete with telescopic sight, and bolts or 'quarrels'. By 1900 the crossbow had virtually ceased to be used as a hunting weapon, and had become the province of the target shooter. The sport would continue to be especially popular in Belgium, but with the exception of Ralph Payne-Gallwey's The Crossbow , of 1903, the subject has been rather neglected in print.

A World War Two picture depicting aircraft worker Connie Dean of Toronto Canada, one of that country's estimated 30,000 'toxophilites', at practice in 1945. Notice the simplicity of the bow, whose only concession to modernity is a small peg-like sight. The shooter wears an arm 'bracer' and finger stalls on her right hand secured around her wrist to protect her from the friction of the string.

Competition shooting is usually against concentrically ringed targets, and the number of arrows shot in any competition is referred to as a round. A York Round in men's competition for example, is composed of six dozen arrows at 100yd (91m), four dozen at 80yd (73m), and two dozen at 60yd (55m). Other entertaining forms of competition include the ancient clout shooting, to a distant patch of ground which acts as the target; archery golf; archery darts; and 'popinjay shooting' at dummy birds. In flight shooting competitors aim purely for length, and in early 1995 the world record was the incredible distance of 1086.69yd (993.32) metres achieved by Alan Webster of Britain.

Amazingly there have been twentieth century western hunters who, though they have had access to firearms, have hunted with the bow. Two of the pioneers were Saxton Pope and Arthur Young, another was Count Ahlefeldt of Denmark who hunted in Kenya in the 1930s, an exploit encouraged by a Danish publishing house. Though he was refused permission to shoot big game, on the grounds of cruelty to the animal rather than the suicidal nature of the venture, he did succeed in shooting impala and gazelle. The American Bob Swineheart did actually hunt big game with the bow in the 1960s, and few dangerous animals were left unshot; amongst his North American trophies were the moose, bear, and shark. In Africa he shot leopard, buffalo, rhinoceros, elephant and lion, the so called 'big five'. The results were not terribly humane, in that the elephant took five arrows to kill, but it did underline the danger to native hunters of earlier years, especially as the elephant succeeded in making a charge, and one arrow from a 100lb (45kg) bow merely bounced off the rhino.

Fencing with swords existed as a training for war since at least the medieval era, and the great schools of fencing in Italy and Spain were developed in the seventeenth and eighteenth centuries. In the eighteenth century fencing was sometimes a practice for the duel, and one form of sword duel, with the Schlager, is still occasionally encountered amongst German student fraternities. Schlager duelling, however, is not designed to inflict death or serious injury, but does involve cuts to the head whilst the eyes and neck are protected. Modern fencing has developed considerably since 1900. In Britain the Amateur Fencing Association was formed in 1902, and from mid-century the sport has had a wide appeal. It is an accepted Olympic discipline, and the international governing body is the Federation Internationale d'Escrime. The three modern fencing weapons are

Target archery being practiced in a manner which would have been familiar to the medieval Englishman. The youth on the right uses a light glass-fibre training bow, whilst the other shooter uses a heavier composite bow.

the foil, epée and sabre. The foil is the lightest and must not exceed 17.63oz (.5kg) in weight and 43.25in (1.1m) in length, and the guard may not be more than 4.75in (121mm) in diameter. The foil was originally developed as a practice sword, and hits are scored with the point, which is finished with a button to prevent wounding. The epée is allowed to be up to 27.13oz (.77kg) and with a guard up to 5.63in (143mm) in diameter, although the overall length restriction is the same as the foil. Hits are again scored with the point.

The sabre is a very light reproduction of the cavalry sabre; it may not exceed 17.63oz (.5kg) in weight or 41.38in (1.05m) in length. It is provided with a knuckle guard and, unlike the other fencing arms, hits are scored with the edge as well as the point. Interestingly the cavalry of the early twentieth century did have another form of practice weapon apart from the fencing sabre; this was the single stick, literally a stick, often inserted into a leather cup or guard, forming a dummy sword with which strokes could be practised. In competition fencing the fencers fight attired in white protective jackets, and masks, on a piste 46ft (14m) long by 6.56ft (2m) wide. Traditionally, scoring was by a jury composed of four judges and a president. Now electronic scoring is common, the jackets and swords being designed to create a circuit and light a bulb when a hit is scored. The system is generally reliable, but it is by no means impossible to cheat by using a modified foil, as has unfortunately been proven in the Olympics. In friendly practice in a club Salle d'Armes or fencing room, the fencers will usually maintain the sporting tradition of acknowledging hits.

The sporting shotgun, like the combat shotgun, was virtually fully developed by 1900. The most common variety was now a hammerless 12-bore with the barrels side by side, though there were still a good number of hammer guns, some of them pinfire, and guns which were 'over and under'. Most of the innovations in non-automatic shotgun design between 1880 and 1920 were to do with details of lock mechanism and the form of the ejector. A very successful hammerless sidelock had been designed by Scott of Birmingham in 1878, with the mechanism mounted on separate plates fitted at the sides of the gun. Hitherto most hammerless actions had been boxlocks, that is with the mechanism mounted in a metal body in the breech. There had been earlier experiments with the automatic ejection of cases, but this became more general from 1881, when Greener patented a new design and applied it to his Facile Principe boxlock gun. Other companies like Anson and Deeley, Boss, Holland and Holland, and Lancaster soon followed suit. Until at least 1860 most shotguns had Damascus or twist bar-

A particularly agile move from Puccini of Italy during an international fencing competition. Notice the umbilical wiring attached to the contestants. Whilst 'close quarter' play is permissible, should the fencers' bodies touch it is determined 'corps-a-corps' and disallowed.

A 'Royal' sidelock ejector 12 bore double-barrelled shot gun, by Holland and Holland of London. The fine quality is apparent especially in the walnut stock and the detail of the lock engraving.

rels. This meant that they were constructed by winding iron and steel around a mandrel, and the pattern thus created often formed a pleasing decorative feature. As the reliability of plain steel barrels improved and the price came down, they were more and more commonly applied to the shotgun. Sometimes these inexpensive plain steel barrels were etched or engraved to mimic the patterns found on Damascus barrels.

Game shooting with shotguns has been popular since at least the eighteenth century, and whilst some shooting is undoubtedly wanton and ill-considered, the organised conservation and rearing of pheasant, grouse, and partridge have certainly aided the preservation of the landscape. Indeed so far as edible game birds are considered, their relatively free lifestyle followed by a swift end is probably more defensible than the battery farming of chickens. In the early part of the century the great shooting parties on the landed estates of Europe were undoubtedly key social events in which place in society was mirrored by role in

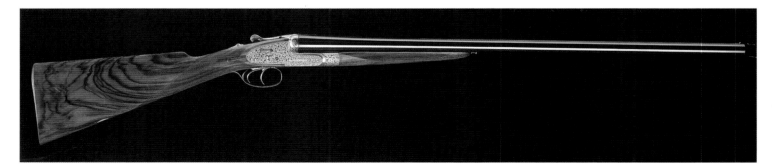

the shoot; those invited would shoot whilst their wives and families would enjoy spectator sport or picnics. Trusted servants would act as loaders and keepers, labourers would act as beaters. When the shooting became competitive incredible bags could be the result: at Abbeystead Lancashire in August 1915, nine 'guns' between them took 5,971 birds in just three days. One of the shooters, who was working with a pair of weapons, experienced such trouble with overheated barrels that he had himself made a pair of silk hand guards for the following day. In contrast, American hunters have tended to follow the game rather than have it driven to them. This requires more physical effort and greater tactical skills on the part of the hunter, and puts a premium on lightweight guns.

Although British firms, like Purdey, Boss, and Holland and Holland led the field in traditional quality, double barrelled, 'side by side' arms, the pump and the automatic were essentially American in inspiration. The pump or slide action, which reloaded and cocked the weapon in one move, was introduced by Winchester in 1892. This had some drawbacks with weight and balance, but its big advantage was in delivering many shots quickly, and this found favour with the police and military. Mauser, Maxim, Mannlicher and others had pioneered semi-automatic arms prior to 1900, but it was not until this century that the principle was commonly applied to shotguns. In 1903 the FN factory at Herstal in Belgium began to produce the Browning-designed five-shot semi-automatic shotgun, and has continued to do so virtually ever since. Other American designers soon latched on to the idea, and companies like Ithaca, Winchester, and Remington have produced semi-automatic models in large quantities.

Since World War Two there have been many new models, if few startling new concepts, and Remington has been one of the most prolific producers. Amongst this company's semi-automatics are the Model II Autoloader, manufactured until 1948; the Model II-48, a .410 gauge produced thereafter; and the Model 58 Sportsman, first designed in the mid 1950s. Perhaps the most popular Remington product of all is the Model 1100. This was first produced in 1963 and is available in three grades, Magnum, Field and Special, with a variety of chokes, barrel lengths and chamber sizes. In Europe the semi-automatic shotgun also gained popularity, with the Russian firm of Baikal, and some of the cheaper Spanish makes covering the lower end of the market, and many of the Italian, French, and the better Spanish guns in more direct competition with the US.

'Rough' shooting with a shotgun. Amongst the accessories carried are shooting jackets, a game bag, and ear defenders. One of the most cost effective avenues for British shotgun enthusiasts is shared rights to a piece of land.

The Browning Superposed B-25 12-bore shot gun, made in Belgium by Fabrique Nationale. This weapon was one of J. M. Browning's last designs, and actually entered full production a few months after his death in 1927. Its full name in Belgium is the 'Fusil a Canons Superposed' 1925, or FCS 25. It has been produced ever since with a variety of minor innovations, and model updates. One of the latest was the deluxe B-25 'Gold', for sporting clays.

A shooter 'follows through' having just blown a clay to fragments at the 'Grouse Flurry', Cottesloe Heath, England. This shooter uses a pair of double barrelled 12-bores, one of which lies on the lip of the pit on top of the gun bag.

One of the most popular European guns is the Italian Beretta S, a well-balanced gun first made in 1955, and with several new variants thereafter, some intended specifically for clays, rather than live targets.

Clay pigeon shooting was first invented in the 1870s, and has since become an important sport in its own right, as well as a practice for game shooting. Whilst in Europe the shooting of game birds like the pheasant or grouse has tended to be the preserve of the rich, and lesser animals and vermin were tackled mainly by the keeper and the countryman, the clay has introduced a mass, and largely class-less, element to the shotgun. The first clay pigeons were in fact of glass, sometimes filled with feathers, and thrown from a crude launcher. Within a decade the flat disc had evolved, but the modern clay pigeon is not really clay but a mixture of chalk and pitch. It has to be strong enough to launch from a trap at speeds of up to 88ft/sec (26.8m/sec), but fragile enough to be easily broken by the gun, as the rules of clay pigeon shooting specify that a visible piece of the target must break off for a hit to be counted. The normal clay has a diameter of 4.68in (120mm), but there are also special varieties with smaller diameters. The 'battue' is a fast and flat disc, and the 'rabbit', being stronger, can be bounced along the ground. Traps also vary considerably. At the inexpensive end of the range are simple spring loaded arms, whilst the top flight traps are fully automatic, magazine fed, and powered by an electric motor.

Most clay shooters adopt a peaked cap and a skeet vest with leather shoulder pads and cartridge loops. Formal training was largely unheard of prior to World War Two, but is now the norm, with schools and clubs often run as commercial businesses. In the British context rules and regulations concerning shotgun ownership were formerly very liberal, but since 1967 have been considerably tightened. By 1990 not only was a shotgun narrowly defined, in the legal sense, as a smooth-bored weapon of not less than 24in (610mm) in the barrel, but limited to a maximum bore of 2in (51mm), and a magazine capacity of two cartridges. Shotgun certificates are required with a photograph of the holder, and the police are entitled to refuse to issue one on several possible grounds. These include the Chief Officer being 'not satisfied' that the person will not be a danger, and that the applicant does not have 'good reason'.

A good deal of clay pigeon shooting is highly competitive. The major disciplines within the sport are Sporting, Skeet, and Trap, each of which is divided into other subdivisions. English Sporting has existed as a championship competition since 1925. Almost any traps will do for this discipline, and a variety of clays may be used, but usually these are shot as pairs; a 'report pair', consisting of a pair where the second target is launched at the sound of the first shot; a 'following pair', where the second clay is launched from the same trap as the first; and the self explanatory but sometimes difficult 'simultaneous pair'. Very often the clays are launched in a manner to emulate the flight of a particular bird. The international clay sporting governing body is the Fédération Internationale de Tir aux Armes Sportive de Chasse (FITASC), whose rules differ somewhat from those normally applied to English sporting.

Skeet is a very different proposition, for the clays are launched from 'houses' one higher than the other, and the shooting stations are arranged in a semi-circle, although only one is occupied at any given moment. Several stands are shot, and the targets may be singles or doubles. There are several varieties of Skeet shooting, including North American, English, and International Shooting Union. Trap shooting similarly has several varieties, Universal Trench, Olympic, Ball and Down the Line, but in all these options the targets are launched from a ground based or entrenched trap ahead of the shooter. Olympic trap, as shot in the games requires no less than fifteen traps, three for each shooter, on a five-shot stand. As

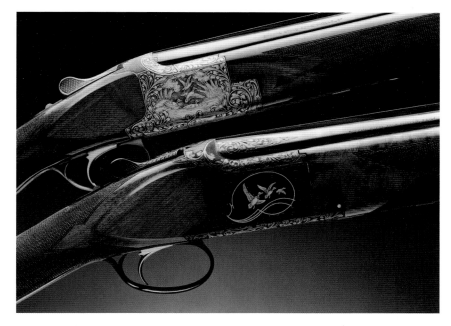

Detail of two Browning Superposed B-25 over-and-under shotguns, made in Belgium. The top example is made to chamber the smaller 20-gauge cartridge, whilst the lower is in the usual 12-gauge or '12-bore'. The 'gauge' of a shotgun an archaic measurement of calibre. It is the number of solid lead balls made to the same diameter as the barrel that are needed to make 1lb (.45kg) weight.

might be expected some of the biggest competitions are sponsored by shotgun manufacturers like Browning or Beretta, though cartridge makers, car and watch manufacturers also take part. 'Combat' shotgunning is totally distinct from clay shooting, and is regarded by many purists as a fringe activity. Combat shotgunning is usually against targets representing humans, and the guns used are identical, or similar, to those used by the police and military.

An interesting adjunct to all shotgun sports is the collecting of cartridges. Military and other cartridges are of course also collected, but shotgun shells have the edge in terms of colour and artistry. The most common are 12-bore, but a good number are also found in 10-, 16-, 20-, and 24-bore, and prior to 1945

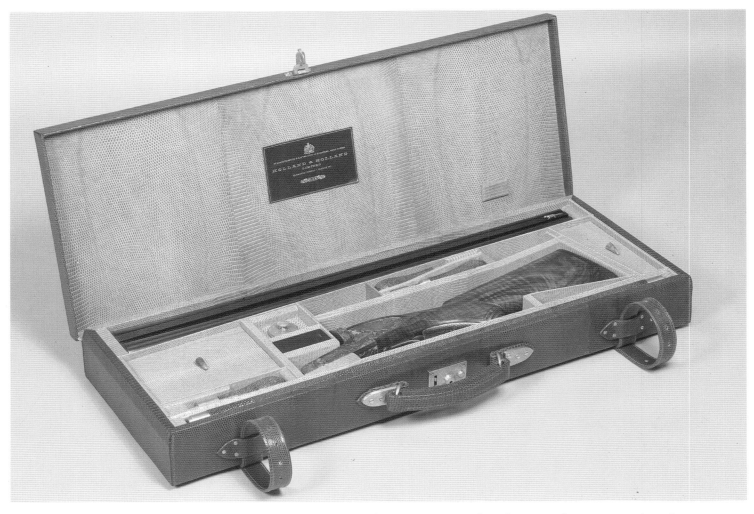

The Holland and Holland 4-bore 'Saurian gun' dismounted for travelling in its elegant carrying case.

there were also significant numbers of pinfire cartridges in use. These last were set off by means of a pin that protruded from the side of the base of the case; the hammer struck the pin, which acted as a striker on the percussion cap. Several manufacturers of shotgun ammunition have long histories; the British firm of Eley for example goes back to at least 1827. This company alone has manufactured literally hundreds of types of cartridge in every conceivable material and colour, and had, or has had outlets in many countries, including the United States, South America, South Africa, Australia, and mainland Europe. Cartridges manufactured by Eley in Britain have included the Tom Thumb, Acme, Grand Prix, Mars, Pergamoid, Rocket, Thor and Vulcan. Kynoch's cartridges are also related to this group, for although the company was started by George Kynoch in 1862 at Witton, Birmingham, they merged with Eley in 1918. At the other end of the commercial scale are gunmakers and iron mongers who retailed only a handful of different cartridges. Amongst these midgets of the ammunition business are counted firms like Freeny's of Galway in the Republic of Ireland who made The Atom, Frank Halls of Chesterfield in Derbyshire, and Mick Simmonds of Sydney, Australia, whose products featured a fallen kangaroo. One of the latest studies lists in excess of 700 makers and suppliers which have existed in the UK alone.

The largest cartridges that the average collector is likely to encounter are the mighty 4-bore, a calibre really only practical for wildfowl and extra long range. As the name suggested the shot weighs 0.25lb (.11kg), and these guns produce massive recoil while being expensive to shoot. Manufacture in both the US and Britain was largely discontinued by about 1930, but there have been one-off guns produced in the calibre since. Perhaps the most amazing of these weapons was Holland and Holland's Saurian Gun a monster exhibition piece of the 1980s; it came not only with a carrying case but a cabinet of curiosities linked to the dinosaur decorative theme of the gun.

The popular idea of a rifle for sport in the twentieth century is likely to be a single-barrelled bolt action magazine rifle like the Mannlicher, Mauser, or Lee Speed. Many hunting rifles for medium, or large, sized game are indeed of this general description, but the century has produced a huge variety of rifled arms, both for target shooting and for different species of game in varied climate and terrain. Target rifles, both small, and full bore, have undergone considerable development. They are now predominantly heavy barrelled with bulky furniture, and fall broadly into three categories, namely prone, free, and International Shooting Union standard. Prone rifles are, of course, designed for use lying down,

Cunz Hector shooting at one of the world-famous competitions at Bisley, England. His bolt action target rifle is heavily customised, and features adjustable cheek and shoulder pieces, and a 'thumbhole grip'. A large wooden rest has been added under the barrel to increase the natural height of the rifle in the standing position with the elbow locked against the body.

Enthusiasts at a revolver shoot. More than one classic Smith and Wesson is visible amongst the smoke.

Martin Millar, Queen's Prize winner at Bisley 1994, is 'chaired' back to the National Rifle Association offices in traditional style. The Queen's prize was first shot in 1860, when it was won by Private E.C.R. Ross of the 7th North Yorkshire Rifle Volunteers. Competition has been yearly ever since, excepting breaks during the World Wars. Only one woman has won the prestigious prize, Marjorie Foster, who achieved it in 1930.

and have a relatively shallow fore end profile, and often a pistol type grip. Free rifles have few restrictions on design, and are therefore often equipped with such subtleties as thumb hole stocks, adjustable palm rests, orthopaedic grips, and hooked butts. ISU standard rifles are limited to 11lb (5kg) in weight, may not have extras like the hook butt, and are intended basically to ensure a uniform standard for international target shooting. Small bore rifles for target use are generally in .22in calibre, but full bore shooting is done in a number of larger, and usually military, or ex-military calibres.

Target rifle actions vary, but over the century American and Continental makers have favoured various bolt actions, whilst those with hinged block Martini-type actions have tended to be British. This long survival of the Martini action is interesting and goes back to the 1890s when the military Martini was going out of army use, and being converted for target and hunting. Many such guns still exist, very often with the names Greener or Bonehill inscribed on their slab sides, indicating which company carried out the conversion. Of the later purpose built target Martinis the majority were made by BSA (Birmingham Small Arms), and one of the last was the Martini International Mark II which weighed a full 14.5lb (6.58kg). Top grade bolt action target rifles are made by many companies amongst which should be numbered Schultz and Larsen, Hammerli, Finnish Lion, and Anschutz. Amongst the German Anschutz models available in the 1990s were the 1913 Super Match, with its adjustable cheek piece and handstop which weighed 15.5lb (7.03kg), and the more manageable 1907, designed to ISU requirements and weighing 10lb (4.5kg). Steyr and Walther produced several competition models in somewhat similar configurations.

Long range match rifles form a separate category, and they are sometimes intended to be fired from the back position with the shooter lying face upward. They may be aided by telescopic or Galilean sights, these last not having the lenses enclosed in a tube. Probably the most famous long range competition is the Queen's Prize shot at Bisley, England, the origins of which go back to 1859 and the Rifle Volunteer movement. The final stages of the Queen's Prize are at 900yd (823m) and 1,000yd (914m) range, but even so this is not the longest competition shoot at Bisley, for parts of the Albert Prize require shooting at 1,200yd (1,097m). Most winners on the ranges at Bisley since 1900 have been equipped with forms of the Lee-Enfield, first in .303in, and then in 7.62mm NATO calibre. Since 1980 more private manufacturers have come on the scene, and in 1986 the Queen's Prize was won by Geoff Cox of the RAF, using a Swing rifle, designed by George Swenson. The Swing used a 7.62mm round, but is distinct from most service rifles in the speed of its action, which operates faster than 1.7 milliseconds. One of the most extraordinary rifles claimed to have a target use is the

A forest of spotting scopes and rifle barrels on the first, 500yd (457m), stage of the Queen's Prize, Bisley. Originally shot for a purse of £250 on the National Rifle Association ground at Wimbledon, the competition was moved to Bisley in 1890. The centenary event was celebrated here 1960.

Texan McMillan M-88. Essentially a long range sniper rifle the M-88 has every appearance of a World War Two anti-tank rifle, and with a .5in calibre, and a weight of 21lb (9.52kg), the bulk to match. The price is also at the heavy end of the scale, retailing at about $3,250 in 1990.

Rifles for game have been even more diverse than rifles for target. The most obvious methods for classifying them are by purpose, calibre, mechanism, and ammunition type. The smallest .22in calibre weapons, which have been in production for most of the century, are often known as 'rook and rabbit' due to their intended target, but are sometimes thought to be not really a sporting arm at all, being somewhat dismissively categorised as vermin guns, or adjuncts to pest control. Calibre alone is not always a reliable guide to power, for next up the scale the recent .223in Remington round has a muzzle velocity of over 3,000ft/sec (914m/sec) and the ability to knock down a moderate sized antelope. Fairly similar in performance is the 30-30 Winchester cartridge, as near a standard for deer as is possible in such a diverse field, and on the market since 1895. In a similar

Traditional Mauser action sporting rifles. Close examination of the elaborate decoration reveals the intended targets, wild boar amongst the oak leaves, and a chamois in the mountains. The double trigger arrangement allows the marksman to take the first heavier pressure and then touch off the shot, leading to greater accuracy.

German Mauser 7.62mm bolt action 'Match' rifles. The latest generations of Mauser bolt actions feature a muzzle brake and a 'short action' bolt. Apart from being marginally quicker the short action saves on space and the shooter's eyes remain on target. Weapons from the basic family have been adapted for sport, target, and military sniping.

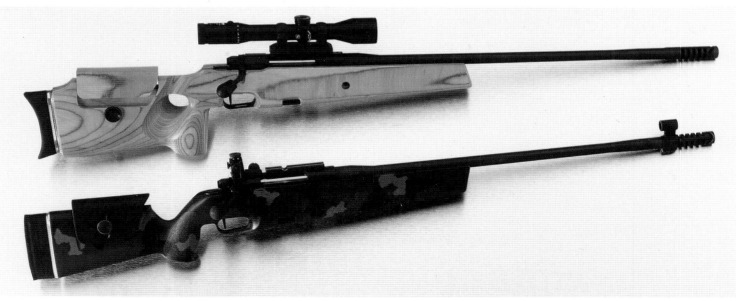

category, but not so fast, was the .33in Winchester round, in production from about 1902 to 1940, and still found occasionally with cartridge reloading enthusiasts. In continental Europe these cartridges and performances were virtually duplicated by various Mauser, Sauer, and Mannlicher rounds for small to medium size game. British sporting rifles for this sort of quarry would often chamber the military .303in, which certainly had advantages in terms of familiarity and supply; but there were also many more specialised rounds for the stalker. One such was the 7mm Rigby Magnum, introduced in 1927, and in use for over 30 years for 'deer stalking and all classes of non-dangerous game'.

At the top of the range come the 'Elephant' and other 'Big Game' rifles and their attendant cartridges. This market was dominated at the turn of the century by the Express Rifle and the Paradox Gun. Whilst the Express Rifle was named after the express train, due to its large high velocity cartridge, the Paradox Gun was an interesting dual-purpose arm, much like a shotgun in general outline. The last few inches of the otherwise smooth barrels were rifled, so that at moderate ranges it could be used with multiple shot, as a shotgun, or with a single bullet as a heavy rifle. There were also a good number of double rifles with ordinary rifled barrels, but set up side by side. More recently the trend has been toward more conventional bolt actions for big game, and falling block mechanisms like the Farquharson and Martini have been eclipsed, but the cartridges still tend to be monsters, whether they rely on the mass of the bullet, or the very high velocity of a necked down cartridge.

Amongst the classic big game cartridges of the century must be numbered the .416in Rigby, designed by John Rigby in 1911 for his Mauser action sporting rifles, and still in production; the .300in Holland and Holland Magnum of 1925; the .300in Weatherby Magnum of 1948; and the .358in Winchester Magnum introduced in 1955. Of particularly stunning power is the .460in Weatherby Magnum, introduced in 1958 which develops even more muzzle energy than the old .600in British Nitro Express. It might be thought that this was more than enough for even the maddest of bull elephants, but by 1990 a British experiment was underway with a .700in calibre Nitro Express, intended to be the most powerful sporting cartridge in the world. Strangely enough the project was initiated by an American, but as one commentator put it, this cartridge is, 'more than adequate for any game animal found anywhere on this planet'. One cannot help thinking that the quest has become one for the most powerful possible, rather than the most practical.

A 10-bore 'Paradox' gun by Holland and Holland, c.1913. In the words of one of the makers' catalogues- 'We need hardly point out to practical sportsmen the great advantages of a weapon which shoots as well as a good cylinder gun, and conical ball up to 100 yards, with the accuracy of a first class Express Rifle. Nor need we refer to the importance of shooting moving objects in jungle with a weapon which one is accustomed to, and which comes to shoulder with the facility and accuracy of an ordinary gun'.

A selection of hunting knives which often form the accompaniment to the game rifle. The Fisk example, bottom, has a traditional stag horn grip, and a blade not unlike the old 'Bowie'. The 'Randall' knife, top row centre, made by the company of Doane Randall at Orlando Florida, takes as its inspiration the Allied fighting knives of World War Two. It is interesting to note that Randall knives have also been carried by pilots, and even into space. The other examples are aimed at the more prosaic tasks of evisceration; but some of them take advantage of modern man-made materials and surface 'Parkerisation'.

A German Sauer 'Dreiling', or 'Drilling', with a rifle barrel mounted under the double smooth-bore shotgun barrels. Although perhaps the most popular of 'combination' long arms, Dreilings were by no means the only configuration. A 'Vierling', as the name suggests had four barrels, usually two rifled and two smooth; the 'Büchsflinte' had one rifled and one smooth, and the 'Expressdreiling' had two rifled barrels and one smooth.

Two variations on the Quackenbush air rifle, which was in production from the 1870s, to about 1930, and helped to bring the idea of the airgun to the masses. Spare parts were available for a further 40 years, but by then the old Quackenbush company had passed on to making nutcrackers and seafood forks.

Modern bolt action hunting rifles suitable for big game include the Weatherby Mark V Safari Grade series; the Kimber African and Big Game; the McMillan Signature Safari; the A-Square Hannibal; the Beeman 600/700; the Heym Magnum Express; and the Whitworth Safari Express, most of which are available in various calibres, and some in left and right hand models. At the top end of the market are the makers who custom build a rifle to the specific requirements of the client. One such company is Auguste Francotte of Belgium, whose bespoke products include choices in terms of sights, stocks, weights, and barrel lengths as well as calibres. Combination and double rifles are also far from dead. Perhaps one of the most interesting is the German Krieghoff Trumpf Dreiling (or Drilling), which as the name suggests has three barrels, a combination of two shotgun barrels and a rifle barrel. Beretta makes a particularly fine double rifle, with sidelock action, .458in Winchester Magnum barrels, silver decoration, and a commensurate asking price of about $20,000.

Though the European and American hunter must bear a large share of blame for the near extinction of certain large mammals, their African brother has, since independence, shown considerable talent in attempting to finish the job. In several war torn, or generally lawless, parts of the continent it is not unknown for poachers with weapons like the AK 47 to indulge in the wholesale slaughter of pachyderms. Undoubtedly the main stimulus for this has been the price of ivory and rhino horn, the one for its decorative, the other for its supposed aphrodisiac, qualities. Commendable international efforts have been made against such trade, but such measures may not be enough. Ironically it is sometimes only the local realisation that big game is a financial resource, whether for the carefully regulated

fee-paying hunter or the almost equally intrusive Nikon-armed tourist, that leads to the conservation of herds and grazing.

Until at least the mid-nineteenth century airguns tended to be expensive hand made items, but with the coming of the industrial era, and falling prices, they became readily accessible to a large segment of society. One of the least impressive airguns, but most important from the point of view of popularisation, was the Quackenbush. The patent for this was issued to Henry Marcus Quakenbush, in June 1876, and though first produced in America the Quakenbush was later made under licence in Germany, and widely marketed elsewhere well into the twentieth century. Despite its crude appearance the

Quakenbush was a reasonably accurate and powerful airgun. In one version the weapon was able to operate as both airgun, firing solid lead slugs, and as a firearm by the removal of a liner, which allowed .22in cartridges to be used. In 1888 the Daisy company entered the field, having been previously employed in the manufacture of windmill equipment. The first Daisy guns, as invented by Clarence Hamilton, were all metal with skeleton stocks, although later models had a more conventional appearance. By the 1950s the American Daisy company was selling in excess of 1,500,000 airguns per year. Probably the most popular and long lived Daisy product was the Model 102 BB (ball bearing), repeater; this first appeared in 1933, and was still in production, virtually unaltered, in the 1990s. The gun has only 13 parts, and has been recommended for children as young as eight. Daisy guns are still found all over the world, but it is interesting to note that until 1930 the biggest overseas market was China.

Another giant of the airgun world was the German company of Mayer and Grammelspacher of Rastatt, which traded under the name Diana. After World War Two the British company of Millard Brothers of Lanark produced many of the Diana models, whilst the German firm, somewhat confusingly, began to retail under the

Airguns remain popular as sporting, target and vermin rifles, especially with young people. In countries with stringent firearm control legislation, an air rifle can permit individuals to shoot cheaply without going to the expense and effort of obtaining a gun licence.

trade name Original. Mayer and Grammelspacher were leaders in the field from about 1920, and even before 1939 had produced many simple models such as the 1, 15, 16, 20, 22, 25 and the Diana Junior in large numbers. After the war, and working under the Original title, the company produced some much more sophisticated and expensive weapons, aimed at accuracy and competitive use. Amongst these was the Model 65, also sold in America as the Hyscore Model 810 Olympic

The BSA underlever 'Airsporter' air rifle. Production of the Airsporter began in 1948, and the design incorporated many of the best features of the old Lincoln Jeffries models. It was available in the standard calibres of .177in and .22in, but the weight of 8lb (3.63kg), and length of 44in (1.12m) varied fractionally from mark to mark.

between 1965 and 1975, and the Model 66 which came in as the old gun went out of production. Germany's importance in the airgun world is underscored by other premier companies, such as Anschutz of Ulm, Weihrauch in Bavaria, Hammerli of Tiengen, and Haenel of Suhl. Haenel in particular has been a dogged survivor, being based within the German Democratic Republic after 1945.

Large scale production of air rifles in Britain began in the late nineteenth century. One of the first models to appear in numbers was the Gem, which was also imported from Germany. Not long after Bonehill of Birmingham entered the market with a gun, similar to the Quakenbush, called the Britannia. Birmingham Small Arms began producing air rifles about 1900, first under licence from Lincoln Jefferies, whose designs they used. Both the Lincoln Jefferies, and the similar BSA improved models which followed it were underlever designs, meaning that the gun was cocked by the stroke of a lever. The barrel did not therefore have to be broken downward, and there were fewer problems with obtaining airtight seals. BSA went on to become one of the world's premier airgun manufacturers, and after World War Two went on to make a range of guns, including the Cadet, Cadet-Major, Club, Merlin and Meteor. One of their best designs was the Airsporter, a robust underlever which went through seven variants, including a special edition limited to 1,000 examples issued in 1982, to commemorate 100 years of the BSA piled arms trademark. The other pillar of the British airgun industry was Webley and Scott, who, having been firearms makers for over a century, first patented an air pistol design in 1911. Serious production of pistols was underway by 1924, and a rifle, the Webley Mk 1, appeared two years later. This gun was rather like the pistols in that it used a pivoted superimposed barrel; it was not terribly popular and was soon replaced by the Service air rifle. Many more models followed; the small Junior of the 1950s and 1960s; the Jaguar of the 1970s, and the full size Hawk and Falcon.

The British 'Lincoln' air pistol. First patented by L. Jeffries and company in 1911, the Lincoln had an air cylinder and plunger in the butt. Cocking was achieved by breaking the barrel downward. Production of the Lincoln is believed to have ceased in the late 1920s, but Jeffries was a prolific inventor and many of his ideas involving levers and pellet-loading gates would subsequently be used by BSA.

Air weapons have also been produced in quantity elsewhere in the world. China for example has not only progressively conquered the toy market, but has become a major airgun producer, with models like the Pioneer and Hunter. The Spanish and Brazilians scored a commercial success with the Paratrooper: this was an interesting departure when it first appeared in 1969, for it appears to have been the first attempt by airgun manufacturers to mimic the plastic furniture and shape of then current military rifles. Though this appearance was largely cosmetic the Paratrooper did have a 25-pellet magazine. The military styling for air rifles caught on, and weapons with assault rifle looks have since been made by many companies, including Crosman in America, and NSP in Sussex England. Perhaps the most extraordinary example of this whole group is the French FA

MAS air rifle, introduced in 1988, which copies the stunted bullpup lines of the French Army's service rifle. Air pistols have also undergone a parallel restyling from about 1970, so that certain models, like the Beeman P1 Magnum, are, in their fantasy cladding, military automatics. In reality the P1 is a .177in, traditional barrel cocking model with a muzzle velocity of about 624ft/sec (190m/sec). Other air pistols, particularly those intended for match use have taken the technological path in style, like the Feinwerkbau Model 100, which boasts not only an adjustable trigger, but an adjustable palm shelf, and left and right hand models.

It is worth noting that although most air weapons work by means of a spring moving in a cylinder and forcing air in front of it, there are other gas systems. The most important of these are pneumatic and CO_2 guns. In the former air chambers are charged with compressed air, usually by pumping, and in the latter cylinders are used, either factory sealed, or recharged from a bottle. It is arguable that the CO_2 guns used for paintball competitions are a new breed of sporting weapon, distinct from the old air pistol and air rifle. True they are not lethal, deliv-

The US Crosman A*I*R* 17 pneumatic air gun. Capable of shooting .177in pellets or ball bearings the A*I*R* 17 consciously mimics the outline of the service M16. Costing only about $40, and weighing just 3lb (1.36kg) this model was introduced in 1986. This is one of many air weapons with military styling, others copy the general outline of the Heckler and Koch G3, the M14, and the FA MAS.

ering only a ball of coated paint, but they look like guns, and use a principle already known in air weapons which fire lead pellets. The ancestor of all paintball guns was the Nel-Spot, a co-operative venture between the firm of Daisy, and the Nelson paint company in the 1960s. This was intended as an easy way to mark timber by shooting an indelible paint pellet at it. Soon there were other guns, and cattle were being similarly treated: before long a rough sport with contestants splatting each other with paint developed. Paintball, as an organised activity with rules, water-based paint, designated playing areas, and protective equipment for the face was in existence in the United States by 1981, and entered Britain within three years.

Within ten years a wide variety of paintball weapons were being produced which mimicked pistols, rifles and SMGs. One of the earliest and most popular pistols is the Splatmaster, a .68in calibre gun, made of plastic and accurate to about 70ft (21.3m), with a muzzle velocity of about 250ft/sec (76m/sec) in the US, and about 170ft/sec (52m/sec) in the UK version. Ten or more balls are held in a magazine which is pushed into the muzzle, and motive power is provided by a small CO_2 bulb in the butt, similar to that found in soda syphons. One bulb will shoot 20 or 30 pellets, but another system was soon devised in which a bigger cylinder is fitted which could be recharged with bottled gas. By 1990 the Splatmaster seemed slow and unsophisticated beside modern paintball guns. Amongst these are exotic sounding weapons like the Razorback, Black Widow, Sheridan Tippman SMG and the WGP Ranger. The Nightmare is a pump-action gun, while the M-85 looks very much like an Uzi SMG, and is capable of fully automatic bursts. Many of these guns have metal frames and barrels and are commensurately expensive. This arsenal of guns is backed by grenades, mines and pyrotechnics, some of which discharge paint and may also be used to score hits on opponents. Playing areas and rules vary considerably from site to site, the smallest games being played inside warehouses, and the largest over huge acreages and include camps, trenches, and vehicles.

Although a number of Eastern martial arts have a long history their techniques and special weapons are predominantly new to the west. Many in the US
and UK became aware of them as a result of the Kung-fu craze in the 1970s, but
it is a fact that the knotted scarf of the Thugee was encountered by the British in
the nineteenth century, and that Jujitsu was practised by scouts and snipers in
World War One. There are many martial arts, at least 23 being recognised in Japan
alone, and devotees often value mental control and elegance of movement as
much as, or more than, prowess with a weapon. What concerns us here how-

The Nunchaku or rice flail in action. Skillfully used the flail is both an offensive and defensive weapon.

A masked paintballer advances through pyrotechnic smoke. 'Head shots' are not normally counted, but most, if not all, sites insist on eye protection to US or British standards. There are also various legal restrictions on weapons, including in Britain a limit to the velocity of the projectile. Most reputable paintball sites will insist on face masks of this type, and some demand throat protection as well. A day's paintball will result in a few bruises, but serious injury is extremely rare, and despite the fearsome image, accidents are actually far more common on the football field. Notice the hefty CO_2 cylinder under the gun; these have become steadily more common as the numbers of semi and full automatic weapons increase.

ever are the weapons which have been deployed in the practice of those arts in the twentieth century. Despite a confusion of terms, schools, and disciplines it is possible to group many of the arms in a relatively few major categories.

Several of these weapons are in fact practice or replica swords, often adopted originally so that sword drills could be executed without serious injury. Foremost amongst these is the Shinai used in the art of Kendo. The length and weight of the bamboo Shinai varies according to the age and experience of the protagonists, who wear four pieces of protective clothing: a helmet (or Men); gloves (Kote); a breastplate (Do); and a stomach guard (Tare). Children as young as three or four are known to practise Kendo in Japan, and since 1928 the sport has been regularised into ten grades, the top of which is Judan. Other forms of dummy sword used in martial arts include the Bokken or wooden sword, and the white stick. Dummy pole arms also make up a significant sub-group within martial arts weapons, the Jo and Bo being nothing more than short and long sticks respectively. The Naginta approximates to the western idea of a halberd, and is traditionally popular with women in oriental martial arts.

Other forms of spear are sometimes known by the generic term of Yari.

Another group of martial arts arms stems from the improvised use of agricultural implements as weapons. Many of these were supposedly developed in Okinawa when it was under Japanese occupation, when the natives were forbidden from practising any martial arts. The Okinawans were forced to practice in secret, and developed skills in using apparently innocent farm tools as weapons. Thus it is that the Kusarigama is a sickle and chain, and the Nunchaku is an articulated rice flail. It is likely that the Chijiriki or ball and chain attached to a rod has a similar derivation. One of the most interesting tools in this category is the Tonfa, an oak rod about 18 to 20in (457 to 508mm) in length, originally used for pounding soya. It has a handle projecting from the side, and is similar to some US police batons. Held by the side handle, it can be spun so that the length runs down the forearm to protect the user from blows, while the short protruding end makes for a powerful jabbing weapon.

Thrown weapons may also be said to form a discrete group. One of the oldest are the hand arrows, or darts, known as Uchine. Shuriken are also like darts or short sticks, usually of metal, and together with the Shaken or throwing stars were favourite weapons of the Ninja, the covert warrior spies of medieval Japan. The art of throwing small objects is known to the Japanese as Shuriken jutsu. The Shaken, sometimes known in the west as death stars, may have anything between four and ten points, and can be holed in the centre to store on a stick, or left plain. Some modern replicas are of the worst possible quality, being fabricated from very poor materials. Despite the bloodthirsty English name, and their banning in Britain, the present writer is aware of no deadly assault which has been perpetrated with them, at least in Europe, in modern times.

A couple of martial arts weapons are very difficult to categorise, although the Sai and the Kyotetsu-koge are probably most similar to small knives and daggers. The Sai is like a long dagger with elongated guards which produce a trident-like outline. Again supposedly derived from a tool used to carry bales of rice, it can be used as a jabbing weapon, or in the same manner as the tonfa, to protect the arm. Armed with a pair of Sai, a skilled user can trap an opponent's sword blade in the guards, and snap it with a sharp twisting motion. The Kyotetsu-koge is a form of double-bladed dagger, usually associated with the Ninja, and attached to the knife part is a length of rope and a heavy ring. Skilled use makes the Kyotetsu-koge a multi-purpose tool and a weapon for grappling, swinging, climbing, stabbing and slashing.

The use of the Tonfa, or soya pounding sticks, as martial arts weapons. In this stance the batons can be used to protect the arms and parry an attack, or jab at the assailant. The Tonfa is the inspiration for the side handled baton used by police forces in a number of countries.

Antiquarian interest in arms and armour of all sorts has burgeoned in the twentieth century, and what was once the province of only the very rich, or very eccentric, has become a commonplace. At the bargain basement end of the market are those who haunt provincial 'arms fairs' simply to collect makers' labels, spent bullets and grenade base plugs: the popular middle ground is occupied by the specialists of bayonet, sword and flintlock: but the true aficionados with leisure and infinite purses are to be found with the top flight contents of the aristocratic gun room, and the medieval armoury. Some of the discerning have collected only weapons with specific forms of decoration, one such specialises in ivory, another in damascene work, and a third in erotic scenes. Such pleasures as are afforded by the best salesrooms and auction houses are justly accorded the accolade of 'art'.

Shooters not only shoot modern weapons but old, and in many cases out of respect for the artefact, or fear of injury, prefer to use reproductions for the purpose. Thus it is that one can find a British or American flintlock made in the 1990s, or a wheelock pistol, hand-crafted by a modern enthusiast. Beyond the simple pleasure of target shooting with real or reproduction antiques lies a whole genre of re-enactment, in which the weaponry is merely a part of a reconstruction of a battle, or a part of a desire to indulge in living history. It can all be indulged with either magpie curiosity, or with a genuine desire to find out more. Both schools of thought have been aided, not only by the improvement of museum displays, but the proliferation of literature on the subject. Perhaps the greatest hothouses of such knowledge are the various 'Arms and Armour' societies, and it is arguable that founded in London in 1950 has propagated more than most.

The 78th Fraser Highlanders firing a volley. Fraser's Highlanders served at Louisberg and Quebec; however this is not the mid-eighteenth century, but the twentieth. The muskets are working reproductions of the famous 'Land Pattern', and the battle is for entertainment and instruction. Weapons often form a cornerstone of battle re-enactment, and its more refined offspring, 'living history'. At Williamsburg in the US the making of guns in the age-old style is itself a major tourist attraction: other armed re-enactors have been thought sufficiently worthy to show in films like the US Civil War epic 'Glory', or the Scottish 'Chasing the Deer'. It is interesting that the public reaction is generally excellent to the portrayal of subjects perceived as 'historic', whilst the recreation of modern subjects are viewed as being in questionable taste. Perhaps some of the terrible events of the twentieth century will themselves be seen one day as nostalgic entertainment.

INDEX

Numbers in *italics* refer to pages with illustrations or captions.

ACR rifle 144
Action Express 191, 192
Adrian helmets 9
Afghanistan war 125–28
AGS 17 grenade launcher 126, 131
airguns 214–17
Airsporter airgun 216
AK5 rifle 140
AK 47 rifle 111, 111–13, 124, 126, 127, 130, 136
AK 74 rifle 125, 126, 130
AKM assault rifle 124, 125, 130, 136
AKSU carbine 126
AMR rifle 166–67
ANC 196
anti-aircraft weapons 167–73
antiquarians 220–21
anti-tank weapons 149–67
AR10 rifle 100–1
AR15 rifle 101
Arab–Israeli wars 115–17
archery 201, 202, 203
Arisaka bayonets 17
Arisaka rifle 16–17, 54, 55, 90, 168
Armed Response Vehicle 187
arrows 201–2
assassination 184–85, 190
AUG rifle 137, 137–38
AVS rifle 74
AWP rifle 145

B–25 shotgun 205, 207
Baikal shotgun 205
Ballester Molina pistol 124
ballistics 182–84, 185
Bankers' Special pistol 178
BAR 49, 66, 94, 107–8
Barnett crossbow 202
batons 175, 188–90, 190
bayonets 43, 80, 81, 95
bazookas 95, 155–57, 156, 158
Beholla pistol 58
Beretta pistols 22, 59, 131, 132, 133, 136, 179, 186
Beretta rifle 145
Beretta SMGs 65, 84
Bergmann guns 31–32, 60
Berka vests 192
Berthier carbine 15
Bisley 209, 210, 211
Blowpipe missile 128, 170–73
BM-59 rifle 50
Bo 219
'Bodeo' revolver 59
body armour:
    Falklands 122–23
    First World War 37–38, 39, 82–87
    police 189, 190–92
    Korean war 96–97
    Vietnam war 109–10
bombs, anti-tank 153–54
bombs, triggers for 193
bomb throwers 40
booby traps 197–99
Borchardt pistol 21
BOSS shotguns 204, 205
bows, types of 201
Boys rifle 151
Brandt mortar 40
breast plates 37–38
Breda machine gun 71
Bren gun 50–51, 51, 70, 96, 107, 121, 169

Bristol body armour 189, 192
Britannia airgun 216
'Brody' helmet 37
Browning machine guns 4, 24, 50, 66, 107, 121
Browning pistols 21, 22, 57, 122
Browning rifles 93, 178
Browning shotgun 205, 207
BSA guns 210, 216
bullpup designs 134–35, 136, 137
Bushman Individual Defence Weapon 142

C8 carbine 120
C96 Mauser 179
car bombs 194
Carl Gustav anti-tank weapon 163
Carl Gustav SMG 116
cartridges 208, 209, 213
Casqué Adrian Modele 1915 37
CETME rifles 140, 140–41
Chassepot rifle 10
Chaucat machine gun 30–31, 31
Chemica Body Shield 38
Chijiriki 220
Claymore mines 194
clay pigeon shooting 206–8
CO$_2$ guns 217
Colt Commando 104, 121
Colt machine gun 24
Colt pistols 20, 21, 57, 79, 109, 124, 178
Commando dagger 81, 81–82
Commando machine gun 108
crime 176–77, 180, 187
crossbows 201, 202

Daisy airguns 215
Dayfield Body Shield 38
De Lisle carbine 74–75
Desert Eagles 142, 191, 192
Diana airguns 215, 216
DP 1928 machine gun 54
Dragon anti-tank weapon 164
Dreilling gun 214
DShK machine gun 71, 126
DUX SMG 64

Eley company 208
EM 2 rifle 134
Energa grenade 162
Enfield Individual Weapon 135
Enfield pistols 56–57
Explosive Ordnance Disposal Suits 192, 193
Express rifle 213

F1 SMG 105–6
F 90 Personal Defence Weapon 143
Facile Principe gun 204
Fairbairn-Sykes knife 81, 81–82
Falcon air rifle 216
Falklands/Malvinas war 119–25
FAL rifle 105, 117, 123
FG 42 rifle 72–73
First World War 9–45
flak jackets 109, 122, 192, 196
flamethrowers 36, 80, 95
forensic science 182–85
free rifles 210
French Nails 44
FR-1, FR-F2 rifles 147
Fusil d'Infantrie Modèle 86/93 43
Fusile Modello 91 rifle 15

G3 rifle 127, 128, 141, 199
G11 rifle 143–44
G98 rifle 10, 14, 16, 30, 36, 39, 55, 72
Galili, Israel 117
Galil rifle 116, 117
game rifles 212–14
game shooting 204–6
Gammon bomb 154
Garand M1 rifle 49–50, 50, 62
gas grenades 187
gas masks 87

Gem airgun 216
Gewehr 41 72
Gewehr 43 72
Glisenti pistols 22, 60
Glock pistols 182, 184, 187
Grail missile 170
Granatenwerfer models 40, 76
'Grease Gun' 61, 110
Greener shotguns 204
Grenade No. 1 33
grenades:
    anti-tank 153
    First World War 33–36
    Korean war 94–95
    Second World War 78
    Vietnam war 108–9, 114–15
guerrillas 194
Gulf wars 119, 128–33, 136
gun control 180–82
gun crime 176–77, 180, 187

Hafdasa pistol 124
Halcon SMG 123–24
handcuffs 188
Handy gun 178
Hawk air rifle 216
Hawkins bomb 154
helmets 36–37, 37, 40, 79, 82–87, 109, 166
Helwan pistol 136
High Coverage Technical Armor 191
Hi Standard pistol 74
Holland and Holland shotguns 204, 205, 208, 209
Holmes shotgun 190
Hotchkiss machine guns 24, 167
human rights 188
hunting knives 213

Imbel pistol 142
incendiary devices 194–95
Ingram Model 10 183
INSAS rifle 141
IRA 196
Israeli-Arab wars 115–17
ISU rifles 210
Ithaca Autoburgler 178
Ithaca shotgun 190, 205

Jaguar air rifle 216
Javelin missile launcher 171, 173
Jeffery rifle 19
Jo 219
Joubert trench dagger 45
Jujitsu 218, 219
Jungle carbine 55, 56
Junior air rifle 216

K98 A2 rifle 30
Kalashnikov rifles 11–13, 126, 127, 197
Kar 98k rifle 52, 55, 58, 84
Karabin rifle 55
'K' bullets 149–50
Kendo 219
Kennedy, President John F. 184–85
Kevlar 190, 191, 192
Kirrikale 144
Kleif flamethrower 36
knives 44–45, 81–82
knuckle knives 45, 79
Korean war 89–98
Krag-Jorensen rifle 11, 12
Krumlauf attachments 74
Kukri 44
Kurz cartridge 73
Kusarigama 220
Kuwait, invasion of 128
Kynoch's cartridges 208
Kyotetsu-koge 220

L1A1 rifle 105, 121, 136
L1A3 bayonet 121
L2A3 SMG 121–22, 122
L4A3 machine gun 121
L7 machine gun 119–20, 121, 169, 171

Gem airgun 216

L34A1 SMG 124
L85A1 rifle 1, 4 135, 136
L86A1 machine gun 135
L96A1 rifle 145
Lancaster shotguns 204
Lanchester SMGs 60
landmines 194
land pattern missile 221
Lange pistols 21, 22
Lanze anti-tank weapon 166
Lanz mortar 40, 42
LAW missile 120, 136, 163, 164
Lebel rifles 14–15, 43
Lee-Enfield rifles 11, 14, 16–17, 55, 80–81, 96, 126, 127, 210
Lee-Metford rifle 11–12
Lee-type weapons 11
Leichte Minenwerfer 40
Lewis guns 28, 29, 31, 65, 151
Liberator pistols 75
Lincoln air pistol 216
Llama pistols 142
long range match rifles 210–12
LRAC 89 rocket 164
Luftschutz helmet 84
Luger pistols 21–22, 57–58, 58

M1 carbine 62, 80, 93
M1 Garand rifle 49–50, 50, 62, 80, 92–93, 94, 99
M1 helmets 68, 85, 109
M1 mortar 76, 78
M2 carbine 93–94, 109
M2 grenades 79
M2 machine gun 4, 66, 68, 86–87, 91, 107, 128, 150
M3 SMG 61, 110, 113
M3 trench knife 80
M4 bayonet-knife 80
M4 carbine 134
M7 assault rifle 138
M7 bayonet 80
M7 grenade launcher 50
M9 pistol 131, 132
M11 charge 194
M14 rifle 99, 100, 192
M16 rifle 4, 6, 100, 100–4, 101, 102–3, 105, 113, 119, 121, 123
M21 rifle 100
M24 rifle 147
M26A1 grenade 108, 109
M40 rifle 147
M42 SMG 61, 70
M44 SMG 64
M52 vest 109
M55 vest 110
M56 SMG 139
M57 anti-tank weapon 166
M60 machine gun 2-3, 4, 89, 100, 106, 106-7, 107, 133
M61 grenade 109
M62 rifle 117
M67 rifle 164
M69 vest 110
M76 rifle 139
M79 grenade launcher 104, 105
M80 rifle 139
M82A1 rifle 147, 167
M-85 paintball gun 217
M-88 rifle 212
M203 grenade launcher 105, 121, 134, 136
M249 machine gun 130, 131, 133
M870 shotgun 132
M950, M-955A SMGs 142–43
M1871 rifle 10
M1888 Mauser 16
M1889 revolver 59–60
M1889 rifle 10
M1903 round 12
M1911A1 pistol 57, 109
M1915 rifle 10
M1916 helmet 37
M1917 knife 45
M1917 machine gun 65
M1917 rifle 17
M1918 'Pedersen device' 32–33
M1919 machine gun 65, 67, 94, 107

M1934 pistol 59
M1935 helmet 84
M1941 machine gun 66
M1951 vest 97–98
machetes 81, 82
machine guns:
  Afghanistan war 128
  Falklands war 119–21
  First World War 23–32
  interwar 53–54, 65–71
  Korean war 91
  Vietnam war 106–8, 114
McNary knife 45
Madsen guns 29–30, *30*
Magnum cartridges 179, 191, *192*, 213
Magnum pistols 179
Makarov pistol 113–14
Malvinas/Falklands war 119–25
Mannlicher-Cacarno rifles *65*, 184, *185*
Mannlicher rifle 16
Mk 2 hand grenade 108
Mark 11A1 grenade 78
Mk 19 grenade launcher 131
martial arts 187, 218–20
Martini-Henrys 126
MAS air rifle 217
MAS rifles *75*, 136
MAS38 SMG 113
MAT 49 SMG 99, 113
Mauser pistols 22, 58
Mauser rifles *10*, 11, *12*, 16, 18, 55, *98*, 140, *150*, *212*
Maxim guns 24, 25, *27, 65, 71, 91*
Mayer and Grammelspacher airguns 215, 216
Meiji pistols 58
Metropolitan police 176, 187, *188, 189*, 192
MG 08 machine gun 28–29, 31, 65
MG 08/15 machine gun 29–30, *30*
MG1 machine gun 71
MG 30 machine gun 53
MG 34 machine gun 53–54, 70
MG 42 machine gun 53–54, *70–71, 168*
Micro-Uzi 142
'Middle East' commando knife 82
MILAN missile 161, 162, 164–66, *166*
MILES system *135*, 137
Millard Brothers 215
Mills bomb 34–35, 78, *79*
Minenwerfer 40, *42*
Minimi machine gun 131, 136
Mistral missile *173*
Mkb42 (H) rifle 73
Model 45 SMG *116*
Model 97 rifle 151–52, *152*
Model 1911 pistol *20*
Moisin-Nagant rifles 15, 16, 55, *56*, 89
Molotov cocktails 194, *195*
Mondragon rifle *10*
mortars:
  3in 77
  2in 76–77,*77*
  First World War 138–43
  Gulf wars 128
  Korean war *94*, 96
  Middle East 117
  Second World War 78–80
  Vietnam war 114
Mossberg shotgun *190*
MP5 machine pistol *189*
MP5 SMG 137, *199*
MP18 SMG 31–32, *32*, 51
MP 28 SMG 51, 60
MP 34, 35 SMGs 51, 53
MP 38 SMG *52*, 53
MP 40 SMG *52, 52, 85*
MP43 rifle 73
MP44 rifle 73, *73*–74, 111
MRC body armour 87

Nagant revolver 57
Naginta 219
Nahrkampfmesser 82
nail bombs 192, *193*
Nails 44
Nambu pistol 58–59
Nanchaku *219*, 220
NATO ammunition *4*, 71, 105, 119, 134
Nel-Spot gun 217
Nightmare gun 217
Ninja 220
Nitro Express rifle 19, 213
No. 2 Mark 1 revolver *56*, 56–57
No. 15 ball grenade 34
Northern Ireland 192, *193, 194, 195, 197*
NSV machine gun 126

Olympic airgun 216

P08 pistol 21, *22*, 57–58, *58*
P7 automatic *180*
P14 Enfield rifle 11, 16
P17 rifle 17
P38 pistol 58
paintball guns 217
PAM SMG 123
Panzerfaust *157, 157*–58, 166
Panzerschreck *158*
Parabellum round 119
Paradox gun *213*
Paratrooper airgun 216
Patchett Mark 5 124
Pattern rifle grenades *35*
Personal Defence Weapon 142
petrol bombs 194, 195
PIAT *154*, 154–55
Pistole 35 57
pistol/SMG hybrids 142
pistols:
  Falklands 124
  First World War 19–23
  Gulf wars and 128, 136
  interwar 55–60
  Korean war 90
  recent designs 142
  Vietnam war 113–14
  Yugoslavia 138
Pitcher grenade 33–34
PKM machine gun *126*
pole arms 219
police arms 175, 177–80, 187–90

PPD SMGs 62–64
PPK pistol 58, 73, 144
PPS SMG 64
PPSh SMG *62*, 64, 90–91, 113
PTRD rifle *152*
PTRS rifle 152

Quackenbush air rifles *214*, 214–15

R4 rifle *141*
Radom pistol 57, 58
Raschen Bag 96
RBS-70 air defence system *173*
Redeye missile 170
Reising SMG 61
Remington round 212
Remington shotgun 190, 205
RG 42 grenade 114
RGD 5 grenade 114
rice flail *219*, 220
Rifle Grenade No. 44 150
rifle grenades 35–36, 153–54, 162
Rifle No. 4 Mk.I *56*
Rigby cartridges 213
Rigby Magnum 213
riot control equipment 196
rockets, anti-tank 155
Ross rifle 17
Royal shotgun 204
RPD machine gun 114
RPG-2 rocket 159
RPG-7 rocket launcher *128, 159, 160*, 166

RPG 16 & 17 160–61
RPG-22 rocket 128
RPK machine guns 114, 126
RUC 192
Ruger Mini rifle *192*

S2-3, S2-6 charges 194
SA-7 missile 128, 170
SA 80 rifle *135*
Sacramento vest 191
SAGGER missile *160*, 161
Sai 220
St Etienne machine gun *29*
'Saurian gun' *201, 208*, 209
Saxhorn missile 161
Schlager sword 202
Schwarzlose machine guns 24, *25*, 65
Second World War 47–87
Seefab bows 201
Semtex 193
Service air rifle 216
SG 43 machine gun 71, *72*, 91, 114, *115*
Shaken 220
Shiki Kikanju machine guns 54
Shinai 219
Short Magazine Lee-Enfield (SMLE) 14, 17, *18, 79*, 97, *127*, 153
shotguns 182, 184, 190:
  cartridge collecting 208
  gauge 207
  pump action 17, 32, 187, *189*, 205
  sporting 204
Shrapnel helmet 37
Shuriken 220
sights *18*, 18–19,*135*, 145, 147, 160, 210
silencers 74–75
Simorov rifle 74, 90
Skeet shooting 207–8
Skorpion super-pistol 142
SKS rifle 74, 113
Smatchet 82
Smith & Wesson revolvers 19, 21, 23, *109*, 178, 179, 187
sniper rifles 17–18, *92*, 130, 138–39, 144–47, 167, 187, 196
Soltam mortars 117
Spanish Civil War 47, *48*, 53, 54
SPAS shotgun 190
Special Weapons and Tactics 187, *188*
Spigot missile 161
spitzer bullets *12*
Splatmaster gun 217
sporting rifles 17, 19, 209–12
sporting shooting 207
Sprengfaust 157
Springfield rifles 11, 12, 17, 32, *92*
SSG 69 rifle 145
Sten gun *60*, 60–61, 74, 96
Sterling guns 124, 136
Sterling pistols 142
Stern Gewehr 16
Stevens Autoshot 178
Steyr pistol *23*
Steyr rifles *35, 38, 137*, 137–38
stick grenade *34, 58*, 78
stiletto 45, *81, 82*
Stinger missile 128, *173*
Stokes mortar *40, 42*, 167
Stoner rifles 108, *109*
Sturmgewehr 44 rifle 72, *73, 73*–74, 111
Sturmgewehr 57 rifle *139*
Sturmgewehr 90 rifle 140
Sturm Ruger 186
sub-machine guns:
  Falklands 121, 123–24
  First World War 31–33
  interwar 47–53, 60–65
  Korean war 90–91
  Middle East *115*
  police squads 177

Vietnam war 105–6, 113
sub-machine gun/pistol hybrid 142
Super Bazooka 158–59
SVD rifle 126, 130, 145
SVT rifle 74
SVT 40 rifle 74
swing rifle 210
sword fencing 202–4
swords 81, *82–83*:
  martial arts 219

T-52-1, T-52-2 vests 97
Taisho machine guns *70*
Taisho pistols 58, *59*
target rifles 209, 210
terrorism 192–96, *197*
thermal charges 195
thermite bombs 195
Thompson sub-machine gun 47–49, *48, 62, 79*, 176–77, *178*
'Three Line Model 1891' 15
throwing stars 220
TM-46 mine 194
TMB-B mines 194
Tokarev pistol 57, 130
Tonfa *220*
TOW missile 128
trench armour 38, *39*
Trialene 194
truck bombs 195
TT33 pistol 90, 113
TTM pistol *90*
Type 1 grenade 114
Type 51 pistol *90*
Type 53 carbine 89–90
Type 53 machine gun 91
Type 54 pistol 113
Type 56 carbine 90, *113*
Type 56 machine gun 114
Type 56 pistol 90
Type 59 pistol 113, 114
Type 63 pistol 90
Type 68 pistol 90
Type 68 rifle *113*
Type 89 mortar 77–78, *78*
Type 91 grenade 78, 80
Type 92 machine gun *70*
Type 94 pistol 59
Type 97 grenade 78, 80
Type 100 SMG 65

Uchine 220
US Enfield rifles 17
Uzi SMG *115*–17, 128

'VB' grenades 35–36
Vektor SP1 pistol 133
Very pistol 16
Vickers-Berthier machine gun 50
Vickers machine guns 24, 27, 29, *32, 67, 96, 168*
Vierling 214
Vietnam war 98–115
Vilar-Perosa gun 32, *33*
VIS-35 pistol 57
Vollmer SMG 53
VZ 27 & 38 pistols 58

Weatherby cartridges 213
Webley & Scott pistols *23*, 216
Webley pistols *19, 20, 22*–23, *95, 175, 176*, 179
Webley rifle 216
Welch knife 45
Welrod pistol 74
Werfgranate M1917 35
Winchester shotgun 32, 205
World War I 9–45
World War II 47–87
WZ 'UR' 150–51

XM207 machine gun *108*

Yugoslavian conflict 138–39

Z-88 pistol 133
ZB machine guns *50*, 54, 128

BIBLIOGRAPHY

Adam, R. *Modern Handguns*. London 1989.
Adams, J. *Know The Game: Archery*. London 1988.
Alm, J. *Eldhandvapen*. 2 Vols. Stockholm 1934.
Amateur Fencing Association. *Fencing*. Wakefield 1974.
Anon. *The Browning Heavy Machine Gun .300 Calibre Model 1917, Made Easy*. Aldershot, c. 1940.
Archer, D.H.R. & Hogg, I.V. (eds) *Jane's Infantry Weapons*. London, many editions.
Armstrong, N.A.D. *Fieldcraft, Sniping and Intelligence*. 1940. Reprinted Brecon 1993.
Baden, M. *Unnatural Death, Confessions of a Forensic Pathologist*. New York 1989.
Baer, L. *The History of the German Steel Helmet*. San Jose, California 1985.
Barker, A.J. *Russian Infantry Weapons of World War Two*. London 1971.
Barlow, J.A. & Johnson R.E.W. *Small Arms Manual*. London 1942.
Barnes, F.C. *Cartridges of the World*. Northbrook, Illinois 1989.
Berger, R.J. *Know your Czechoslovak Pistols*. Chino Valley, Arizona 1989.
Berger, R.J. *Know Your Broomhandle Mausers*. Chino Valley, Arizona 1985.
Blair, C. (ed) *Pollard's History of Firearms*. New York 1985.
Buerlein, R.A. *Allied Military Fighting Knives*. Richmond, Virginia 1984.
Burrard, G.B. *The Identification of Firearms and Forensic Ballistics*. London 1934.
Byron, D. *The Official Guide to Gun Marks*. Brecon 1990.
Canfield, B.N. *A Collectors Guide to the M1 Garrand and the M1 Carbine*. Lincoln, Rhode Island 1988.
Canfield, B.N. *Winchester in the Service*. Lincoln, Rhode Island 1991.
Carter, A. *German Ersatz Bayonets*. Brighton 1976.
Carter, A. *German Bayonets*. 4 Vols. Norwich 1984-1994.
Clapp, W.M. *Modern Law Enforcement Weapons and Tactics*. Northbrook, Illinois 1987.
Clutterbuck, R. *Terrorism and Guerilla War*. London 1990.
Cooke, R. *Paintball*. London 1991.
Cormack, A.J.R. *Astra Pistols and Revolvers*. Windsor 1972.
Cornfield, S. *The Queen's Prize, the Story of the National Rifle Association*. London 1987.
Davidson, I.D. *Bayonet Markings, a Guide for Collectors*. Brighton 1973.
Dean, B. *Helmets and Body Armour in Modern Warfare*. 1930, new edition New York 1977.
Dewar, M. *Weapons and Equipment of Counter Terrorism*. Poole 1987.
Dowell, W.C. *The Webley Story*. Leeds 1962.
Dugelby, T.B. *The Bren Gun Saga*. Toronto 1986.
Dunstan, S. *Flak Jackets*. London 1984.
Edmiston, J. *The Sterling Years*. London 1992.
Ellis, J. *The Social History of the Machine Gun*. London 1975.
Escritt, L.B. *Rifle and Gun*. London 1953.
Ezell, E.C. *Small Arms of the World*. Harrisburg 1983.
Ezell, E.C. *Handguns of the World*. New York 1981.
Farnell, G.C. & M. *Target Shooting*. Wakefield 1972.
Farrar-Hockley A. *Infantry Tactics 1939-1945*. New Malden 1976.
Finn, M. *Art of Shuriken Jutsu*. Leeds 1983.
Fleischer, W *Panzerfaust*. Atglen 1994.
Gander, T. *Field Rocket Equipment of the German Army 1939-1945*. London 1972.
Gander, T. *Guerilla Warfare and Weapons*. Wellingborough 1989.
Gazette des Armes Magazine. Paris 1974-1990.
Goldsmith, D.L. *The Devil's Paintbrush*. Toronto 1989.
Guns Review Magazine. London continuing.
Harms, N.E. & Feist, U. *Weapons of the German Infantry During World War Two*. Buena Park, California 1968.
Hatcher, J.S. *Textbook of Pistols and Revolvers*. Marines, North Carolina 1935.
Hiller, D.E. *The Collectors Guide to Air Rifles*. Euxton 1985.
Holland & Holland. *Gun and Rifle Manufacturers, the Illustrated Catalogue*. London 1904.
Hogg, I.V. & Weeks, J. *Military Small Arms of the Twentieth Century*. Many editions, London 1973 onwards.
Hogg, I.V. *The Encyclopedia of Infantry Weapons of World War Two*. London 1977.
Hughes, G. & Jenkins, B. *A Primer of Military Knives*. Two parts, Brighton 1973 and 1981.
Isby, D.C. *War in a Distant Country, Afghanistan: Invasion and Resistance*. London 1989.
Jacklin, G. & Whipp, D. *The Lewis Gun*. London 1941.
Jarrett, A. *Shooting at Clays*. London 1991.
Jinks, R.G. *History of Smith and Wesson*. North Hollywood, California 1977.
Johnson, H.E. *Small Arms Identification and Operation Guide - Eurasian Communist Countries*. Defence intelligence, Washington 1977.
Kirkland, K.D. *Remington*. London 1988.
Ladd, J. & Melton, K. *Clandestine Warfare, Weapons and Equipment of the S.O.E. and O.S.S.* London 1988.
Latham, S. *Knives and Knifemakers*. New York 1973.
Long, D. *Modern Ballistic Armour*. Boulder, Colorado 1986.
Longstaff, F.V. & Atteridge *The Book of the Machine Gun*. London 1917.
Mantoan, N. *Bombe A Mano Italiane 1915-1918*. Place of publication not given, 1980.
Markham, G. *Japanese Infantry Weapons of World War Two*. London 1976.
Marshall, S.L.A. *Infantry Operations and Weapons Usage in Korea*. 1953, reprinted London 1988.
McFarland, J.D. (ed) *AR-15, M 16, Assault Rifle Handbook*. El Dorado, Arizona 1985.
Melton, H.K. *O.S.S. Special Weapons and Equipment*. New York 1991.
Nelson, T.B. *The World's Submachine Guns*. Cologne 1964.
Owen, J.I.H. *Nato Infantry and It's Weapons*. London 1976.
Patents for Inventions *Class 119, Small Arms, 1855-1930* (London). Reprinted Oceanside, California 1993.
Phillips, R & Knapp, J. *Sir Charles Ross and His Rifle*. Ottawa 1969.
Radom, M. *The Martial Arts*. London 1977.
Riling, R. *Guns and Shooting a Bibliography*. New York 1951.
Rosser-Owen, D. *The Vietnam Weapons Handbook*. Wellingborough 1986.
Rutterford, K. *Collecting Shotgun Cartridges*. London 1987.
Scott, J.D. *Vickers a History*. London 1962.
Skennerton, I. *The British Service Lee*. Margate, Queensland 1982.
Skennerton, I. *The British Sniper*. Margate, Queensland 1984.
Skennerton, I. *British Small Arms of World War Two*. Margate, Queensland 1988.
Skennerton, I. *An Introduction to British Grenades*. Margate, Queensland 1988.
Skennerton, I. & Richardson, R. *British and Commonwealth Bayonets*. Margate, Queensland 1984.
Smith, W.H.B. *Gas, Spring and Air Guns of the World*. New York 1957.
Stamps, M & Skennerton, I. *.380 Enfield No 2 Revolver*. London 1993.
Stevens, F.J. *Fighting Knives*. London 1980.
Stevens, R.B. *U.K. and Commonwealth F.A.L.s*. Toronto 1980.
Sweeting, R.C. *Modern Infantry Weapons and Training*. Aldershot 1962.
Textbook of Smallarms. London 1929.
Thompson, L. *Commando Dagger*. Boulder, Colorado 1985.
Truby, J.D. *The Lewis Gun*. Boulder, Colorado 1976.
Ulrich, A.L. *A Century of Achievement, Colt 1836-1936*. Hartford, Connecticut 1936.
U.S. Army. *Handbook on German Military Forces*. Washington 1945.
U.S. Army. *Field Manual 23-30, Grenades and Pyrotechnics*. Washington 1959.
U.S. Army. *Field Manual S-31, Boobytraps*. Washington 1965.
U.S. Army. *Vietnam Primer; Lessons Learned*. Washington 1967.
U.S. Army. *Operator's Manual, Pistol, Semi automatic 9mm, M9*. Washington 1985.
Venner, D. *Carbines et Fusils de Chasse*. Paris 1973.
Wallace, W.B. *Textbook of Small Arms*. Enfield 1904.
Walter, J. *The German Rifle*. London 1979.
Walter, J. *The Luger Book*. London 1986.
War Office, and MOD, *Official Weapons training manuals-Anti Tank Rifle* ,1937. *Light Machine Gun*, 1939. *2inch Mortar MkII*, 1939. *Anti Tank Mines*, 1940. *Browning Automatic Rifle*,1940. *Grenade*, 1942. *Bayonet*, 1942. *Light Machine Gun*, 1948. *Anti-Tank Grenade, No. 94, (Energa)*, 1953. *GPMG*, 1966.
Ward, D.M. *The Other Battle; Being a History of the Birmingham Small Arms Co. Ltd.* York 1946.
Warner, K.(ed) *Gun Digest*. Many editions, Northbrook, continuing.
Weeks, J. *Men Against Tanks*. Newton Abbot 1975.
Weeks, J. *Recoilless Anti Tank Weapons*. London 1973.
Wilkinson, F. *Sporting Guns*. London 1984.
Woodend, H. *British Rifles*. London 1981.

ACKNOWLEDGMENTS

Project Editor was Graham Smith. All pictures were researched and provided by TRH Pictures, apart from those supplied by Stephen Bull. The publishers also wish to thank Mr Herbert Woodend and the staff of the MOD Pattern Room, Nottingham, for their assistance.

PICTURE CREDITS

1: TRH; 2/3: US Navy; 4/5: US Army; 6: Airman Magazine; 8/9: Robert Hunt/IWM; 10: (top) Robert Hunt, (bottom) e.t. archive/Forrester/Wilkinson; 11: Stephen Bull; 12/13: Robert Hunt/US Signal Corps; 14: Robert Hunt; 15: Stephen Bull; 16: Robert Hunt; 17: (top) Robert Hunt/IWM, (bottom) e.t. archive/Forrester/Wilkinson; 18: Robert Hunt/IWM; 19: Robert Hunt/IWM; 20: (top) TRH, (bottom) e.t. archive/Forrester/Wilkinson; 21: (both) e.t. archive/Forrester/Wilkinson; 22: (top) e.t. archive/Forrester/Wilkinson, (bottom) TRH/MOD Pattern Room; 23: (top) TRH/MOD Pattern Room, (bottom) e.t. archive/Forrester/Wilkinson; 24: Robert Hunt; 25: (both) Robert Hunt; 26/27: Robert Hunt; 28: (top) Robert Hunt, (bottom) TRH; 29: (both) Robert Hunt/IWM; 30: (top) Robert Hunt, (bottom) Robert Hunt/IWM; 31: Robert Hunt/US National Archives; 32: (top) TRH, (bottom) TRH/MOD Pattern Room; 33: Robert Hunt/IWM; 34: Robert Hunt/IWM; 35: Robert Hunt; 36: (top) Robert Hunt, (bottom) Robert Hunt/IWM; 37: TRH; 38: (both) Robert Hunt; 39: (left) Robert Hunt/IWM, (right) TRH; 40: (left) Robert Hunt, (right) Robert Hunt/IWM; 41: Robert Hunt/IWM; 42: (top) Robert Hunt/IWM, (bottom) Robert Hunt; 43: Robert Hunt; 44: TRH; 46/47: TRH48: (top) Robert Hunt, (bottom) US National Archives; 49: US Army; 50: (top) e.t. archive/Forrester/Wilkinson, (bottom) TRH/MOD Pattern Room; 52: Robert Hunt; 53: TRH; 54: Robert Hunt; 55: (top) TRH/MOD Pattern Room, (bottom) TRH; 56: (from top) TRH/MOD Pattern Room; TRH; Robert Hunt; TRH; 57: e.t. archive/Forrester/Wilkinson; 58: (top) e.t. archive/Forrester/Wilkinson, (bottom) Robert Hunt; 59: (both) e.t. archive/Forrester/Wilkinson; 60: TRH/MOD Pattern Room; 61: (top) Robert Hunt/IWM, (bottom) TRH/MOD Pattern Room; 62: US Army; 63: Robert Hunt/IWM; 64: TRH/MOD Pattern Room; 65: (top) US Army, (bottom) TRH; 66: TRH/IWM; 67: TRH/MOD Pattern Room; 68/69: US DoD; 70: (top) USMC, (bottom) Robert Hunt; 71: Robert Hunt; 72: TRH/MOD Pattern Room; 73: (top) Robert Hunt, (bottom); e.t. archive/Forrester/Wilkinson; 74: TRH/MOD Pattern Room; 75: (top) TRH/MOD Pattern Room, (bottom) TRH; 76: (left) Robert Hunt, (right) US Army; 77: TRH; 78: TRH/MOD Pattern Room; 79: (top) US National Archives, (bottom) TRH/IWM; 80: US Army; 81: (top) e.t. archive/Forrester/Wilkinson, (bottom) TRH; 83: US Navy; 84: TRH; 85: TRH; 86: US Army; 88/89: US DoD; 90: TRH; 91: (top) TRH/MOD Pattern Room, (bottom) US Army; 92: USMC; 93: US Army; 94: US DoD; 95: US Army; 96: UN; 97: UN; 98: US Navy; 99: TRH; 100: (top) US Army, (bottom) TRH/MOD Pattern Room; 101: US Army; 102/103: US DoD; 104: US Army; 105: (both) TRH/MOD Pattern Room; 106: US Army; 107: US DoD; 108: US Navy;109: (top) TRH/MOD Pattern Room, (middle) US Army, (bottom) US DoD; 110: US Army; 111: (top) e.t. archive, (bottom) US DoD; 112: Robert Hunt; 113: USAF; 114: (top) TRH/MOD Pattern Room, (bottom) e.t. archive; 115: (both) TRH; 116: (top) US DoD, (bottom) UN; 118/119: US DoD; 120: (top) USAF, (bottom) TRH; 121: (top) UK MOD, (bottom) TRH; 122: (both) TRH; 123: TRH; 124: (both) TRH/MOD Pattern Room; 125: UK MOD; 126: (top) TRH/MOD Pattern Room, (bottom) UK MOD; 127: (top) TRH/T.A. Davis, (bottom) TRH/SOF; 128: TRH/MOD Pattern Room; 129: US Navy; 130/131: (both) USMC; 132: (top) USAF, (bottom) US Navy; 134: US Navy; 135: (both) TRH; 136: FN Herstal; 137: (top) USAF, (bottom) TRH; 138: TRH/J-P. Husson; 139: TRH/Yves Debay; 140: US Navy; 141: TRH; 142: (top) e.t. archive/Forrester/Wilkinson, (bottom) Calico; 143: FN Herstal; 144: Ian Hogg/H&K; 145: (top) TRH, (bottom) Accuracy International; 146: (top) US Army, (bottom) FN Herstal; 147: TRH/MOD Pattern Room; 148/149: TRH; 150: (top) TRH/MOD Pattern Room, (bottom) FN Herstal; 151: (top) TRH/MOD Pattern Room, (bottom) Robert Hunt/IWM; 152: (both) TRH/MOD Pattern Room; 153: TRH; 154: TRH/MOD Pattern Room; 155: Robert Hunt/IWM; 156: US Army; 157: TRH; 158: TRH/MOD Pattern Room; 159: (top) UK MOD, (bottom) TRH/MOD Pattern Room; 160: (left) UK MOD, (right) NATO; 162: (top) UK MOD, (bottom) FN Herstal; 163: (top) TRH/MOD Pattern Room, (bottom) Hunting Engineering; 164: US Army; 165: McDonnell Douglas; 166: (left) TRH/J-P Husson, (right) TRH; 167: (top) TRH/SOF, (bottom) Robert Hunt/IWM; 168: (top) Robert Hunt/IWM, (bottom) TRH; 169: (left) TRH, (right) TRH/Fox; 170: TRH/J-P Husson; 171: Shorts Bros.; 172: General Dynamics; 173: Bofors; 174/175: TRH; 176: e.t. archive/Forrester/Wilkinson; 177: FBI; 178: (top left & right) Aldino, (bottom) TRH/MOD Pattern Room; 179: (both) TRH/MOD Pattern Room;180: TRH; 181: TRH; 182: Metropolitan Police; 183: (top) TRH/MOD Pattern Room, (bottom) Glasgow Herald; 185: Popperfoto; 186: US Navy; 187: TRH/M. Roberts; 188: (top) TRH, (bottom) Metropolitan Police; 189: Metropolitan Police; 190: (top) ASP, (middle) e.t. archive/Forrester/Wilkinson, (bottom) TRH/MOD Pattern Room; 191: TRH; 192: (top) TRH/MOD Pattern Room, (bottom) TRH; 193: (both) TRH; 194: USAF; 195: Pacemaker Press;196: (top) Stephen Bull/Greater Manchester Police Museum, (bottom) TRH/MOD Pattern Room; 197: (top) Pacemaker Press, (bottom) TRH; 198: FBI; 200/201: Holland & Holland; 202: (top) Barnett, (bottom) TRH; 203: Barnett; 204: (top) TRH, (bottom) Holland & Holland; 205: (top) Holland & Holland, (bottom) Browning; 206: TRH/P. Hicks; 207: Browning; 208: Holland & Holland; 209: TRH/P. Hicks; 210: (top) TRH, (bottom) TRH/P. Hicks; 211: TRH/P. Hicks; 212: (both) Mauser; 213: (top) Holland & Holland, (bottom) TRH; 214: (top) Sauer, (bottom) Atkins Collection; 215: N. Allen; 216: (top) TRH, (bottom) Atkins Collection; 217: TRH; 218: TRH/Bedlam; 219: P. Lewis; 220: P. Lewis; 221: TRH;